THE RISE AND FALL OF A MEDIEVAL FAMILY

THE DESPENSERS

THE RISE AND FALL OF A MEDIEVAL FAMILY

THE DESPENSERS

KATHRYN WARNER

PEN & SWORD
HISTORY

AN IMPRINT OF PEN & SWORD BOOKS LTD.
YORKSHIRE - PHILADELPHIA

First published in Great Britain in 2020 by
Pen & Sword History
An imprint of
Pen & Sword Books Ltd
Yorkshire - Philadelphia

ISBN 978 1 52674 493 7

A CIP catalogue record for this book is available from the British Library.

Printed and bound in England
By TJ Books Limited.

Pen & Sword Books Ltd incorporates the Imprints of Pen & Sword Archaeology,
Atlas, Aviation, Battleground, Discovery, Family History, History, Maritime,
Military, Naval, Politics, Railways, Select, Transport, True Crime, Fiction,
Frontline Books, Leo Cooper, Praetorian Press, Seaforth Publishing,
Wharncliffe and White Owl.

For a complete list of Pen & Sword titles please contact
PEN & SWORD BOOKS LIMITED
47 Church Street, Barnsley, South Yorkshire, S70 2AS, England
E-mail: enquiries@pen-and-sword.co.uk
Website: www.pen-and-sword.co.uk

Or

PEN AND SWORD BOOKS
1950 Lawrence Rd, Havertown, PA 19083, USA
E-mail: uspen-and-sword@casematepublishers.com
Website: www.penandswordbooks.com

Contents

Contents

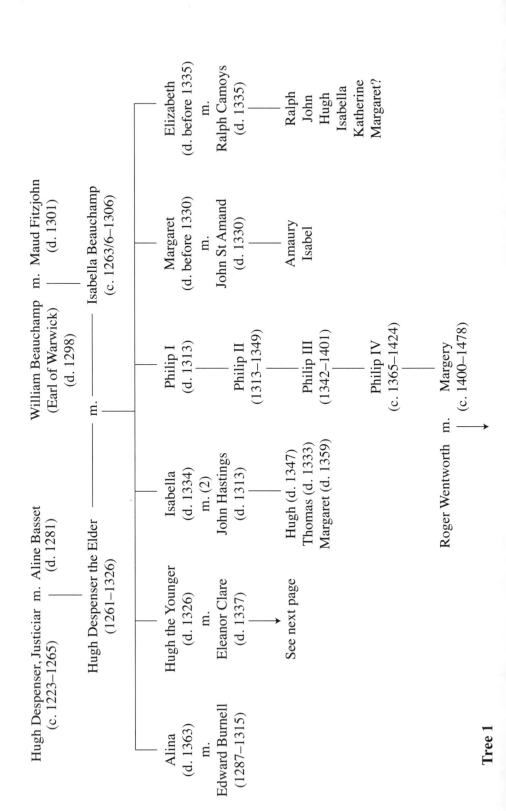

Hugh Despenser, Justiciar m. Aline Basset
(c. 1223–1265)   (d. 1281)

William Beauchamp m. Maud Fitzjohn
(Earl of Warwick)   (d. 1301)
(d. 1298)

Hugh Despenser the Elder   m.   Isabella Beauchamp
(1261–1326)   (c. 1263/6–1306)

Alina
(d. 1363)
m.
Edward Burnell
(1287–1315)

Hugh the Younger
(d. 1326)
m.
Eleanor Clare
(d. 1337)
→
See next page

Isabella
(d. 1334)
m. (2)
John Hastings
(d. 1313)

Hugh (d. 1347)
Thomas (d. 1333)
Margaret (d. 1359)

Philip I
(d. 1313)

Philip II
(1313–1349)

Philip III
(1342–1401)

Philip IV
(c. 1365–1424)

Margery
(c. 1400–1478)

Roger Wentworth m.   →

Margaret
(d. before 1330)
m.
John St Amand
(d. 1330)

Amaury
Isabel

Elizabeth
(d. before 1335)
m.
Ralph Camoys
(d. 1335)

Ralph
John
Hugh
Isabella
Katherine
Margaret?

Tree 1

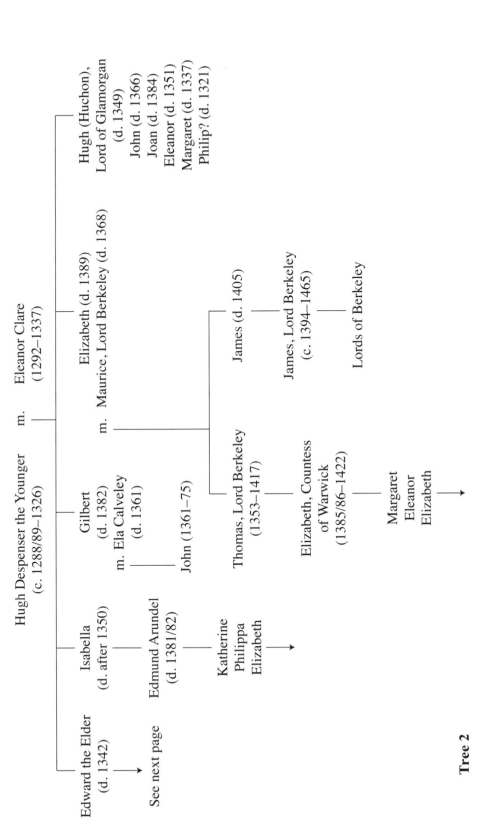

Hugh Despenser the Younger
(c. 1288/89–1326)

m.

Eleanor Clare
(1292–1337)

Edward the Elder
(d. 1342)

See next page

Isabella
(d. after 1350)

Edmund Arundel
(d. 1381/82)

Katherine
Philippa
Elizabeth

Gilbert
(d. 1382)
m. Ela Calveley
(d. 1361)

John (1361–75)

Elizabeth (d. 1389)

m. Maurice, Lord Berkeley (d. 1368)

Thomas, Lord Berkeley
(1353–1417)

Elizabeth, Countess
of Warwick
(1385/86–1422)

Margaret
Eleanor
Elizabeth

James (d. 1405)

James, Lord Berkeley
(c. 1394–1465)

Lords of Berkeley

Hugh (Huchon),
Lord of Glamorgan
(d. 1349)
John (d. 1366)
Joan (d. 1384)
Eleanor (d. 1351)
Margaret (d. 1337)
Philip? (d. 1321)

Tree 2

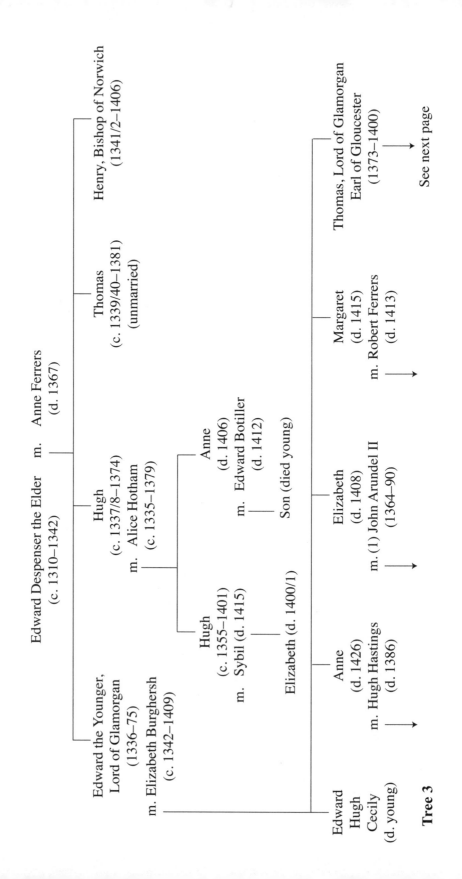

Edward Despenser the Elder m. Anne Ferrers
(c. 1310–1342) (d. 1367)

Hugh
(c. 1337/8–1374)
m. Alice Hotham
(c. 1335–1379)

Thomas
(c. 1339/40–1381)
(unmarried)

Henry, Bishop of Norwich
(1341/2–1406)

Edward the Younger,
Lord of Glamorgan
(1336–75)
m. Elizabeth Burghersh
(c. 1342–1409)

Hugh
(c. 1355–1401)
m. Sybil (d. 1415)

Anne
(d. 1406)
m. Edward Botiller
(d. 1412)

Son (died young)

Elizabeth (d. 1400/1)

Anne
(d. 1426)
m. Hugh Hastings
(d. 1386) →

Elizabeth
(d. 1408)
m. (1) John Arundel II
(1364–90) →

Margaret
(d. 1415)
m. Robert Ferrers
(d. 1413) →

Thomas, Lord of Glamorgan
Earl of Gloucester
(1373–1400)

→ See next page

Edward
Hugh
Cecily
(d. young)

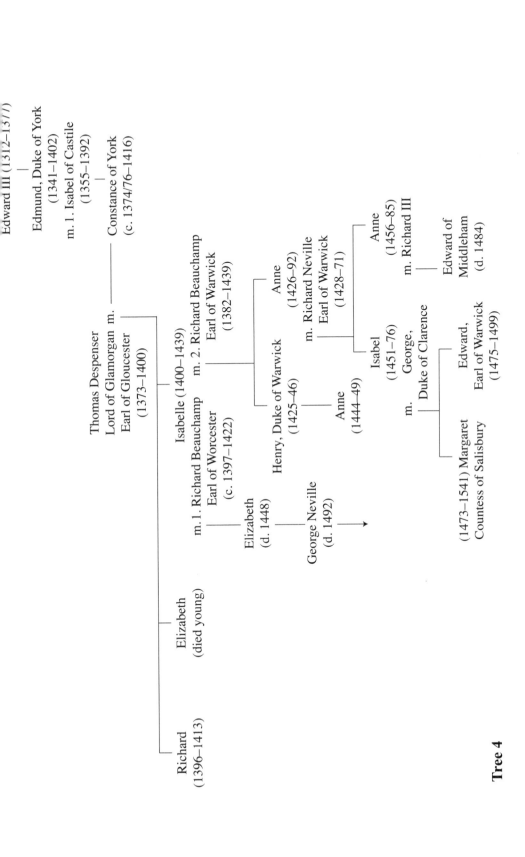

Tree 4

Introduction

A historian has called the Despensers 'one of the fourteenth century's most reviled families'. [1] This is perfectly true, and the Despensers' story from the thirteenth century to the early fifteenth is almost impossibly dramatic. Of the seven chief Despenser lords between 1265 and 1400 – Hugh the justiciar, Hugh the Elder, Hugh the Younger, Hugh the Younger's eldest son Hugh known as 'Huchon', Edward the Elder, Edward the Younger, and Thomas – three were executed, two died in battle, one probably died of plague, and only one died of natural causes. The Despenser men generally failed to die peacefully in their beds.

They did, however, have a knack for making excellent marriages which elevated the family's fortunes in each generation. Hugh the justiciar (d. 1265) married the heiress Aline Basset, and their son Hugh the Elder (d. 1326) married the Earl of Warwick's daughter Isabella Beauchamp. Hugh the Younger (d. 1326) married Edward I's eldest granddaughter Eleanor Clare, who eleven years after their wedding brought him one-third of her late brother's earldom of Gloucester, the greatest windfall the Despenser family ever received. Huchon (d. 1349) married the Earl of Salisbury's daughter Elizabeth Montacute. Edward the Younger (d. 1375) married the heiress Elizabeth Burghersh, and their son Thomas (d. 1400) made the most impressive match of all by marrying Constance of York, granddaughter of the kings of England and Castile and daughter of the first Duke of York. Finally, Thomas's daughter and heir Isabelle Despenser (d. 1439) married two earls, Worcester and Warwick. These excellent Despenser marriages made the family close kin to the kings of England, yet despite this and despite all their wealth and influence, the family came close to disaster on several occasions. Hugh the justiciar was killed fighting against Henry III and his son the future Edward I in 1265, and the greed, despotism and corruption of Hugh the Younger and his father in the 1320s brought down King Edward II and almost destroyed the

Despenser family as well. Thomas Despenser was summarily executed by a mob in 1400 after rebelling against the new king, Henry IV, in favour of the old one, Richard II.

In other areas, at least, the picture is somewhat rosier, and the family may have been patrons of some of the greatest authors of medieval England. The poet William Langland (*c.* 1325/30–*c.* 1387/1400), who authored *The Vision of Piers Plowman,* one of the great works of medieval English literature, was the son of Eustace 'Stacy' Rokele or Rokayle. Stacy himself was the son of a loyal Despenser adherent, Peter Rokele, undersheriff of Buckinghamshire in the 1320s, and an inscription in a manuscript of *Piers Plowman* calls William Langland the son of Stacy Rokayle, 'a tenant of the Lord Spenser [i.e. Despenser] in the county of Oxfordshire'. In 2001, a writer postulated that the Despensers were connected to the author of the great poems *Gawain and the Green Knight* and *Pearl* in the second half of the fourteenth century. [2] And Isabelle Despenser, countess of Worcester and Warwick, commissioned the court poet John Lydgate (*c.* 1370–*c.* 1450) in the late 1420s to translate *The Fyfftene Joyes of Our Lady,* a devotional poem to the Virgin, from Latin into English. Lydgate dedicated his work to 'the worshipfull Pryncesse Isabelle nowe Countasse of Warr[ewyk], Lady Despenser'. [3]

The Despensers: The Rise and Fall of a Medieval Family tells the story of this most fascinating of dynasties from the baronial wars of the 1260s until the 1430s, through the forced abdications of two English kings, the Hundred Years War, the Black Death, and the Great Uprising of 1381.

*

A Note on Names

The Despensers were exceptionally conservative with given names, and most of the male members of the family were called Hugh or Philip. This was, unfortunately and often extremely confusingly, the case with most noble English families of the Middle Ages. On top of all the Hugh and Philip Despensers, the father-in-law, husband, eldest son and grandson of Elizabeth Despenser (d. 1408) were all called John Arundel; the son, grandson and great-grandson of Isabella Despenser (d. 1334) were all called Hugh Hastings; Isabelle Despenser (d. 1439) married two men called Richard Beauchamp; and Isabelle had a daughter and a stepdaughter both called Elizabeth Beauchamp, who married two Neville brothers. I have endeavoured to differentiate the many people with the same name as clearly as possible in the text and have erred on the side of aiding the reader rather than being entirely consistent. At the front of each of the six sections are lists of the main people discussed in that section, and there are family trees at the start of the book, also intended to aid the reader.

The name Beauchamp is pronounced 'beecham', and Bohun is 'boon'. The name Despenser was written 'le Despenser' in the Middle Ages, and female family members were called 'la Despensere'. I have omitted the 'le' and 'la', and also the 'de' (meaning 'of' in French) in the names of noble families such as de Clare and de Vere. I have also modernised given names, e.g. Eleanor rather than the usual medieval spelling of Alianore, Philippa for Philippe, Edmund for Esmon, Joan for Johane, and so on.

A Note on Money

A pound consisted of twenty shillings or 240 pence, and a mark was two-thirds of a pound and consisted of thirteen shillings and four pence or 160 pence. A fourteenth-century labourer earned about two pence per day or around three pounds per year, and the richest men in England in the fourteenth century – the Despensers' cousin Henry, first duke of Lancaster, and his son-in-law John of Gaunt – had an annual income of about £12,000.

*

Part 1

Rising from the Ashes:
Hugh the Elder, 1261–1306

Dramatis Personae

Hugh Despenser (b. *c*. 1223), justiciar of England: son and heir of Hugh Despenser (d. 1238) and a mother whose identity is uncertain

Aline Despenser, née Basset (b. 1240s): Hugh the justiciar's wife, probably his second wife; only surviving child and heir of Philip Basset

Philip, Lord Basset of Wycombe (d. 1271), third son and heir of Alan Basset and Aline Gai; and **Hawise** (d. before November 1254), daughter of either Matthew Lovaine or Ralph Hastings: parents of Aline Despenser

Ela Longespée (d. 1297): daughter of William Longespée, earl of Salisbury; marries Philip Basset in 1254; Aline's stepmother

John Despenser (d. 1275): Hugh the justiciar's first cousin

Hugh Despenser 'the Elder' (b. 1 March 1261): only son of Hugh the justiciar and Aline, and the Despenser/Basset heir; also heir to his father's cousin John Despenser

Joan, Eleanor and possibly **Anne** and **Hawise Despenser**: daughters of Hugh the justiciar; Joan marries Thomas Furnival, Eleanor marries Hugh Courtenay (b. 1249); Hawise, who marries Ralph Basset of Drayton (d. 1299), may be Hugh's daughter

King Henry III (b. 1207, r. 1216–72), and his son **Lord Edward**, later King Edward I (b. 1239, r. 1272–1307); Henry's brother **Richard**, earl of Cornwall (1209–72), and Richard's son and heir **Edmund**, earl of Cornwall (1249–1300)

1

Simon Montfort, earl of Leicester (b. *c.* 1208): French nobleman, married to King Henry's sister Eleanor (1215–75)

Roger Bigod, earl of Norfolk (b. *c.* 1245): second husband of Aline Despenser; stepfather of Hugh Despenser the Elder; marries secondly Alicia of Hainault in 1290

Isabella Chaworth, née Beauchamp (b. *c.* 1263/6): eldest daughter of William Beauchamp, earl of Warwick; widow of Patrick Chaworth (d. 1283); marries Hugh Despenser the Elder in or soon before December 1285

Maud Chaworth (b. 1282): Isabella's only child from her first marriage; Hugh Despenser the Elder's stepdaughter; marries Edward I's nephew Henry of Lancaster (b. 1280/81) in 1297

William Beauchamp, earl of Warwick (b. *c.* 1240) and **Maud FitzJohn**: parents-in-law of Hugh the Elder; their son and heir is **Guy Beauchamp**, earl of Warwick (b. *c.* 1271/5)

Hugh Despenser the Younger (b. *c.* 1288/9): second child and first son of Hugh the Elder and Isabella; the Despenser/Basset heir behind his father

Alina (b. *c.* 1286/7), **Isabella** (b. *c.* 1290/92), **Philip** (b. *c.* 1292/4), **Margaret** (b. *c.* late 1290s) and **Elizabeth** (b. *c.* early 1300s) **Despenser**: the other children of Hugh the Elder and Isabella

Leonor of Castile (b. *c.* 1241), first queen of Edward I, and their son **Edward of Caernarfon** (b. 1284), prince of Wales, duke of Aquitaine, earl of Chester and count of Ponthieu, heir to his father's throne; and Edward of Caernarfon's stepmother **Marguerite of France** (b. 1278/9), who marries Edward I in 1299

Chapter 1

Evesham, Worcestershire, 4 August 1265

It was called a battle, but in fact it was a slaughter. Simon Montfort, earl of Leicester, had spent over a year ruling England after defeating his brothers-in-law King Henry III and Richard, earl of Cornwall, and his nephew Lord Edward, at the battle of Lewes in Sussex in May 1264. Edward, heir to the English throne, escaped from captivity and raised an army, and on 4 August 1265 annihilated his uncle Simon's forces in the town of Evesham in Worcestershire. Simon himself was one of the many men killed during the battle, soon after seeing his eldest son Henry Montfort cleaved almost in half. Much of his army was cut down or wounded and taken prisoner, and his second son Simon the younger arrived at the battlefield with reinforcements in time to see his father's head carried past on a spike. The great earl of Leicester's body was mutilated and dishonoured: his head and testicles were sent to Maud, Lady Mortimer at Wigmore Castle in Herefordshire, as a macabre gift from her husband Roger.

Another man killed at the battle of Evesham, one of Simon Montfort's closest and most loyal allies, was the Leicestershire baron Sir Hugh Despenser. Despenser was the son and heir of another Hugh Despenser, who was seriously ill in October 1237 when Henry III sent his physician Master Thomas to tend him, and who died between 23 February and 30 May 1238. The younger Hugh was probably born in 1223, and was placed in the custody of his uncle Geoffrey Despenser after his father's death. [1] Hugh was knighted on 1 January 1245, and King Henry sent him two casks of wine for his celebratory feast afterwards. [2] In the thirteenth century, the name 'Despenser' was often written as *Dispensator* or *Dispensarius*, and this gives a clue to the family's origins: they were the stewards or 'dispensers' of the earls of Chester in the twelfth century, and had originally come to England after the Norman Conquest. [3]

Hugh Despenser was a lawyer, and was appointed justiciar of England in 1260. [4] In April/May 1257, he had been one of the men who accompanied Henry III's brother Richard of Cornwall to Aachen for his coronation as King of Germany. [5] Hugh was a long-term associate and friend of Simon Montfort, a French nobleman who arrived in England around 1230 and married Henry and Richard's sister Eleanor in 1238. Simon's uneasy relationship with his brother-in-law the king exploded into war in the 1260s, after he led a group of barons who in 1258 imposed the Provisions of Oxford on Henry. The Provisions were a radical set of propositions which limited the executive powers of the king and made him little more than a figurehead. They were soon overturned, but during the period when he controlled the English government between May 1264 and the battle of Evesham fifteen months later, Simon Montfort held two parliaments and invited representatives from the shires and towns for the first time, and is remembered today as one of the progenitors of the English parliament. Despite his long association with Henry III and Richard of Cornwall, Hugh Despenser enthusiastically supported Montfort's reforms of Henry's government. When the papal legate in England, Montfort's countryman Gui Foucois (soon to become Pope Clement IV), excommunicated Montfort and his followers in 1264, he named them as 'Simon, earl of Leicester, Hugh Despenser, and others their accomplices'. As well as this obvious indication of Despenser's deep involvement with the earl's reforms, Simon Montfort appointed Hugh as one of the executors of his will on 1 January 1259, a clear sign of his trust in Despenser. [6]

England slid slowly towards war between the royalist party and the baronial party led by Montfort in the early 1260s. In March 1264, Hugh Despenser – then constable of the Tower of London – led a group of rioters who attacked the Isleworth manor of Richard of Cornwall, whose coronation in Germany he had attended seven years previously. [7] His cousin John Despenser, son and heir of his uncle and former guardian Geoffrey, shared his allegiance to Montfort and was said to be 'against the king', as did a rather more distant cousin, Adam Despenser. Both John and Adam were captured by Roger Mortimer of Wigmore, a staunch ally of the king and rival of the Despensers, in 1264. [8]

4

Hugh Despenser married Aline Basset, who was much his junior, born sometime in the 1240s. Her father gave the couple his Northamptonshire manor of Barnwell when they wed. [9] Aline is likely to have been Hugh's second wife; Henry III had granted Despenser permission to 'marry where it shall seem best for his promotion' as far back as February 1238 when he was 14 or 15, and it seems unlikely that he would have waited for as long as twenty years to do so, though the identity of his presumed first wife is not recorded. King Henry gave Despenser a cask of wine on 12 February 1259, which possibly reveals the date of his and Aline's wedding. [10] Aline was one of the two daughters of Philip, Lord Basset, and became her father's sole heir when her sister Margery FitzJohn died before 1271. Philip himself was the third son and ultimate heir of Alan Basset (d. 1232), lord of High Wycombe in Buckinghamshire; Philip's eldest brother Gilbert died childless in 1241, and his second brother, Fulk (d. 1259), was bishop of London. [11] Philip Basset, Hugh Despenser and another baron, Hugh Bigod, alternated the office of justiciar of England in the first half of the 1260s.

Philip was married to Hawise, daughter either of Sir Matthew Lovaine or Sir Ralph Hastings, and they named one of their two daughters Aline after Philip's mother Aline Gai. The Bassets owned lands in Suffolk, Cambridgeshire, Essex, Oxfordshire, Surrey, Buckinghamshire, Wiltshire and Hampshire, all of which passed to the Despenser family via Aline's marriage. Philip was a royalist baron who was badly wounded and captured at the battle of Lewes in May 1264, fighting for Henry III and Henry's son Edward and brother Richard against his Despenser son-in-law and Simon Montfort. Even pro-Montfort chroniclers commented on the 'glory' Philip won on the battlefield, and the Worcester annalist stated that Hugh Despenser tried to save his father-in-law, but Basset refused to surrender while he could still stand and received more than twenty wounds. [12] Despite his bravery, he, with King Henry and Henry's brother and son, were captured at Lewes and held in comfortable captivity for over a year while Montfort and his allies ruled the country.

Philip's daughter Aline was certainly the mother of Hugh Despenser the justiciar's only son Hugh 'the Elder', who was her and Philip's heir as well as her husband's. Hugh the justiciar also had daughters Joan, Eleanor and possibly Anne and Hawise, though it is not entirely clear whether Aline or Hugh's unknown first wife was their mother. Joan Despenser married Thomas Furnival and gave birth to her son Thomas the younger in the early 1290s or soon before (he was aged either 40 or '40 and more' in 1332), and almost certainly was Aline's child. Eleanor Despenser married Hugh Courtenay of Okehampton, and her only son Hugh Courtenay the younger, earl of Devon, was born in September 1276. [13] Eleanor might also have been the grandmother of Richard, Lord Grey of Codnor, born in the early 1280s, via one of her daughters. Grey was addressed as 'dearest cousin' by Hugh Despenser the Younger (b. *c.* 1288/9), Hugh the justiciar and Aline Basset's grandson, in 1324. [14] If Eleanor did become a grandmother in the early 1280s, it is impossible that Aline Basset, who was no more than about 40 years old then and perhaps younger, could have been her mother.

William, Lord Ferrers of Groby in Leicestershire, who was born about 1240 and was the younger brother of the earl of Derby, married a woman called Anne, stated by the *Complete Peerage* to have been Despenser the justiciar's daughter. Their eldest child William Ferrers the younger was born in January 1271. Assuming her identification is correct, Anne seems much more likely to have been born to Hugh's first wife than to Aline. [15] It is possible that Hugh and Aline had a daughter called Hawise, who married Ralph Basset, son and heir of Ralph Basset of Drayton in Staffordshire, an ally of Hugh Despenser who was also killed fighting for Simon Montfort at Evesham. Ralph Basset the son (d. 1299) married a woman called Hawise whose parentage is uncertain, but as Aline's mother was also called Hawise, it is likely that she and Hugh would have given one of their daughters this name. Basset (d. 1299) and Hawise had a son inevitably also named Ralph Basset (d. 1343), who was addressed as 'dearest cousin', 'fair cousin' and 'beloved cousin' in the 1320s by Hugh Despenser the Younger. Hugh also talked of 'the honour of you and all of us who are of your lineage' in a 1324 letter to Basset. Unless Basset's mother was a Despenser, the two men would have been fifth cousins or thereabouts (the Bassets of Drayton were only rather distantly related to the Bassets of Wycombe, Aline's family), a relationship which seems a little tenuous for Hugh to talk to Ralph about 'all of us who are of your lineage'. Finally, a petition which relates to a raid on Sempringham Priory in Lincolnshire in 1312 mentions 'the support of Sir Hugh Despenser [the Elder] and his sisters, ladies in the said priory'. [16] Apparently Hugh the justiciar had two or more daughters who became nuns, or at least retreated into a priory for a while.

The man known to posterity as Hugh Despenser the Elder, his parents' only son and heir, was born on Tuesday, 1 March 1261, probably at one of his father's Leicestershire manors or at one of his grandfather Philip Basset's Buckinghamshire manors. In 1275, the Leicestershire jurors at the inquisition post mortem of Hugh the justiciar's cousin John Despenser knew Hugh the Elder's exact age and date of birth, and in 1281 the Buckinghamshire jurors at his mother Aline's inquisition post mortem were the only ones in the seven counties where she held lands who knew this information. [17] Eight months after little Hugh's birth, shortly before 11 November 1261, Sir Matthew Lovaine – perhaps the father of Hawise, late wife of Philip Basset – died. [18] If this identification is correct, Matthew was the little Hugh's maternal great-grandfather. Hawise Basset herself had died sometime before November 1254, when Philip received papal permission to marry his second wife, Ela, dowager countess of Warwick and a granddaughter of Henry II (r. 1154–89) via Henry's illegitimate son William Longespée, earl of Salisbury (d. 1226). Ela's first husband died in 1242, and she was a first cousin of Henry III. Unusually, she retained her maiden name; both Henry III's son Edward and her step-grandson Hugh Despenser the Elder addressed her as 'Ela Lungespeye'. [19]

Little Hugh the Elder was just 3 years old when his father fought at the battle of Lewes in May 1264. Lord Edward, heir to the throne, escaped from his uncle Simon Montfort's captivity a few months later and raised an army against Montfort, and trapped Simon and his forces in the Worcestershire town of Evesham. Hugh the justiciar refused to abandon his friend Simon before the battle, even though Montfort supposedly begged him to flee from the town and save himself on account of his 'great age'. This is a curious remark given that Despenser was fifteen or so years younger than Montfort and only about 42, and the comment was probably somewhat misreported by a chronicler. Despenser replied 'My lord, my lord, let it be. Today we shall all drink from one cup, just as we have in the past'. [20] Montfort's respect for Despenser's abilities is clearly revealed by his comment to the younger man shortly before the battle that 'you will leave behind you hardly anyone of such great value and worth'. [21] Little is known of Hugh Despenser the justiciar personally, but this assessment of him by one of the great men of the Middle Ages reveals that he was an immensely able and intelligent person, admired and respected by his peers. Despenser was a capable lawyer, administrator and estate manager, and his son Hugh the Elder inherited his abilities and added a great talent for diplomacy to the list. Hugh the Elder's son Hugh the Younger was also clever and able, though in his case his intelligence and common sense came second to his almost pathological greed, which in the 1320s brought about his own destruction, his father's and King Edward II's, and came close to destroying the Despenser family.

Despenser the justiciar was – literally, not metaphorically – stabbed in the back during the final stages of the battle of Evesham. The dagger which killed him was possibly wielded by Roger Mortimer of Wigmore, the man who sent Simon Montfort's head and testicles to his wife Maud after the battle, and who had captured Despenser's cousins John and Adam in 1264. At any rate, decades later the justiciar's grandson Hugh the Younger swore revenge on Mortimer's son and grandson for his death at Evesham. The justiciar was buried alongside Simon Montfort and Simon's son Henry before the high altar in the abbey church of Evesham. [22] He left his young widow Aline, at least two and perhaps four or more daughters, and his 4-year-old son and heir. Hugh had so much trust in Aline that he left her in command of the Tower of London when he went to fight at Evesham, and one chronicler commented on the 'inconsolable grief' she felt at the loss of her husband. [23]

Chapter 2

Fortunately for Aline Despenser, her father was a friend of the king, and two months after Evesham, Henry III gave her the three Leicestershire manors which had belonged to her husband and would ultimately pass to their son, 'in consideration of the service of Philip Basset'. [1] Philip died on 29 October 1271 leaving his daughter as his sole heir, and Aline inherited thirteen manors in seven counties, a figure which does not include the third of the Basset lands held in dower by her stepmother Ela, who outlived her by sixteen years. [2] By the time of Philip's death, Aline had married her second husband, Roger Bigod, earl of Norfolk. Born *c.* 1245, he was close to her own age, and was the nephew of the childless Roger Bigod (d. 1270), the previous earl of Norfolk, and the son of Hugh Bigod, who had alternated the office of justiciar with Philip Basset and Hugh Despenser. Aline used her first husband's name throughout her second marriage. Even the earl called his wife by the name of her previous husband, and a grant of pasture land to her in 1280 named her 'Lady Alyne la Despensere, countess of Norfolk'. [3] Noblewomen of the thirteenth and fourteenth centuries tended to use the name of the highest-ranking of their husbands, and as an earl, Roger Bigod was of higher rank than Hugh Despenser had been. This indicates that Aline had found her first marriage a happy one, and wished to honour Hugh's memory. She and Roger had no children, and Roger had no offspring from his second marriage either and was the last of the Bigod earls of Norfolk.

Aline's son Hugh the Elder was 10 years old when his Basset grandfather died in 1271, and 11 when King Henry III died in November 1272 to be succeeded by his son Edward I, then 33. Edward and his Spanish wife Leonor of Castile were on crusade in the Holy Land and did not return to England until August 1274. Their coronation took place at Westminster Abbey that month, and 13-year-old Hugh may have attended with his mother and his stepfather the earl of Norfolk. One of the earliest occasions when Hugh appears on record came after the death of his father's cousin John Despenser in 1275, when Hugh was named as the heir to John's three manors, Martley, Beaumanor and Arnesby. He was allowed to take possession of the manors on 3 March 1282, two days after he turned 21 and thus came of age. [4]

Hugh attended a jousting tournament in Compiègne in 1278, aged 17, and was said in a government record of 1280, wrongly, to be the 'son and heir of John Despenser'. In 1282, the king, going on campaign to North Wales, ordered Hugh to stay in England with the royal cousin Edmund, earl of Cornwall, 'for the preservation of the king's peace'. Also in 1282, Edward I asked Hugh to build two gates in his park at Barrow, Cheshire, to enable the king's carts to pass through more easily on the way to Rhuddlan, North Wales. Hugh took part in the king's Welsh wars the following year, under the earl of Cornwall's command. [5] He was first summoned to parliament in 1283 when he was 22 years old, and appears again on record on 3 November 1284 when he was given permission to take thirty cartloads of wood annually from a forest in Leicestershire. [6] As he grew up, Hugh the Elder decided to follow an entirely different career trajectory to his father, and was a loyal royal servant for all his long life, faithfully serving Edward I and his son Edward II for more than forty years.

Shortly before 11 April 1281, Aline Despenser, countess of Norfolk, died at the age of no more than 40 and perhaps younger. [7] Her son, now 20 years old, was her heir, but her inheritance was sizeable enough (though part of it was still in the hands of Aline's stepmother Ela) that her widower the earl of Norfolk tried to gain control of it after her death. A medieval custom called 'the courtesy of England' allowed a man to keep hold of all his late wife's inheritance until his own death, provided that they had at least one child together. Roger Bigod claimed that Aline had borne him a child at her manor of Woking in Surrey and that it had lived long enough to take a breath before dying. Hugh Despenser vigorously challenged his stepfather, and Bigod was forced to give up his claim; Aline's inheritance passed intact to her son. [8] As well as the Basset lands Hugh inherited from his mother and grandfather Philip, and three manors from John Despenser, he held several manors which had belonged to his father the justiciar: Loughborough, Hugglecote and Freeby in Leicestershire, Ryhall in Rutland, Parlington in Yorkshire and Alkborough and Sibsey in Lincolnshire.

Edward I allowed Hugh to have full possession of his mother's lands on 28 May 1281, a few months before he came of age, on acknowledgement of a due payment of 500 marks. The rights to Hugh's marriage were granted to William Beauchamp, earl of Warwick, also on 28 May 1281, but Hugh bought the rights for 1,600 marks. [9] Warwick was in his early forties in 1282, the same age as King Edward, and was married to Maud FitzJohn, a first cousin of Hugh's stepfather Norfolk. Maud had previously been married to Gerard, Lord Furnival, who died in October 1261; the couple had no children, and Gerard's ultimate heir was his nephew Thomas Furnival, husband of Hugh's sister Joan. Earl William of Warwick was a towering figure in English politics and warfare in the last three decades of the thirteenth century, though little now is known of him personally, other than a macabre anecdote. His father died in 1268 and was buried in Worcester, but in 1276, rumours came to the earl's ears that another man had been interred in his father's stead. William had the body exhumed, whereupon he and his younger brothers realised that it was indeed their father. William was excommunicated for this sacrilege. [10]

Despenser's association with the earl of Warwick would result in his marriage to William's eldest daughter Isabella some years later, though in 1281/2 she was married to her first husband Patrick Chaworth, and around 2 February 1282 bore him a daughter whom she named Maud after her mother. Patrick died shortly before 7 July 1283. His and Isabella's 1-year-old daughter Maud Chaworth was heir to his lands, which included the lordships of Kidwelly and Carmarthen in South Wales and sixteen manors in five English counties. [11] Isabella was 20 or 21 years old at most when she was widowed in 1283, perhaps only 17 or 18.

Hugh Despenser was one of the young noblemen knighted by the king in Winchester on 8 September 1285 when he was 24. [12] Perhaps now that he was a knight at last, he decided that it was time to venture into marriage as well. Sometime in late 1285, Hugh wed the widowed Isabella Chaworth without royal permission, in what is likely to have been a love-match. Edward I seized Hugh and Isabella's lands and goods on 21 December 1285 because of their unlicensed marriage, and they received them back on 30 November 1286. On 27 January 1287 Hugh acknowledged a fine of 2,000 marks for his misdemeanour, though Edward I respited the sum. In the meantime, the king had raised £400 from selling Hugh's goods. [13] As well as Hugh's brief association with

Isabella's father the earl of Warwick in 1281, she held nine manors in four counties as dower and jointure from her marriage to Patrick Chaworth, and four of the nine lay in Wiltshire, close to some of the many manors Hugh inherited and owned in that county. [14] There is much evidence that Hugh always resided in Wiltshire when he was not on royal business, and this local connection might also explain how he and Isabella came to know each other.

Chapter 3

Over the next few years, Hugh and Isabella Despenser had six children, two boys and four girls. Alina, named after her grandmother the countess of Norfolk, was born *c.* 1286/7 and married in May 1302; Hugh, the first son and the Despenser heir, was born *c.* 1288 or 1289 and married in May 1306; Isabella was born around 1290 or 1292 and probably also married in 1306; Philip, named after his father's grandfather Philip Basset, was born before 24 June 1294 and married in June 1308; Margaret was born around the late 1290s and married in December 1313; and Elizabeth the youngest was probably born around 1300, and married before June 1316. There was apparently something of an age gap between the four eldest Despenser siblings and the two youngest, Margaret and Elizabeth, given the gap of five and a half years between Philip's wedding in June 1308 and Margaret's in December 1313.

The name Elizabeth was quite an unusual one in England at the time, so the youngest Despenser daughter may have been named in honour of Edward I and Queen Leonor's fifth daughter Elizabeth (b. 1282), who married the Count of Holland in January 1297 and her second husband the earl of Hereford in November 1302. 'Margaret' was not a name found in the Despenser or Beauchamp families, and Margaret Despenser was perhaps named after Edward I's third daughter Margaret (b. 1275), who moved to the continental duchy of Brabant in 1297 to join her husband Duke Jan II, or after Edward's second queen Marguerite of France, whom he married on 8 September 1299. It is also possible, however, that she was named after a godmother. Alina Despenser's name was spelt in her own lifetime as Alyne or Eleyne, and the name Hugh was often spelt Hughe, Hug, Hugg, Huge, Hue, Huwe and other variations.

All the Despenser children had children of their own, except Alina the eldest. Hugh Despenser the Elder and Isabella Beauchamp had about twenty-two grandchildren, Hugh the Younger contributing ten to the total, and Isabella had another seven grandchildren via her daughter Maud Chaworth. Almost nothing is known about the childhoods of the next generation of Despensers, not even their dates of birth, though they can be narrowed down by reference to the dates of their marriages. Hugh the Elder spent much time abroad in the late 1280s, 1290s and early 1300s, and Isabella probably accompanied him on at least some of his many visits overseas, though would certainly have returned to England to give birth. Until 1351, English law held that anyone who inherited lands had to be born within the allegiance of the king of England, that is, in England itself, Wales, Ireland or the great duchy of Aquitaine in south-west France. In addition to this legal requirement, English landowners preferred their children and heirs to be born in one of their own lordships, if possible.

Hugh the Elder spent a lot of time at his manor-house of Vastern in Wiltshire, and it was by far his favourite residence; whenever his location can be determined, and he was not at court or attending parliament or overseas on the king's business or taking part in a military campaign, he was at Vastern. [1] It stood on a ridge near the village of Wootton Bassett, and was called Fasterne in the Middle Ages. In 1293 Hugh enclosed thirty acres of wood adjoining his two deer-parks there, in 1300 gained Edward I's permission to enclose another wood next to his parks which was part of the royal forest of Braydon, and in 1320 enlarged the parks. [2] When Hugh inherited the manor from Aline in 1281, the parks of Vastern consisted of 789 acres, and Hugh himself added another 600 acres. One of the parks was called *Lytelpark*, 'Little Park', and at nearby Wootton Bassett Hugh owned pasture called *Wyndmulleshulle*, 'Windmill Hill'. [3] Philip the miller of Wootton Bassett gave Hugh permission in 1294 to build a fence or hedge along a ditch in a wood that he owned near Vastern, from *Wodebrugge* ('woodbridge') to *Northcoumbe*, and in exchange Hugh promised to give him five quarters of barley annually and feeding for twenty pigs. The miller's son, Philip of Wootton Bassett, demised his land and tenements by the manor of Vastern to Hugh in 1316 in exchange for 50 shillings yearly and a new robe at Christmas. [4]

Given that Hugh spent so much time at Vastern, it seems highly likely that at least some of his children were born there, and that they grew up there. Hugh himself may also have spent much time at Vastern in childhood and adolescence, as his grandfather Philip Basset and mother Aline sometimes stayed there in the 1260s and 1270s, and in

1267 when Hugh was six, Philip received permission to make two deer-leaps in his new park at Vastern and his old park at nearby Wootton. Aline was at Vastern on 16 June 1280, a few months before her death. [5] Hugh's great-grandfather Alan Basset first built Vastern's park and stocked it with game. Alan's eldest son Gilbert built the manor-house in the 1230s, and his third son Philip built a private chapel there in the 1260s and founded a hospital at nearby Wootton in 1266. [6] Vastern had two 'high towers' covered with lead, a great hall with at least one fireplace, a kitchen, grange, bakehouse, brewhouse, drains, a water-tank, fishponds, a gatehouse with its own latrine, a cellar, and rooms called *Shyngledechamber* (meaning 'shingled', i.e. the room had a tiled roof) and *Haloneschamber*. Between 1415 and 1431 the dowager duchess of York held a third of Vastern in dower, and she had twelve chambers, a 'small chapel' and a tower there. [7]

Chapter 4

As of late 1285, Hugh Despenser the Elder was the son-in-law of the earl of Warwick as well as the stepson of the earl of Norfolk. As such, and in possession of a sizeable inheritance across England and of his wife's dower and jointure lands in Wiltshire, Hampshire, Gloucestershire and Berkshire, he was a man of some substance. Perhaps in an effort to win the king's favour after he married Isabella without permission, Hugh witnessed his first royal charter on 1 January 1286, and was 'going beyond seas' on Edward I's service on 27 May that year. He expected to be away until early November 1286 and appointed two attorneys to take care of his affairs while he was away. [1] He went abroad again on 10 April 1287, until November that year, this time joining the king personally in Gascony in south-west France. [2]

A somewhat mysterious letter from Edward I's eldest two daughters Eleanor (b. 1269) and Joan of Acre (b. 1272) still exists, dated c. 1287, which reveals that Hugh was involved in a feud of some kind with Sir John Lovel, John Lovel 'the bastard' and Ralph Gorges. [3] Ralph Gorges was a long-term Despenser adherent so presumably took Hugh's side in the matter. In October 1288, Hugh was one of the men, with his father-in-law and stepfather, ordered by the regent of England, the earl of Cornwall – Edward I remained overseas until August 1289 – not to ride about the country with an armed force or to disturb the king's peace. Some of the other men to whom this order was sent were the earl of Warwick's brother-in-law Richard FitzJohn, and Gilbert 'the Red' Clare (1243–95), earl of Gloucester, whose daughter Eleanor would marry Hugh's first son and heir Hugh the Younger a few years later. [4] Hugh the Younger was born sometime in the late 1280s, perhaps at Vastern in Wiltshire.

In October 1289, Hugh the Elder went to the county of Hainault in modern-day Belgium in the company of his stepfather Norfolk, to arrange the earl's second marriage. Despite Norfolk's attempts to claim Hugh's inheritance in 1281 and Hugh's threats of legal action to prevent this, it seems that the two men were quite close: Hugh visited his stepfather on several occasions, at least once in the company of the earl's brother Ralph. [5] Hugh witnessed Norfolk's assignment of dower to his second wife Alicia, daughter of the count of Hainault, on 12 June 1290, as did John Bigod, another of the earl's younger brothers. [6]

Norfolk and Alicia married at the royal manor of Havering-atte-Bower in Essex on 24 June 1290, and Hugh almost certainly attended, probably with Isabella and their small children Alina and Hugh the Younger. [7] Havering lay just ten miles from Hugh the Elder's Essex manor of North Weald Bassett, though he rarely if ever spent time there, and in 1296 was described as a knight who owned lands in Essex but was non-resident in the county. [8] Later in 1290, the Spanish queen of England, Leonor of Castile, died at the age of 49, and Hugh and Isabella, and his stepfather Norfolk and father-in-law Warwick, surely attended her funeral in Westminster Abbey on 17 December 1290. Leonor left her five daughters and her only surviving son, Edward of Caernarfon, born in April 1284 and heir to his father's throne.

A Richard Nugent gave his house in London, on Bishopsgate opposite the Benedictine priory of St Helen, to Hugh the Elder on 15 March 1290. In August 1320 Hugh still owned a house in London, presumably this one. [9] Hugh was very well-off, and in February 1291 shortly before his thirtieth birthday lent the large sum of £500 to the young earl of Arundel, Richard Fitzalan, who was perpetually short of cash and in massive debt to the Crown. [10] This was an early connection between the Despenser and Arundel families, and in the fourteenth and early fifteenth centuries they would intermarry several times. Hugh made plenty of other loans between the 1290s and 1320s as well, on one occasion in 1309 lending the enormous sum of £4,000 (a few million in modern terms). [11] He is not easy to find on record in the early 1290s, except that in June 1292 Edward I sent him a gift of six bucks hunted in the royal forest of Whittlewood, and in November that year Hugh and numerous other English noblemen including his father-in-law Warwick set out on a military campaign to Wales. [12] Perhaps Hugh lived quietly with Isabella and their young children at Vastern much of the time. Their second daughter, named after her mother, was probably born in the early 1290s.

In June 1294, Edward I appointed Hugh the Elder keeper of the royal castle of Odiham in Hampshire, an appointment his son Hugh the Younger would receive in 1320 as well. [13] Also in June 1294 and again in 1296/7, Hugh the Elder received one of his most important commissions from the king when he was sent, with the archbishop of Dublin and the bishop of Durham, as an envoy to the German king Adolf of Nassau (r. 1292–98) and Siegfried von Westerburg, archbishop of Cologne (r. 1275–97). [14] Hugh and Isabella's fourth child and second son Philip Despenser was born before 24 June 1294, probably not too long before, and on that date Hugh gave Philip his manors of Alkborough in Lincolnshire and Parlington in Yorkshire and all the goods and chattels in them. He had inherited these manors from the father he could surely remember barely if at all, Hugh the justiciar. [15] Hugh and the other envoys left England for Germany soon after this grant, and he was back at Vastern by 19 November 1294. He was in England on 1 September 1295 when he complained that deer in two of his Essex manors had been hunted and stolen, and on 30 November 1295 when he witnessed a royal charter with his stepfather and his father-in-law. [16]

Edward I appointed Hugh and two other men to consult with the cardinals and to seek a peace settlement with France on 17 November 1295; the two kingdoms had gone to war the year before when the young king of France, Philip IV (r. 1285–1314), confiscated Edward's land of Gascony in south-west France (the part of the duchy of Aquitaine ruled by the kings of England, who named themselves dukes of Aquitaine). [17] On 7 December 1295, the powerful Gilbert 'the Red' Clare, earl of Gloucester and Hertford, died at the age of 52. He left his 4-year-old son Gilbert as his heir and three daughters from his second marriage to the king's daughter Joan of Acre, including 3-year-old Eleanor, future Lady Despenser.

Hugh the Elder went overseas on this latest mission soon after 3 January 1296. [18] His wife Isabella and their children Alina, Hugh, Isabella and Philip must have grown accustomed to his frequent absences abroad. On 30 July 1296 Hugh was back in London, and attended parliament in Bury St Edmunds, Suffolk that November. He witnessed the chancellor of Scotland swearing fealty to Edward I on 28 August 1296 with his stepfather and father-in-law, and between September and December adjudicated on 'petitions of Scottish women' with three other men. [19] Hugh, the bishop of Durham and Sir Walter Beauchamp, uncle of Hugh's wife Isabella and steward of the king's household, were appointed to travel to Flanders on 13 December 1296. They were instructed to settle the proposed marriage between one of the daughters of Guy, count of Flanders (either Philippa or Isabella) and Edward I's 12-year-old son and heir, Edward of Caernarfon. [20] Hugh was, however, in England on 5 and 9 February, 15 April, 27 May, 3 June, 14 and 24 July and 6 August 1297, so seems not to have departed on this occasion, and the proposed England-Flanders marriage never took place. [21] Edward I made Hugh justice of the forest south of the River Trent on 12 February 1297, a position he would hold for much of the next three decades. [22] That same month, Hugh's step-grandmother Ela died when she must have been over 70, and he came into his entire inheritance when the portion of Philip Basset's lands Ela had held in dower reverted to him as Basset's heir.

Chapter 5

Isabella Despenser née Beauchamp's daughter from her first marriage, Maud Chaworth, turned 15 in early 1297 and married Edward I's nephew Henry of Lancaster shortly afterwards. [1] Presumably Hugh the Elder and Isabella, and Maud's Despenser half-siblings, attended the wedding. Henry of Lancaster was the second son of the king's brother Edmund, earl of Lancaster and Leicester, who died in June 1296, and was equally royal on his mother Blanche of Artois's side: she was a niece of Louis IX of France (r. 1226–70) and was married firstly to Enrique I (r. 1270–4), king of Navarre in northern Spain. Blanche's only child with Enrique, Jeanne (b. 1273), Henry of Lancaster's half-sister, was queen of Navarre in her own right and was married to Philip IV, king of France. Maud Chaworth herself probably lived with her mother and her Despenser siblings until her marriage, but would have been deemed old enough at 15 – Henry, born in 1280 or 1281, was slightly older – to set up home with her new husband.

Edward I, at war with Philip IV since 1294, went on military campaign in Flanders against Philip in August 1297. The adolescent heir to the throne, Edward of Caernarfon, remained in England as nominal regent. Hugh Despenser the Elder is frequently named in Edward I's correspondence in this difficult, crisis-ridden year as one of the king's most important supporters, and was among the great magnates of the realm who swore fealty to Edward of Caernarfon in London on 14 July. [2] Hugh's stepfather Roger Bigod, earl of Norfolk, had a famous altercation with Edward I about the earl's unwillingness to go overseas on the king's latest military campaign, and Hugh's father-in-law William Beauchamp, earl of Warwick, claimed poverty and did not take part in the Flanders campaign either. Warwick remained in England as a member of the regency council advising Edward of Caernarfon.

Hugh sailed to Flanders with the king on 24 August 1297. [3] His sojourn on the Continent, however, was short, and although Edward I himself remained overseas until March 1298, Hugh was in England on 3 and 8 November 1297. [4] In June 1298 his father-in-law Warwick died in his late fifties, and his brother-in-law Guy, born sometime between 1271 and 1275, succeeded him as earl. William Beauchamp was buried at the Greyfriars' church in Worcester, and left items in his will to his wife Maud FitzJohn, his son Guy and two of his daughters who were nuns, but nothing to his eldest daughter Isabella Despenser or any of her children. Maud FitzJohn was buried next to him when she died three years later. The new earl of Warwick and his Despenser brother-in-law fought with Edward I at the battle of Falkirk in July 1298, an English victory during the long wars of Scottish independence.

In December 1298, one Saer Barber of London was arrested and incarcerated in Newgate prison in the city for saying that Hugh Despenser the Elder was 'unworthy of praise' and 'kept more robbers with him than any other man in England'. Barber added 'it was a great wonder that [Hugh] had not lost his hood in Ghent going into Flanders', presumably a reference to Hugh's rather brief participation in Edward I's Flanders campaign of 1297, though the meaning of this expression is obscure. [5] This is an early piece of evidence for Hugh's sinister reputation, and he was castigated by chroniclers for his corruption and brutality, especially as justice of the forest. The author of the *Vita Edwardi Secundi* or 'Life of Edward II' commented *c*. 1313: 'the whole land has turned to hatred of him. Few would mourn his downfall. As an unjust official he did harm to many.' Some years later, the same chronicler complained again about Hugh's 'harshness', and stated that he was 'brutal and greedy' and had wronged many people and 'vilely disinherited' others. [6]

There seems little doubt that Hugh the Elder was guilty of viciousness and corruption during his long career, and both he and his son Hugh the Younger were hugely greedy for land and money. Hugh the Elder was none too scrupulous about adding to his already large inheritance. In the early 1300s he acquired the Hertfordshire manor of Bushey supposedly by falsely accusing its owner of various felonies in his capacity as justice of the forest and imprisoning him, and forcing him to hand over the manor. He was accused of abusing his position to acquire the village of Barnsley in Gloucestershire as well: Hugh arrested John FitzHerbert at Leckhampstead after John killed a stag in Windsor forest, and refused to free him until John handed over his manor to him. [7] Hugh was also, however, like his father Hugh the justiciar, a capable and intelligent man, and a talented diplomat and estate administrator. Two of his Wiltshire manors, Vastern and Wootton Bassett, were jointly valued at £53 when his mother Aline died in 1281, and in 1402 the three manors of Vastern, Wootton Bassett and Berwick Bassett were jointly valued at £66. While Hugh the Elder was in possession of them, Vastern and Wootton Bassett were separately valued at £60 and £56. [8]

Hugh's brother-in-law Warwick attended the wedding of 60-year-old Edward I and his 20-year-old second wife Marguerite of France in Canterbury on 8 September 1299, and most probably Hugh and Isabella were there as well. Marguerite was the younger half-sister of Philip IV, and her marriage to the English king was intended to end the war between England and France which had begun in 1294. Philip IV's only daughter, 4-year-old Isabella, was betrothed to Edward of Caernarfon for the same purpose. Queen Marguerite became pregnant immediately and gave birth to her first son, Thomas of Brotherton, on 1 June 1300. Her second, Edmund of Woodstock, followed on 5 August 1301.

Hugh Despenser witnessed a royal charter at St Albans in Hertfordshire on 3 November 1299 with his stepfather Norfolk, brother-in-law Warwick and his stepdaughter Maud's teenaged husband Henry of Lancaster, the king's nephew, and he was at Vastern on 21 November. On 10 December, his second cousin Robert Keynes gave Hugh his manors of Chelworth in Wiltshire and nearby Somerford Keynes, just over the Gloucestershire border. [9] Hugh then travelled to London and Westminster, where parliament was held in March 1300. The funeral of the king's brother Edmund, earl of Lancaster and Leicester, who had died almost four years before, was belatedly held at Westminster Abbey on 20 March 1300, and almost certainly Hugh attended; he was in London and Westminster on 22 and 28 March. [10]

Subsequently Hugh rode north with the king and most of the English nobility to Scotland, where Edward I besieged the castle of Caerlaverock in south-west Scotland from 10 to 15 July 1300. The heralds wrote a poem (in French) praising the English noblemen who took part in the siege of Caerlaverock, and called Hugh 'the good Hugh Despenser, who loyally on his courser knew how to disrupt a melee'. [11] Sixteen-year-old Edward of Caernarfon, who would be made Prince of Wales the following February, was also present at the siege, though Hugh Despenser the Younger, who many years later became involved in a long, intense and probably sexual relationship with Edward, was only about 11 or 12 in 1300. Hugh the Younger's father must have sent him to live and serve in the household of a nobleman or noblewoman, as was customary for the sons of the nobility, though which one is unknown. Possibly Hugh served his maternal uncle Guy Beauchamp, earl of Warwick, who was one of the hundreds of English noblemen and knights at Caerlaverock in July 1300, and perhaps was also present at the siege as one of his uncle's squires. [12] A decade or so younger than his sister Isabella Despenser, Earl Guy was in his mid or late twenties in 1300, and his son and heir Thomas was not born until February 1314.

Although King Edward remained in Scotland until the second week of October 1300, Hugh the Elder travelled south soon after the siege of Caerlaverock. He was in London on 9 August 1300 and again on 6 June 1301, though by 17 June 1301 had travelled to Vastern in the Wiltshire countryside. [13] He turned 40 on 1 March 1301. Probably he, Isabella and their children, except presumably Hugh the Younger, lived at Vastern much of the time in the early 1300s, and the youngest Despenser child, Elizabeth, may have been born around 1300 or soon afterwards. Hugh the Elder was sent to the 'court of Rome', i.e. to Pope Boniface VIII, in September 1300. He was appointed on 25 April 1302 – the eighteenth birthday of Edward of Caernarfon, now prince of Wales – as one of the envoys to the pope 'touching the re-establishment of peace with the king of France'. [14]

Hugh was at Vastern in March/April 1302 before he departed from England yet again. A witness to a grant made to him at this time was his sister or half-sister Eleanor's 25-year-old son Sir Hugh Courtenay, future earl of Devon, visiting his uncle at Vastern. [15] In the late 1200s and early 1300s, Despenser made a concerted effort to increase his landholdings in Wiltshire, and was particularly interested in manors which lay close to Vastern. He acquired Marston Meysey, Seend, Chelworth, Somerford Keynes and lands in Compton Bassett (which he already owned), all within twenty miles of Vastern, and received royal permission to impark part of the royal forest of Melksham, also under twenty miles away. John Meysey complained after Hugh's death that Hugh took Marston Meysey from him specifically because it adjoined Vastern, and claimed that after he tried to get Marston back, Hugh falsely accused him of taking part in a rebellion against the king; John had to flee abroad and did not dare return to England while Hugh was alive. Hugh acquired Lydiard Tregoze five miles from Vastern later as well, by typically dubious means: the owners' son was imprisoned, and they handed over their manor to Despenser in exchange for his securing the young man's release. Even though Hugh's grandfather Philip Basset was buried in Stanley Abbey in Wiltshire, Hugh forced the abbot and convent of Stanley to release their manor of Berwick Bassett, eight miles from Vastern, to him, or so they claimed after his downfall. Probably also after Hugh's death, Henry atte Hook stated that he had purchased land near Vastern, but Hugh forcibly occupied his land and imprisoned Henry for a week at Vastern. This reveals that Hugh had a prison or at least a room with a secure lock, and also that he refused to tolerate anyone else holding land close to his favourite residence. [16]

Chapter 6

Prior to his departure for Rome, Hugh surely attended a wedding: shortly after 3 May 1302, the eldest of his six children married. Alina Despenser wed the young nobleman Edward Burnell, who was probably born on 22 July 1287 and hence was 14 going on 15; she was the same age or perhaps slightly older. [1] Edward's mother Maud was the sister of Richard Fitzalan, earl of Arundel, and his father Philip Burnell (1264–94) was the nephew and heir of the influential Robert Burnell (d. 1292), bishop of Bath and Wells, chancellor of England and a close ally of Edward I. Hugh the Elder had been granted the rights to the boy's marriage on 1 January 1296 and paid 1,000 marks (£666) for it, so must have planned the wedding to his daughter for some years. Edward Burnell had previously been the ward of Henry III's half-brother William Valence, earl of Pembroke (d. 1296), and in 1296/7, a year when Valence's widow Joan's accounts survive, Joan looked after Edward and bought him clothes, shoes, gloves and reins for his horse. [2]

Edward Burnell came into a large inheritance with lands in nineteen counties, though his father Philip contrived to leave massive debts at his death, and on several occasions between 1308 and 1312, Edward had to borrow money. [3] The young Despenser/Burnell couple were to have no children so it is impossible to say when they began cohabiting, and a petition from Edward's mother Maud presented to the summer parliament of 1302 implies that her son was then in her custody, shortly after he married Alina Despenser. [4] Certainly they would have lived together when they were both 16, if not before. Sometime after he came of age, Burnell settled seven of his own manors in Gloucestershire, Shropshire and Norfolk jointly on himself and Alina, and she held them for the rest of her long life. [5] On 12 February 1313 Burnell granted his father-in-law the reversion of his manor of Sheen, west of London, and Despenser must have given Sheen to Edward II very soon after Burnell's early death in August 1315, as the king referred to it as his own manor in December 1315. [6] Sheen later became known as Richmond Palace and was a royal residence for centuries.

Hugh the Elder was back in England after his latest visit to the papal court by 26 July 1302, was at Vastern that September though spent much of the rest of the year 1302 at court, and in January 1303 was yet again at Vastern. In August 1303, he received a gift of the Buckinghamshire manors of Fulmer and Datchet from Edmund Pinkeny. After Hugh's downfall and execution in 1326, he was accused of having 'unjustly removed and ejected' Pinkeny from Datchet, and the manor was restored to the latter. [7] Given the pattern of Hugh's and his elder son's behaviour over many years, this charge may well be true. In early 1306 Hugh also acquired the Hampshire manor of Bedhampton, though on this occasion not by dubious methods; he paid John FitzReynold £1,000 for it. [8]

Hugh travelled to Scotland later in 1303, and spent Christmas there with Edward of Caernarfon, prince of Wales. Hugh and his wife Isabella's first cousin Richard Burgh, earl of Ulster, were the two envoys sent by King Edward to meet John 'the Red Comyn', lord of Badenoch and one of the Guardians of Scotland, in February 1304, and Hugh and his brother-in-law Warwick dined with Edward of Caernarfon in Perth on 21 February. [9] John of Pontoise, bishop of Winchester, who was French or at least of French origin, granted Hugh the Elder all his lands in France on 15 September 1304. Pontoise died on 4 December following, and Hugh was one of his executors. [10] Mention is made in 1308 of houses in Paris and elsewhere in France which Hugh owned, presumably from the bishop, and which he gave to Amadeus, count of Savoy. [11] John of Pontoise founded a college dedicated to St Elizabeth of Hungary (d. 1231) close to his palace of Wolvesey in Winchester in 1301/2, and Hugh Despenser the Younger evidently took an interest in it, as in 1313 he interceded with the king on the college's behalf on three occasions. [12]

Edward of Caernarfon sent Hugh the Elder a number of letters in 1304/5 (in French), a year when his correspondence fortuitously survives. One letter relates how Hugh had sent him a gift of raisins and wine which, Edward declared, could not have arrived at a better time, and another states that Hugh was one of the members of the king's council who was also a friend of the prince. Hugh was twenty-three years Edward's senior, and perhaps something of a father figure to him. One of the young prince's closest companions, alongside the Gascon nobleman

Piers Gaveston who had been placed in his household by the king *c.* 1300, was Gilbert Clare, lord of Thomond in Ireland, who would become one of Hugh's sons-in-law, probably in 1306. [13]

Hugh Despenser the Elder managed the difficult task of remaining close to both the king and his son in the last years of Edward I's reign. Edward I and Edward of Caernarfon had a furious row in August 1305 and another in early 1307, and Hugh's ability to walk the tightrope and to remain trusted by both men should not be underestimated. His talent for diplomacy and his loyalty to the Crown raised the Despenser family high, and forty years after Hugh the justiciar fought with Simon Montfort against Henry III and his son Edward I, the justiciar's grandson was to marry Edward I's eldest granddaughter.

Part 2

Bringing Down a King:
Hugh the Younger, 1306–1326

Dramatis Personae

Hugh Despenser the Elder (b. 1261), made earl of Winchester 1322; son and heir of Hugh Despenser, justiciar of England (d. 1265) and Aline Basset, countess of Norfolk (d. 1281)

Isabella Despenser, née Beauchamp (b. *c.* 1263/6), elder sister of Guy Beauchamp, earl of Warwick; married to Hugh the Elder since *c.* December 1285

Hugh Despenser the Younger (b. *c.* 1288/9): elder son of Hugh the Elder and Isabella; father of Hugh ('Huchon'), Edward, Gilbert, John, Isabella, Joan, Eleanor, Margaret and Elizabeth Despenser

Eleanor Despenser, née Clare (b. 1292): eldest granddaughter of King Edward I; daughter of Gilbert 'the Red' Clare, earl of Gloucester (1243–95); marries Hugh the Younger in May 1306

Alina Burnell, née Despenser (b. *c.* 1286/7): eldest child of Hugh the Elder and Isabella; marries Edward Burnell (b. *c.* 1287) in 1302; has no children

Isabella Hastings, née Despenser (b. *c.* 1290/92): third child and second daughter of Hugh the Elder; marries 1) Gilbert Clare of Thomond (b. 1281) *c.* 1306, 2) John Hastings (b. 1262) *c.* 1308/9, and 3) Ralph Monthermer (b. *c.* 1262) in 1318; mother of Hugh (b. *c.* 1310), Margaret and Thomas Hastings; stepmother of John Hastings (b. 1286)

Philip Despenser I (b. *c.* 1292/4): fourth child and second son of Hugh the Elder; marries Margaret Goushill (b. 1294) in 1308; father of Philip Despenser II (b. 1313)

Margaret St Amand, née Despenser (b. *c.* late 1290s): fifth child of Hugh the Elder; marries John St Amand (b. *c.* 1276/83) in 1313; mother of Amaury (b. 1315) and Isabel St Amand

Elizabeth Camoys, née Despenser (b. *c.* early 1300s): sixth and youngest child of Hugh the Elder; marries Ralph Camoys (b. 1273 or earlier) in or before 1316; mother of Ralph, John (b. *c.* 1320), Hugh (b. *c.* 1322/4), Isabella, Katherine and possibly Margaret Camoys; stepmother of Thomas Camoys (b. 1290s or early 1300s)

Maud, née Chaworth (b. 1282): stepdaughter of Hugh the Elder and older half-sister of the six Despenser siblings; marries Edward I's nephew Henry of Lancaster in 1297; mother of Henry of Grosmont, first duke of Lancaster (b. *c.* 1310/12), and great-grandmother of King Henry IV

Edward I (b. 1239): king of England from 1272 to 1307; marries 1) Leonor of Castile in 1254 and 2) Marguerite of France in 1299

Edward of Caernarfon, prince of Wales (b. 1284): son of Edward I and Queen Leonor; succeeds his father as King Edward II in July 1307

Isabella of France (b. *c.* 1295): daughter of Philip IV, king of France, and Jeanne I, queen of Navarre; marries Edward II in 1308

Edward of Windsor, later King Edward III (b. 1312): eldest child of Edward II and Isabella of France; Hugh Despenser the Elder's godson

John of Eltham (b. 1316), **Eleanor of Woodstock** (b. 1318) and **Joan of the Tower** (b. 1321): younger children of Edward II and Isabella of France

Piers Gaveston, earl of Cornwall (b. *c.* late 1270s): nobleman of Béarn, beloved of Edward II; marries Margaret Clare, sister of Eleanor Despenser, in 1307

Guy Beauchamp, earl of Warwick (b. *c.* 1271/5): uncle of the Despenser siblings

Gilbert Clare, earl of Gloucester and Hertford (b. 1291): eldest grandchild of Edward I; brother-in-law of Hugh Despenser the Younger; marries Maud Burgh in 1308; has no children and his sisters Eleanor Despenser, Margaret and Elizabeth are his heirs

Thomas of Lancaster, earl of Lancaster and Leicester (b. 1277/8): nephew of Edward I and first cousin of Edward II; and his brother and heir **Henry of Lancaster** (b. 1280/1), married to Maud Chaworth and brother-in-law of the Despenser siblings

Chapter 7

Hugh Despenser the Younger, now 17 or 18 years old, was knighted in Westminster Abbey on Sunday, 22 May 1306. So were 266 other men including the 22-year-old prince of Wales, Edward of Caernarfon, and Hugh the Younger's future brothers-in-law Gilbert Clare, heir to the earldom of Gloucester, Gilbert's namesake first cousin Gilbert Clare, lord of Thomond, and Ralph Camoys. Another young man who shared the occasion with Hugh was 19- or 20-year-old Roger Mortimer of Wigmore, whose grandfather of the same name had fought against Hugh's grandfather the justiciar at the battle of Evesham in 1265 and perhaps killed him personally. A splendid banquet was held afterwards in Westminster Hall during which numerous minstrels entertained the new knights. One of the many dozens of performers was Janin of Brabant, who played the vielle (a stringed instrument not unlike a modern violin), and who was in the household of Hugh Despenser the Elder. [1]

Four days after he was knighted, on 26 May 1306, Hugh the Younger married. His bride was Eleanor Clare, eldest of the three daughters of Edward I's second daughter Joan of Acre and her first husband Gilbert 'the Red' Clare, earl of Gloucester, the mightiest of all English noblemen in the late thirteenth century. Eleanor, born in October 1292, was 13 and a half, about three or four years younger than her new husband. Marriage to the king's eldest granddaughter was the greatest match Hugh could have made, and Edward I himself arranged it and attended the wedding in his private chapel in the Palace of Westminster. Eleanor Clare's uncle Edward of Caernarfon, prince of Wales, duke of Aquitaine, earl of Chester and count of Ponthieu, also attended, and Hugh Despenser the Elder witnessed one of the prince's charters at Westminster the day before. [2] Hugh the Elder's loyalty to the king and his decades of royal service had reaped great rewards for his son. Hugh the Younger's grandfather the justiciar died fighting against the king and his father;

now Edward I deemed Hugh a suitable husband for his granddaughter, and paid Hugh the Elder £2,000 for his son and heir's marriage. [3] This was considerably more than the £666 Hugh the Elder himself paid for the marriages of two of his sons-in-law, Edward Burnell and John St Amand.

Hugh the Elder promised the king that he would give his son and daughter-in-law an annual income of £200, and assigned them the revenues from six of his manors. Hugh did not give the young couple the manors outright, at least at first, and in 1310 they were all still officially in his own possession. [4] Although Hugh the Younger was set to inherit the Despenser/Basset lands when his father died, it is perhaps revealing that Hugh the Elder gave two of his manors to his younger son Philip in 1294 for Philip to hold for the rest of his life, but gave none to his elder son, or at least, not until Hugh the Younger was in his early twenties or older. The Despenser brothers' uncle the earl of Warwick, who had no son until 1314 when he was over 40, arranged in 1306 for his lands to pass ultimately to Philip Despenser, not to Hugh the Younger. [5] Again, this may simply be because Warwick knew that his nephew Hugh would one day come into a sizeable inheritance and thus had no need for his lands, but might mean that he favoured Philip over Philip's elder brother.

Isabella, second of Hugh the Elder's four daughters, married Eleanor Clare's Irish cousin Gilbert Clare, lord of Thomond, almost certainly also in 1306. Gilbert was born in Limerick on 3 February 1281, and was around ten years older than his new wife. [6] He was the son and heir of Thomas Clare (c. 1245–87), Eleanor's uncle (her father's younger brother), and his mother Juliana (d. 1300) was the daughter of Maurice FitzGerald, lord of Offaly. (Confusingly, Eleanor's elder brother, heir to the earldom of Gloucester, was also called Gilbert Clare.) Gilbert 'the Red', earl of Gloucester, had been granted the rights to his namesake nephew's marriage in 1292, and it is highly likely that his widow Joan of Acre arranged Gilbert's marriage to her son-in-law Hugh the Younger's sister. [7] The Despenser-Clare wedding had probably taken place or had at least been arranged by 10 April 1306, when Hugh the Elder was named first in a list of men attesting letters of protection for Gilbert of Thomond. [8]

Nothing is known about Isabella and Gilbert's very short marriage. Later in 1306, Gilbert went on campaign to Scotland with the king, on 6 February 1307 was said to be 'staying in England', and on 22 June 1307 was on his way to Scotland again on the king's service, so Isabella may never have seen her husband's native Ireland before his death later in 1307. Gilbert and his father-in-law were among the men appointed to accompany Edward of Caernarfon to France in March 1307, a visit which ultimately never took place. [9] He was a member of Edward of Caernarfon's household and, with Piers Gaveston, was one of Edward's closest companions, as revealed by several of the prince's letters in 1304/5. [10]

Just after Hugh the Younger's wedding to the king's granddaughter, at this moment of great triumph for the Despenser family, his mother passed away. Isabella Beauchamp died a little before 30 May 1306 when the writ for her inquisition post mortem was issued, and may even have died on the day of her son's wedding. She was probably only in her early forties and was already a grandmother when she died, via her eldest child Maud Chaworth: Maud's daughter Blanche of Lancaster (d. 1380), Lady Wake, had been born by 1306. Isabella's youngest child Elizabeth Despenser was perhaps only about 5 or 6 years old when she lost her mother. Isabella and Hugh the Elder had been married for just over twenty years, and Hugh outlived his wife by another twenty years, but never remarried. In early December 1306, Hugh's stepfather Roger Bigod, earl of Norfolk, also died, in his early sixties. Roger left no children, and in 1312 Edward II gave the earldom of Norfolk to his 12-year-old half-brother, Thomas of Brotherton.

The widowed Hugh the Elder and his newlywed son went to Scotland and the north-east of England in the late summer and autumn of 1306, taking part in a savage military campaign led by Edward of Caernarfon. Hugh the Younger was given letters of protection on his wedding day to accompany his father to Scotland, and Hugh the Elder sent letters from Dunipace near Falkirk, Kildrummy in Aberdeenshire and Newbottle near Durham on 13 August, 15 September and 4 October 1306. [11] Now that the younger Hugh was a knight and a husband, he was deemed old enough to take part in a military campaign. Although he was a keen jouster, and competed in tournaments held at Dunstable in 1309 and on the Continent in 1310, he was not one of the twenty-two young knights who deserted from the 1306 campaign to joust overseas. His brother-in-law Gilbert Clare of Thomond was one, as were his cousin Ralph Basset, two of his Beauchamp cousins, and John Haudlo of Kent, a long-term Despenser adherent. The Béarnais nobleman Piers Gaveston, beloved companion and probably lover of Edward of Caernarfon, and soon to marry Hugh's sister-in-law Margaret Clare, was another. [12]

By the end of November 1306, Hugh the Elder was back at Vastern in Wiltshire, though on 12 April 1307 witnessed one of Edward I's charters at Carlisle, just south of the Scottish border and 300 miles north of Vastern. [13] His brother-in-law Thomas Furnival, husband of his sister Joan, was 'staying in Scotland with Hugh Despenser' on 28 June 1307. [14] Hugh the Younger's whereabouts are uncertain. Given his wife Eleanor's youth, the couple may not have lived together at first. Eleanor turned 14 in October 1306 while her husband was in Scotland or the far north of England, and gave birth to their eldest child in 1308 or early 1309, so was 15 when she first conceived.

Eleanor's mother Joan of Acre, countess of Gloucester, died on 23 April 1307, only in her mid-thirties, and a few weeks later Joan's father, the king, followed her to the grave. Edward I died on 7 July 1307 at the age of 68, in Burgh-by-Sands near Carlisle. He had been leading a campaign against Robert Bruce, formerly earl of Carrick, who had stabbed his rival John 'the Red Comyn' to death in February 1306 and had himself crowned king of Scotland a few weeks later. Edward of Caernarfon, now 23, succeeded as King Edward II, and heard the news of his father's death in or near London on *c.* 11 July. One piece of evidence suggests that Hugh Despenser the Elder was with Edward of Caernarfon at Byfleet in Surrey on 25 June 1307, though as noted above, there is contradictory evidence which places him hundreds of miles away in Scotland with Thomas Furnival at this time. A charter granted by Edward of Caernarfon is dated at Byfleet '25 June, 35 Edward I' (i.e. 1307), and 'Hugh le Despenser' is named third among the eight witnesses. [15] Perhaps this means Hugh the Younger, though he is not otherwise known to have witnessed any charters of Edward II's before 1316, and was always called 'Hugh son of Hugh Despenser' or 'Hugh Despenser the son'.

Chapter 8

Whether he had been with Edward I when he died or was with the new king in the south, Hugh the Elder was certainly in Edward II's company when he was proclaimed king in Carlisle on 20 July 1307, and accompanied Edward when he took his army over the Scottish border. [1] Edward soon returned to England. His inability to deal with Robert Bruce would become one of the defining features of his reign, as would his infatuation with the young Gascon nobleman Piers Gaveston, whom his father, deeply concerned about the two men's relationship, had sent into exile some months before. Edward recalled Gaveston as soon as he could, and made him earl of Cornwall in early August 1307.

Hugh the Elder attended the new king's brief first parliament at Northampton in October 1307. [2] Perhaps rather curiously, however, he did not attend Piers Gaveston's wedding to Margaret Clare, younger sister of his daughter-in-law Eleanor and one of Edward II's nieces, at Berkhamsted Castle on 1 November; he was then in London. [3] It is possible that Hugh the Younger was present at the wedding of his sister-in-law Margaret to the new earl of Cornwall, but he was so insignificant and powerless for the first half of Edward II's reign that no-one bothered to note his presence. Probably Hugh the Younger also attended the funeral of King Edward I, held at Westminster Abbey just five days before the Gaveston-Clare wedding. As the former king's grandson-in-law, Hugh was, rather astonishingly, one of the senior male members of the royal family, though his high rank did not bring with it the slightest political influence whatsoever at this stage.

By the standards of his class and his family, Hugh the Younger was impoverished, with an annual income of around £155; by way of comparison, his brother-in-law the earl of Gloucester earned close to £7,000 a year. Hugh's income came from the revenues of six manors – Oxcroft in Cambridgeshire, Kersey and Layham in Suffolk, and North

Weald Bassett, Lamarsh and Wix in Essex – assigned to him and Eleanor by his father in 1306 and formerly, except Layham, all held by his great-grandfather Philip Basset. Hugh the Elder had promised Edward I to give his son and daughter-in-law £200 a year in land, but the six manors' revenues fell short. [4] Possibly, Hugh the Younger and Eleanor lived on one or several of these manors for the first few years of their married life. Sometime after March 1310, Hugh the Elder gave Kersey to his son outright rather than merely assigning its revenues to him, and probably did the same with the other five manors. The two Hugh Despensers were later accused of deliberately holding Layham between them so that no-one could know which of the two was the rightful tenant and have their proper legal rights against him. [5] Before 1318, Hugh the Elder gave his son his Rutland manor of Ryhall, which he had inherited from his father the justiciar and his grandfather Hugh Despenser (d. 1238). This grant brought Hugh the Younger's annual income to rather more than the promised £200. [6]

Wix, Oxcroft, Lamarsh and North Weald Bassett all had manor-houses with gates, fishponds, rabbit warrens and deer-parks, and Hugh the Younger kept partridges and cattle in them. The manor-house of Kersey had an acre and a half of gardens around it. Henry III had given Kersey to Philip Basset in 1243, and in 1252 granted him the right to hold a market there every Monday. [7] Wix Priory, a house of eight or ten Benedictine nuns, stood on the top of a hill within the manor of Wix, and in the 1330s Hugh the Younger's fifth and youngest daughter Elizabeth Despenser lived there for a while before she married. Small Augustinian priories stood in the villages of Kersey and North Weald Bassett (Latton Priory) as well. [8] Oxcroft, in the parishes of Balsham and West Wratting ten miles south-east of Cambridge, was called *Oxecrofthalle* or 'Oxcroft by Balsham' in the fourteenth century, and Hugh the Younger was accused of ejecting the sisters Alice and Avice Boys from their home there and of imprisoning the older sister. He was also accused of forcibly occupying a house and three acres of pasture in Kersey which should have belonged to Joyce Weyland and her husband Thomas Curzon. Lamarsh, near the River Stour, contained a park, a wood and a piece of land called *Buggelond*, and Wix had a 'park with many wild animals', woods called *Shottele* and *Litleshottele* and a piece of land called *Parkhalle*. [9] In the 1310s North Weald Bassett had forty-six inhabitants who owed homage and service to Hugh the Younger, six women and forty men, including the prior of Latton, a hayward, a cutler, a baker, two brewers, a weaver, two carters, a shepherd, two cowherds and 'Simon of Ireland'. [10] After 1317, Hugh Despenser the Younger made himself the richest and most powerful man in England and Wales. Until he was 30, however, for all the illustriousness of his wife's royal connections and his father's wealth, Hugh was a very minor lord whose sphere of influence was restricted to a handful of small manors in East Anglia.

Hugh's sister Isabella was widowed in November 1307 when Gilbert Clare, lord of Thomond, died aged 26. Isabella was only about 15 or 17 and had no children from her short marriage to Gilbert; his heir was his brother Richard, born c. 1283/5. [11] In 1308 or 1309 Isabella married her second husband, John, Lord Hastings, who was born in May 1262 and was just fourteen months younger than her father, and three decades older than she. Hastings had five children from his first marriage, and his two eldest sons William and John the younger were born in 1282 and 1286 and were a few years older than their new stepmother. This has caused endless confusion among some modern writers, especially as John the elder's first wife (d. 1305) was also called Isabella. John Hastings' marriages to two women with the same given name also caused confusion among his descendants at the end of the fourteenth century, and in 1397 his and Isabella Despenser's 62-year-old granddaughter was asked to give formal testimony on the question of which Hastings relatives descended from which wife. [12] John was already a grandfather when he married the teenaged Isabella Despenser; his elder daughter Joan, called Jonete or Jonetta, gave birth to her son Roger Huntingfield around 1 August 1306, and bore her second son John Huntingfield before her death in 1307. John Hastings' third son, Henry, was a scholar at Oxford or Cambridge in 1310 and became a canon of Lincoln in 1312. [13] Isabella used the Hastings name for the rest of her life rather than her first husband's prestigious name of Clare, perhaps an indication that her second marriage was a happy one, and John was the father of her three children. In 1300 when he was 38, Hastings was called 'he who all honour displays', and was said to be 'in deeds of arms daring and reckless' but 'mild and gracious' to those around him. [14]

Isabella and John had a son named Thomas who died childless and apparently unmarried on 11 January 1333, and their other son, Sir Hugh Hastings, was 24 years old in February 1335 and therefore was born in 1310 or early 1311. [15] Hugh Hastings, named after his Despenser grandfather, married the heiress Margery Foliot and had children; his grandson, Hugh Hastings III, married back into the Despenser family in 1376. Isabella and John Hastings' only daughter was Margaret (d. 1359); she married William Martin (d. 1326) and secondly Robert Wateville (d. 1330), but had no children. To confuse matters, however, in 1397 Isabella's granddaughter Maud de la Mare (her son Hugh's daughter) claimed that Isabella had only two children, Hugh and Thomas, and that Thomas Hastings died soon after his baptism. Maud also stated that 'at the birth of Thomas her grandmother's womb was torn within so that she might no longer bear children'. [16] Evidently Maud had forgotten about her aunt Margaret Wateville, and an entry on the Patent Roll makes it apparent that Thomas Hastings was still alive as an adult on 6 July 1332, so Maud was wrong on that point. [17] Perhaps, though, she was correct that Thomas was Isabella's youngest child and that she was, owing to a very difficult birth, unable to bear more children afterwards. She was to have none with her third husband.

Edward Burnell, husband of Isabella's elder sister Alina, was allowed to take possession of his large inheritance in numerous counties on 6 December 1307 though he was probably only 20 and therefore a few months underage, and had already performed homage to the king. [18] Edward II spent the first Christmas of his reign at Westminster, and scandalously appointed Piers Gaveston as regent of his kingdom while he travelled to France to marry Philip IV's daughter Isabella in January 1308. The royal couple wed in Boulogne and returned to England on 7 February; Hugh Despenser the Elder travelled abroad with the king and was one of two men with Edward in his barge as he came ashore at Dover on his return, a sign of the highest favour. [19] John, Lord Hastings was another of the barons who accompanied Edward to France and travelled with him through Kent to London in February 1308 (the king and queen's coronation took place at Westminster Abbey on 25 February), and was also with the king and Despenser in March 1308. [20] Perhaps he and Despenser discussed Hastings' marriage to Despenser's daughter Isabella, a few months after Gilbert of Thomond's death, though as a widow, Isabella herself surely had more say in her second marriage than in her first. Edward II appointed John Hastings as his seneschal of Gascony, the large territory in south-west France he had inherited and ruled, in October 1309, and Isabella went there with her husband and may have given birth to her children there. Tragedy struck the Hastings family when her stepson William Hastings died in early 1311, and left his younger brother John as the Hastings heir. [21]

Despenser the Elder's loyalty to the king continued throughout 1308, while his brother-in-law Guy Beauchamp, earl of Warwick, and others demanded the exile of Piers Gaveston, sick of Edward II's excessive favouritism towards him. On 12 March 1308, Edward made Despenser custodian of the Wiltshire castles of Marlborough and Devizes, and the *Vita Edwardi Secundi* specifically names him as the king's only important noble supporter in that difficult year. [22] This was not entirely true – Edward's powerful cousin Thomas, earl of Lancaster and John Hastings were some of the others – but is a mark of how close Hugh was known to be to Edward II. His son and heir Hugh the Younger, however, seems to have followed the political lead of the barons hostile to the king and Gaveston including his uncle the earl of Warwick, perhaps as a deliberate policy so that one of the Despensers would always be on the winning side. Edward was forced to consent to Gaveston's exile from England for the second time, and appointed him lord lieutenant of Ireland. Gaveston departed in late June 1308, taking his 14-year-old wife Margaret Clare with him, but Edward had no intention of accepting his beloved's absence, and spent the next year scheming to bring him back. It worked.

Hugh the Elder's second son Philip Despenser married sometime before 29 June 1308, and his bride was the Lincolnshire heiress Margaret Goushill, whose family took their name from the village of Goxhill in Lincolnshire. Margaret was born on 11 or 12 May 1294, so was close to Philip's age; his date of birth is not known, though he is first mentioned on record on 24 June 1294, and may recently have been born then. [23] Probably, it was a marriage of two 14-year-olds, and Edward II permitted them to enter the lands Margaret had inherited from her father Ralph Goushill on 29 June 1308, in Bristol where he had just waved Piers Gaveston off to Ireland. For Hugh the Elder to find a wife for his son who also owned lands in Lincolnshire made good sense, and Alkborough, one of the manors Philip held from his father in the same county, lay close to Margaret's manors of Goxhill, Halton and Immington. All was not well, however, between Hugh and his younger son: sometime before November 1312, Hugh brought a writ of covenant against Philip, i.e. a claim for damages for breach of promise, regarding the lands of Margaret Goushill's inheritance. [24]

Philip's elder brother Hugh the Younger became a father sometime in 1308 or perhaps in early 1309 when Eleanor gave birth to their first child, a boy; she was 15 or 16 and Hugh about 19 or 20 when they became parents. Inevitably their son was also named Hugh, though he always appears in Edward II's accounts as Huchon or Huchoun, obviously his family nickname, and the name by which he will be called throughout this book. The *Anonimalle* chronicle referred to him as Hughelyn or 'little Hugh'. [25] Hugh 'Huchon' Despenser was Edward I's eldest great-grandchild and Edward II's eldest great-nephew (the king was only 24 years old in 1308), and became the Despenser heir behind his father from the moment of his birth.

Piers Gaveston returned to England in late June 1309, a year almost to the day after he had left, and the infatuated king restored him to his earldom of Cornwall. Hugh Despenser the Elder attended the parliament held at Stamford, Lincolnshire in August 1309 which restored Gaveston, and his son Hugh the Younger for once was also in the king's presence when he successfully requested a favour for a Despenser adherent from Edward on 5 August, though he was not one of the barons summoned to parliament. He probably met the king in his father's company, as Hugh the Elder requested various favours from Edward also on 5 August. [26] In or a little before September 1309, two men broke into Hugh the Elder's park at Vastern and hunted deer, but were caught and arrested. One of the men was Master Nicholas Stratton, parson of Garsdon church nine miles away. [27] Hugh lent the king £37 to buy eleven tuns (12,595 litres) of wine sometime in 1308 or 1309; Edward, bequeathed massive debts of £200,000 by his father, was perpetually short of money for the first few years of his reign, and often borrowed it from Hugh. [28]

Chapter 9

Hugh Despenser the Younger spent much of the year 1310 jousting on the Continent, despite an order by Edward II at the end of 1309 that no English noblemen or knights were permitted to leave the country to do so. The infuriated king confiscated Hugh's six manors, but gave them back two months later when he learnt that they in fact belonged to Hugh the Elder. [1] Probably Eleanor accompanied her husband abroad, and may have given birth to their second son, Edward Despenser, shortly before 21 October 1310, when the king paid a messenger for bringing him news of Eleanor. [2] Eleanor turned 18 around 14 October 1310 and it seems that she and Hugh had two sons already, and perhaps they named their second after the king to assuage his anger with Hugh for jousting overseas. Hugh the Elder, still high in the king's favour despite his son's breaking of Edward's prohibition, was with Edward II in Windsor on 8 June 1310. He was in London nine days later when John Mare assigned his manor of Ashmore to him, a grant witnessed by some of Despenser's long-term adherents such as Ralph Camoys and Ingelram Berenger. [3]

The king spent the period from late 1310 until September 1311 at the port of Berwick-on-Tweed on the far north-east coast, trying and failing to deal with Robert Bruce, king of Scotland. Edward was accompanied by his wife Queen Isabella, his nephew the earl of Gloucester, his nephew-in-law the earl of Surrey, and Piers Gaveston, earl of Cornwall and also Edward's nephew-in-law. Hugh the Elder did not go north with the king, and charter witness lists reveal that he witnessed only three of Edward's sixty-four charters issued between 8 July 1310 and 7 July 1311 (Edward's fourth regnal year), all of them on 16 July 1310. On 6 December 1310, Hugh was, as so often, in Vastern. [4] Perhaps his family joined him there for the festive season, including his eldest daughter Alina and son-in-law Edward Burnell, and his son Hugh the Younger, Hugh's wife Eleanor, and their two infant sons. Hugh the Elder's second daughter Isabella gave

41

birth to her son Hugh Hastings sometime in 1310 or the beginning of 1311, most likely in the south-west of France where she and her husband John lived for some years, and his younger son Philip Despenser probably spent most of his time in Lincolnshire with his wife Margaret Goushill. Margaret turned 16 in May 1310 and Philip was also 16 or a little more, so they were old enough now to set up home together. The two youngest Despenser children, Margaret and Elizabeth, were not yet married and perhaps still lived with their father. Hugh the Elder's stepdaughter Maud Chaworth (b. 1282) gave birth to her only son around 1310 or 1312; he is known as Henry of Grosmont after his birthplace in Wales, became the first duke of Lancaster in 1351, and was the grandfather of King Henry IV (b. 1367). Maud also had six daughters, Blanche, Isabella, Maud, Joan, Eleanor and Mary of Lancaster.

A group of earls, bishops and barons who called themselves the Lords Ordainer issued a series of reforms of the king's household and government, the Ordinances, in September 1311, and the king was forced to consent to them. One of the Ordinances demanded the exile of Piers Gaveston from England for the third time. The Lords Ordainer also demanded that several men who were alleged to have left court with the specific intention of assaulting Hugh Despenser the Younger – Sir Robert Darcy, Sir Edmund Bacon and unnamed others – should be removed from the king's household. [5] For all the elder Despenser's loyalty and closeness to the king, members of the royal household decided that it was a good idea to beat up his son, perhaps even on Edward II's own orders (though this is uncertain). As Hugh the Younger, however, was to be arrested in 1316 for repeatedly punching a baron in the face and in 1326 was involved in a brawl in Northamptonshire, he was doubtless capable of giving as good as he got.

Hugh the Elder departed from court again for a few months in late 1311 and 1312: he witnessed one of Edward II's charters at Westminster on 27 December 1311, and the next on 17 July 1312 at the start of the sixth year of Edward's reign. In this regnal year, which ran from 8 July 1312 until 7 July 1313, Hugh witnessed all but one of Edward's sixty-eight charters, and therefore must have been at court most of the time. [6] Despenser was busy at the other end of the country in early 1312, indulging in reprehensibly lawless behaviour. He sent a large group of men to abduct Elizabeth Hertrigg 'with force and arms' from the custody of her guardian George Percy at Wambrook in Dorset on 22 February 1312.

Edward II had granted the rights to Elizabeth's marriage to George Percy in December 1309, and around the same time gave custody of the lands of her late father John Hertrigg to Hugh the Elder. Elizabeth, born around 2 February in either 1303 or 1304, was only 8 or 9 years old. A few months later, the king ordered an official to deliver to Hugh the Elder 'the bodies of the heirs whose marriages have been assigned to him, as he complains that certain of them are eloigned in diverse places so that he cannot have the profit of their marriages'. [7]

While Hugh the Elder was busy kidnapping a young girl in Dorset, momentous events occurred at the other end of the country. Piers Gaveston returned to England from his third exile at the start of 1312. Perhaps he came back only temporarily for the birth of his and Margaret Clare's daughter Joan – Hugh the Younger and Eleanor Despenser's niece, and Gaveston's only legitimate child and heir – but Edward II restored the earldom of Cornwall to him. King and favourite skulked in the north while Edward's furious barons plotted to capture Gaveston. He was besieged at Scarborough Castle in May 1312 by some of Edward's disgruntled barons, and surrendered to Aymer Valence, earl of Pembroke. As Pembroke was taking Gaveston south to his own castle at Wallingford, Gaveston was abducted from Deddington in Oxfordshire, a manor which belonged to Hugh Despenser the Elder, on 10 June 1312 by Despenser's brother-in-law Guy Beauchamp, earl of Warwick. Beauchamp led Gaveston to his castle at Warwick thirty miles away and imprisoned him in the dungeons there, and after the earls of Lancaster, Hereford and Arundel arrived they led Gaveston out on to the road towards Kenilworth, on the earl of Lancaster's lands, and executed him.

News reached the king and his four-months pregnant wife Isabella of France in York a week later. Edward travelled south, leaving the queen behind in York out of the way of possible danger, and met Hugh Despenser the Elder and other advisers in London on 14 July 1312. Edward had already re-appointed Hugh as justice of the forest five days before Gaveston's death, a reward for his loyalty to him, and the very wealthy Hugh lent Edward £2,000 for the expenses of the royal household sometime before November 1312. In exchange, Edward promised him 'all custodies and marriages in the king's hands' until the debt was paid off. [8]

The king was furious at the murder of his beloved Gaveston, as well as shocked and bereaved, and the matter was a personal one for Hugh the Elder too: Gaveston had been abducted by his brother-in-law from one of his own manors. The queen's father Philip IV of France sent negotiators to England to mediate between Edward and Gaveston's killers, and Hugh the Younger's brother-in-law the earl of Gloucester also negotiated between them. They managed to avert a civil war, and the earls of Lancaster, Warwick and Hereford submitted to the king on their knees. Queen Isabella gave birth to her and Edward II's eldest child at Windsor Castle on Monday, 13 November 1312. It was a boy, named Edward after his father and grandfather, and he immediately became heir to the throne. Several chroniclers comment that the king's joy at the birth of his son went some way to assuaging his terrible grief over Gaveston's death, and Edward chose Hugh Despenser the Elder as one of Edward of Windsor's seven godfathers, a very great honour. [9]

Hugh was with the king at Windsor from late October 1312 until the following February, and evidently had access to ready cash while he was there, as he lent Edward £100 on 5 November, £40 on 13 November and £200 on 25 November, and lent 1,000 marks (£666) to a John Marshall of Guildford on 26 December. He also paid for large quantities of wheat and barley to feed the king's household. His son Hugh the Younger joined him at Windsor in early February 1313, and made one of his very few intercessions with Edward II (on behalf of the college of St Elizabeth of Hungary in Winchester) before he became the king's favourite and probably lover in 1318/19. [10]

Chapter 10

A man called Nicholas Litlington was born around 1312 or 1315, and most probably he was the illegitimate son of either Hugh the Elder or Hugh the Younger. Nicholas used the Despenser coat of arms, was closely associated in later decades with Hugh the Younger's grandsons Edward and Henry Despenser, and named his parents as Hugh and Joan. He became prior of Westminster in 1362 and its abbot in 1374, and died in 1386, leaving a number of items marked with the coronet of the Despensers. Not long before his death, he commissioned a missal (a book containing all the texts and instructions to celebrate Mass throughout the year) which displays the Despenser arms in numerous places, and he fed the poor on the anniversary of Edward II's death. [1] It is beyond question that Nicholas was a member of the Despenser family. It is likely that he was Hugh the Younger's son from a relationship with a mistress, though it is not impossible that he was an illegitimate son of Hugh the Elder, and therefore a much younger half-brother of Hugh the Younger. Hugh the Elder lived the last two decades of his life as a widower, and it is certainly possible that he had a mistress.

Hugh the Elder went to Ponthieu in northern France with Edward II and Aymer Valence, earl of Pembroke, a half-nephew of King Henry III and another of the infant Edward of Windsor's godfathers, in December 1312. Edward II had a week-long series of meetings with his father-in-law, Philip IV of France. On 22 January 1313, Hugh was at his manor of Speen in Berkshire, and later the same day travelled the thirty-five miles to Westminster and was still there on 9 and 22 February. The king was also at Westminster at the end of January and in February. [2] Hugh seems to have spent all of March 1313 at court, and on the 25th Edward II pardoned him all the debts he and his ancestors owed to the Exchequer, also pardoned 'all accounts and reckonings' which Hugh should have presented in Edward I and Edward II's reigns in his capacity as a royal official, and granted that any future acquisitions of land by Despenser would never incur any charges at the Exchequer. The king also forgave 'all [Hugh's] trespasses committed in the king's forests'. [3] These were huge favours, and a clear sign of the great affection and gratitude the king felt towards Despenser.

Edward and Queen Isabella spent two months in her native France between May and July 1313. Both Hugh Despensers were among the many English nobles who went with them, and Hugh the Younger's brother-in-law Gilbert Clare, earl of Gloucester, the 29-year-old king's 22-year-old nephew, remained in England as regent. [4] Beginning c. 1313, Edward's clerks started referring to Hugh the Elder as 'Hugh Despenser the father' or as 'Hugh Despenser senior', rather than merely 'Hugh Despenser' as they had almost always done before. This was a tacit acknowledgement that Hugh the Younger existed, at least, but apart from a couple of small favours Edward granted at his nephew-in-law's request in 1312/13, he almost entirely ignored Hugh the Younger while showing great affection to Hugh's wife Eleanor and his father, a rather startling revelation given the king's later dependence on Hugh.

Hugh the Elder's son-in-law John, Lord Hastings died on 10 February 1313, three months before his fifty-first birthday, leaving Isabella Despenser a widow for the second time in her early twenties. John was buried in the Greyfriars' church in Coventry with his parents Henry Hastings and Joan Cantelou, his first wife Isabella Valence, and their daughter Jonete and her son John Huntingfield. The Hastings Chapel in the Greyfriars church – which has long since vanished – displayed the arms of Hastings, Cantelou, Valence and Despenser. John's heir was his second son John, aged 26, and his and Isabella Despenser's three children were mere infants when they lost their father. [5]

Isabella's nephew Philip Despenser II, the only child of her brother Philip and Margaret Goushill, was born in Lincolnshire on 6 April 1313. Philip the father, only about 19 or 20 years old, died shortly before 24 September 1313 of unknown causes. [6] The manors of Parlington and Alkborough, given to him by his father, passed back to Hugh the Elder, though were later held by Philip's descendants. Philip Despenser II had a son, Philip III, born in 1342, and himself died in 1349. Philip III lived until 1401, leaving yet another son called Philip, born around 1365. Philip Despenser IV died in 1424 and left his daughter Margery Wentworth née Despenser as the heir to this cadet branch of the Despenser family, and Parlington and Alkborough were among the manors that passed to her. [7] Margery was the great-great-grandmother of Henry VIII's third queen Jane Seymour (*c.* 1508–37), whose mother was also called Margery Wentworth.

Margaret Goushill, widowed in September 1313, married her second husband Sir John Ros, younger son of William, Lord Ros of Helmsley in Yorkshire, sometime before 22 April 1314. Evidence suggests that Margaret's brother-in-law Hugh Despenser the Younger was not pleased about her second marriage just months after Philip's death: at the Lincoln parliament of February 1316, Hugh punched John Ros in the face over and over until Ros was bloody. Allegedly this was because Ros had tried to arrest Hugh the Elder's household retainer Sir Ingelram Berenger, a man Hugh the Younger must have known for most of his life, though Ros's marriage to Philip Despenser's widow might have been another reason. [8]

Sometime soon after 4 December 1313, a few weeks after losing her brother Philip, Hugh the Elder's third daughter Margaret (b. *c.* late 1290s) married Sir John St Amand, a nobleman of Bedfordshire who also owned lands in Ireland. The marriage cost Hugh the Elder 1,000 marks, the same amount he paid in 1302 for the marriage of his first son-in-law Edward Burnell, and St Amand promised to grant his new wife Margaret lands in three English counties and in Ireland worth £300 a year. [9] This was a larger sum than the annual income Hugh the Elder allowed to his son and heir Hugh the Younger. John St Amand was much Margaret Despenser's senior, born sometime between 1276 and 1283, and was the heir of his brother Amaury (b. 1268) when the latter died childless in July 1310. Another St Amand brother, Guy, was the elder twin of Amaury and was named as their father's heir in 1285, but died before November 1287. Their sister Hawise St Amand married Simon Montacute and became a grandmother in or before the late 1290s, and her grandson William Montacute (b. *c.* 1301) became earl of Salisbury in 1337. [10] Although he was at least 30 and possibly 37 when he married Margaret, John seems not to have been married before, and had perhaps taken minor orders in the church until his brother died and made him a landowner. Various entries in the chancery rolls call him 'Master John St Amand', meaning that he had a bachelor's or master's degree in law from Oxford or Cambridge, a qualification he had attained by February 1301. [11] Edward I pardoned John in 1305 for helping an Alice Droys to escape from Oxford Castle and for 'detaining the castle against the king's will' with at least five other men. John's great-grandfather Amaury St Amand (d. 1241) had been chosen as Edward I's godfather in 1239. [12]

Margaret and John's son Amaury (whose name also often appears as Emery, Aymer or Almaric), the St Amand heir, was born on 20 February 1315, fourteen months after their wedding. On the day of Amaury's birth, at the request of Margaret's brother Hugh Despenser the Younger, Edward II gave permission for John St Amand to settle two of his own manors on himself and Margaret jointly. [13] This grant should probably be interpreted as John's reward to Margaret for giving him a son and heir. They also had a daughter, named after Margaret's late mother Isabella Beauchamp, who married Richard Haudlo. Richard was the eldest son of the long-term Despenser retainer Sir John Haudlo, whose second wife Maud was the sister and heir of Hugh the Elder's son-in-law Edward Burnell: an example of how members of the Despenser affinity intermarried, even after the catastrophic downfall and disgrace of the two Hugh Despensers in 1326. Margaret St Amand is rather obscure, and like her brother Philip Despenser, seems to have died young. The date of her death is not recorded, but she was already dead when John St Amand passed away in January 1330, as there is no record of her receiving widow's dower and she was not an executor of his will. She may have been dead as early as 25 July 1322, when John leased out one of his holdings to a couple called William and Alice Bythewatere, and Margaret is not mentioned in the grant. [14]

Edward II had inherited a war in Scotland from his father, after Robert Bruce crowned himself king in 1306 against the wishes of Edward I and his son, who considered themselves rightful overlords of the northern kingdom. Edward II's inability to deal with Bruce had enabled the latter to entrench his position over the previous few years and to gain a considerable number of powerful allies, and the English king's long sojourn in Berwick-on-Tweed in 1310/11 achieved nothing. In 1314 Edward finally took an army north, hoping to defeat Bruce once and for all, but the battle of Bannockburn fought near Stirling Castle on 23 and 24 June 1314 has gone down in history as one of England's most humiliating military defeats ever, and the king's eldest nephew Gilbert Clare, earl of Gloucester, was killed. Gloucester's brother-in-law Hugh Despenser the Younger and Hugh's father fought at Bannockburn, and were both among the knights who accompanied Edward II during his long and desperate gallop to the safety of Dunbar Castle to evade capture after the battle. [15] The long-term Despenser adherent Ralph Camoys, soon to marry Hugh the Elder's youngest daughter, also fought at Bannockburn, as did Hugh's son-in-law Edward Burnell. Eleven men are named as accompanying Hugh the Younger to the battle. [16] Edward II's defeat in Scotland weakened his political position at home, and his cousin and enemy Thomas of Lancaster, one of Piers Gaveston's killers in 1312, took the opportunity to assert his dominance over the English government. Lancaster forced Hugh Despenser the Elder, whom he disliked, to leave court. [17]

The earl of Gloucester left his widow Maud, one of the many daughters of Richard Burgh, earl of Ulster, and a second cousin of Hugh Despenser the Younger and his siblings. Although Countess Maud claimed to be pregnant with her late husband's son, she was not, and Gloucester's heirs therefore were his sisters: Eleanor, Hugh's wife; Margaret, widow of Piers Gaveston; and Elizabeth, widow of the earl of Ulster's eldest son John (d. 1313). Gloucester had been one of the richest men in the kingdom, and now Hugh the Younger and Eleanor were set to inherit one-third of the vast Clare inheritance (minus the dowager countess's dower) with lands in England, Wales and Ireland. This was the greatest windfall the Despenser family would ever receive; it made their fortune. Hugh and Eleanor would, however, have to wait for almost three and a half years before they saw any of their lands.

Chapter 11

On or soon before 20 May 1315, disgruntled that the king had not yet ordered the Clare inheritance to be given to the late earl of Gloucester's co-heirs, Hugh Despenser the Younger seized Tonbridge Castle in Kent, one of the earl's castles. Almost certainly he did this simply to make a point, as he surrendered possession of the castle after only a few days, and was never punished for it. His dramatic action did not, however, have the desired effect of forcing Edward to begin the division of the Clare inheritance eleven months after his nephew Gloucester's death.

Alina Burnell, Hugh the Elder's eldest child, was widowed on 23 August 1315 when Edward Burnell died at the age of 28. Alina received her dower and the lands she had held jointly with her husband on 3 February 1316, and an inquisition revealed that she held four manors in three counties by gift of her father's adherent Sir Ingelram Berenger. [1] As the couple had no children, Burnell's heir was his younger sister Maud, widow of Sir John Lovell, who was killed at Bannockburn. Not long after her brother's death, Maud married her second husband, the Despenser adherent Sir John Haudlo, without Edward II's permission. Maud's first cousin and nearest surviving male relative Edmund Fitzalan, earl of Arundel, imprisoned Haudlo at various castles in Shropshire from 9 October to 26 December 1315, presumably to express his dissatisfaction with their marriage. [2] Guy Beauchamp, earl of Warwick, Hugh the Elder's brother-in-law, also died in August 1315, leaving his 18-month-old son Thomas as his heir.

Hugh the Elder spent almost all the period from August 1314 until May 1316 away from court. He made a short visit to the king in early July 1315 when Edward was at Westminster, and most probably also attended the funeral of Piers Gaveston when Edward finally had him buried at Langley Priory in Hertfordshire at the beginning of 1315. [3] It seems that Edward and Hugh had little option but to consent to the earl of Lancaster's demand that Hugh be removed from court. Hugh was, as so often, at Vastern on 11 September 1315 when he received a letter from Edward. The king requested that Hugh travel to Paris at the end of November regarding 'the accomplishment of the peace' between Edward and the king of France. Edward's father-in-law Philip IV had died on 29 November 1314 and the king of France was now Philip's son Louis X (b. 1289), eldest of the three brothers of Edward's queen, Isabella. The matter to be discussed in Paris related to Edward's duty to travel to France to pay homage to Louis as his new overlord for his French territories of Gascony and Ponthieu. (As it happened, Louis X died on 5 June 1316 after a reign of only a year and a half, and Edward managed to avoid having to pay homage to him.) Hugh sent back a non-committal reply: he promised that 'if God give me life and health' he would travel to Westminster in early October 1315 to discuss the situation with the archbishop of Canterbury and other members of the royal council, and thereafter 'they will advise you and I will advise you of what can be done in the business'.

Edward II wrote to his chancellor and his treasurer complaining that 'the said Hugh has not promised outright that he will attend to the business,' and asked them to ascertain 'if the said Hugh can be induced to undertake the charge of the business'. [4] Edward's referring to Hugh by his first name without 'Sir' was rather discourteous and reveals his irritation with the older man, and the matter indicates that although Hugh the Elder served Edward I and his son loyally for four decades, he was not merely a sycophant who jumped every time the king snapped his fingers, but felt confident enough to turn down a royal request if he did not wish to do it. Possibly the king was rather annoyed with Hugh in 1315 anyway, as on 28 February and again on 13 July he ordered investigations into Hugh's conduct as justice of the forest, with reference to 'frequent complaints of acts of oppression alleged to have been committed' in his capacity there (unless they were ordered by the earl of Lancaster, battling with his cousin Edward for control of the government). [5]

Edward continued to refuse to partition the lands of his late nephew the earl of Gloucester, on the grounds that Gloucester's widow Maud was pregnant. Hilariously, the pretence continued for two and a half years after the earl's death at Bannockburn; the king wished his nephew's vast income to pour into his own coffers for as long as possible and therefore delayed the partition of Gloucester's lands, and he did not trust

Hugh Despenser the Younger at all. The king took a month's holiday in September/October 1315 and went swimming and rowing in the Fens with 'a great company of common people', according to the Westminster chronicle *Flores Historiarum*; he was at Fen Ditton when he sent his irritated letter about Hugh the Elder to his chancellor and treasurer. Three weeks later, Edward received a visit at Impington in the Fens from Hugh the Younger, who demanded that his wife Eleanor's share of her late brother's inheritance be given to them. Hugh was fobbed off; he subsequently sent a petition setting out the reasons why he and Eleanor should have their lands. The king refused again, claiming via his lawyers that 'the case was novel and hitherto unseen in the realm'. [6] Even Edward's great affection for his eldest niece Eleanor was not enough to persuade him to hand her lands over to her and her husband.

Hugh the Younger went before the king again at the Lincoln parliament of January/February 1316 and demanded his and Eleanor's share of the Clare inheritance. He was so infuriated at the refusal and the ongoing pretence that Countess Maud was going to bear her husband's son twenty months after his death that he beat up Sir John Ros, second husband of his brother Philip's widow Margaret Goushill. He was arrested and admitted liability for a massive fine of £10,000, of which he never paid a penny. Hugh the Younger witnessed his first-ever charter of Edward II's at Westminster on 14 May 1316, and as of *c.* late 1315 there is evidence that he was at court much more often than previously. Roger Mortimer of Chirk (b. *c.* 1256) and his nephew Roger Mortimer of Wigmore (b. 1286/7), men Hugh the Younger loathed and allegedly swore revenge on for his grandfather's death at Evesham in 1265, witnessed the same charter, and so did Hugh the Elder, finally back at court after his long absence. [7]

At an uncertain date before 13 June 1316, Hugh the Elder's fourth daughter and youngest child Elizabeth (b. *c.* 1300) married one of her father's loyal adherents: Ralph, Lord Camoys. [8] As well as Camoys' long-term service in Despenser's retinue, there was a family connection: he was a cousin of Ralph Goushill, whose daughter and heir Margaret married Elizabeth Despenser's elder brother Philip in June 1308. Ralph Camoys did homage for a manor in Norfolk and was granted royal permission to enter it in November 1294, and must have been at least 21 then, so he was born in November 1273 at the latest. He was knighted in May 1306 with Edward of Caernarfon and his future brother-in-law

Hugh the Younger, and owned lands mostly in Sussex. [9] Ralph was more than twenty-five years Elizabeth Despenser's senior and over 40 when they married, and had a son, Thomas, from his first marriage to Margaret Brewes, who was old enough to fight in a battle in March 1322. [10]

By 3 February 1321, Elizabeth Despenser had three or perhaps four children: Ralph, John and Isabella Camoys, and possibly Margaret. [11] Elizabeth must have named her daughter Isabella after her late mother, and Isabella Camoys became abbess of Romsey Abbey in Hampshire in 1352 and held the position until her death in 1396. As Margaret was the name of Ralph Camoys' first wife, it is possible that Margaret Camoys was Elizabeth's stepdaughter, not her daughter. John Camoys, probably Elizabeth's second son, was said to be 40 years old in 1360, and died sometime before April 1372. [12] When Elizabeth's husband Ralph Camoys died in 1335, his heir was his eldest son Thomas, Elizabeth's stepson, who died in April 1372. As Thomas's only son died before him, the Camoys heir in 1372 was Elizabeth's grandson Thomas Camoys the younger, her son John's son, who was born *c.* 1350. (Her eldest son Ralph died without children.) Thomas lived long enough to command the rearguard of the English army at the battle of Agincourt in October 1415 when he was about 65, and his second wife, Elizabeth Percy née Mortimer (b. 1371), was a great-great-granddaughter of Edward II. [13] Thomas Camoys was the grandfather of William, Lord Hastings (b. *c.* 1430), a close friend of Edward IV who was executed by Edward's brother Richard, duke of Gloucester, in 1483.

Elizabeth's second or third daughter Katherine Camoys was born sometime after February 1321, and was betrothed in September 1324 to William, born January 1321, son and heir of Ralph, Lord Greystoke (1299–1323). [14] William Greystoke ultimately married someone else, so probably Katherine died young. Elizabeth's third son Hugh Camoys, named after her father, first appears on record on 29 July 1324. [15] Hugh Camoys was a member of Edward III's household in 1345, was given a manor by his first cousin the earl of Lancaster in 1350, and witnessed one of Lancaster's grants in 1359. Hugh witnessed another grant of land, meadow and wood to his sister Isabella, abbess of Romsey, in 1376. He married a woman named Joan, and was still alive in October 1387 and dead by July 1394. [16]

Hugh Despenser the Younger does not seem to have been close to any of his brothers-in-law except Ralph Camoys. In February 1320, Ralph was made constable of Windsor Castle on the same day that Hugh was made constable of Odiham Castle in Hampshire, almost certainly as a result of Hugh's new influence with Edward II, and that summer Hugh appointed Ralph as his attorney when he went to France as part of Edward's large retinue. [17] Another indication of Hugh and Ralph's closeness dates to April 1319. Hugh, Ralph and Elizabeth were all pardoned by Edward for acquiring 'the bailiwick of the forestership' of the royal forests of Alice Holt and Woolmer in Hampshire from a Richard Venuz for Camoys and his heirs, without the king's licence. Somewhat peculiarly, on the same day as the pardon, Ralph Camoys was appointed with two other men to investigate the sudden death of Richard Venuz in Hampshire. [18]

A knight who almost became yet another of Hugh the Younger's brothers-in-law was Peter Ovedale or Uvedale, who inherited lands from his maternal grandfather and from his father John Ovedale (d. 1322), a Despenser associate. Peter (b. 1290) made an indenture with Hugh in London on 30 August 1316 that he would serve in Hugh's retinue with ten men-at-arms 'in peace and war in England, Scotland and Wales', and 'further, should he take to wife Lady Hastings, the said Hugh's sister, he should pay the said Hugh 400 marks.' Ultimately, however, the planned marriage did not go ahead. It is perhaps significant, given that either Hugh the Younger or Hugh the Elder most probably fathered Nicholas Litlington from an extramarital relationship, that one of the manors the Ovedale family held was Litlington in Cambridgeshire, which lay twenty miles from the Despenser manor of Oxcroft. [19]

Chapter 12

In May 1317, Edward II finally gave up his pretence that the dowager countess of Gloucester would bear a posthumous child to her husband two years and eleven months after his death. He ordered Gloucester's vast inheritance to be divided into three parts for his sisters Eleanor Despenser, Margaret Gaveston and Elizabeth Burgh. Just weeks before, he had married Margaret and Elizabeth to his two current court favourites, Sir Hugh Audley and Sir Roger Damory, and in November 1317 the partition of the Gloucester lands was finally ready. Eleanor and Hugh the Younger received the lordship of Glamorgan in South Wales and other estates in England to a value of over £1,400 a year, and when the dowager countess of Gloucester died in 1320 and the third of the Clare estates she had held as dower was shared among the three sisters, the Despensers' total income increased to well in excess of £2,000 a year. Finally, Hugh the Younger was rich, and the great lordship of Glamorgan would belong to the Despenser family for generations.

Hugh the Younger and Eleanor built a large family. By October 1310, they almost certainly already had two sons, and their eldest daughter was named after Hugh's late mother; Isabella Despenser was 8 when she married the earl of Arundel's 7-year-old son in February 1321, so was born in 1312 or the beginning of 1313. [1] Joan, the second daughter, named after her maternal grandmother Joan of Acre, countess of Gloucester, may have been born around 1314/15. In 1323, Joan Despenser was betrothed to John FitzGerald, son and heir of the earl of Kildare, who was born in 1314 but died shortly after his betrothal. [2] Joan subsequently became a nun at Shaftesbury Abbey in Dorset. The third son, Gilbert, was probably the fifth Despenser child and was perhaps born around 1316/17, though does not appear on record until July 1322. Some writers have wrongly stated that Gilbert was one of the children of Hugh the Younger and Eleanor's second son Edward, but several entries on the Charter Roll in

1322 clearly state that he was Hugh and Eleanor's son, and they named him after Eleanor's father and brother. Gilbert Despenser did not die until 1382, a fact which may have led some writers to conclude wrongly that he came from a younger generation of Despensers. Even the chronicler of Tewkesbury Abbey, the Despenser mausoleum, misidentified Gilbert. [3] Gilbert's sister Joan, nun of Shaftesbury, lived a long life as well, and died in November 1384 when she was 70 or almost. She has also sometimes been identified as the daughter of Hugh the Younger and Eleanor's son Edward, but was certainly their own second daughter.

Hugh and Eleanor's youngest surviving son was John Despenser, for whom Edward II bought a saddle in November 1324. [4] As John was then old enough to ride, he must have been born in the early 1320s at the latest. A fifth Despenser son died at the end of 1320 or beginning of 1321, probably very soon after birth. Edward II bought cloth to drape over the coffin or tomb of 'the son of Sir Hugh Despenser junior', unnamed, on about 13 January 1321. [5] A survey of London in 1603 listed the people buried in the house of the Austin Friars in the city, including 'Philip Spencer sonne to Sir Hugh Spencer, Dame Isabell daughter to Sir Hugh'. [6] The wording makes it apparent that Philip and Isabella were siblings, and both Hugh Despenser the Elder and Hugh the Younger had daughters named Isabella. Philip Despenser I, second son of Hugh the Elder, was a landowner in Lincolnshire, and it therefore seems very unlikely that he would have been buried in London on his death in 1313. As the 'Philip Spencer' interred in the Austin Friars was not given the title 'Sir', and Philip Despenser I was a knight, this Philip was most probably a son of Hugh the Younger. Although the name of the Despenser boy who died at the beginning of 1321 does not appear in any fourteenth-century record yet discovered, it is likely that Hugh and Eleanor would have named one of their sons after Hugh's late brother. Hugh spent part of January 1321 in London and Westminster, so it makes sense that his little son would have been buried in the city.

The third Despenser daughter was Eleanor, named after her mother. She was betrothed in or before July 1325 to the future earl of Pembroke, Laurence Hastings, who was born in March 1321. [7] It is unlikely that she was much older than he and must have been born in the late 1310s or early 1320s, and was raised with her mother's cousins, Edward II's daughters Eleanor of Woodstock (b. June 1318) and Joan of the Tower (b. July 1321). It is possible that the little Despenser boy who died soon after birth and was apparently called Philip was a twin of either John or Eleanor. The fourth daughter, Margaret, was born at the royal manor of Cowick in Yorkshire on or just before 2 August 1323, and the fifth daughter and youngest Despenser child, Elizabeth, was most probably the infant born to Eleanor at the royal manor of Sheen on or shortly before 14 December 1325. [8]

Nine children of Hugh the Younger and Eleanor survived childhood and at least one did not. There is every reason to suppose that Hugh and Eleanor's marriage was a successful one, and where Eleanor's itinerary can be established in and after 1318 she was almost always at court with her husband and her uncle the king. It seems probable that Hugh and Edward II had a sexual relationship from the late 1310s onwards, and as Eleanor was almost always with them, she can hardly have been unaware of it. She can hardly have failed to be aware of her husband's penchant for extortion and false imprisonment in the 1320s either, but she remained one of his and her uncle's most faithful supporters until both men were brought down in 1326/7.

Hugh the Younger's rise to influence began when he and Eleanor were granted their share of her late brother's enormous wealth in late 1317, but it was the appointment bestowed on him around August or October 1318 which really catapulted him to great power. The English magnates made him Edward II's chamberlain, the man responsible for controlling access to the king, apparently against Edward's own wishes. After Hugh became royal chamberlain and spent most of his time with Edward, the king became infatuated with or in some way dependent on him. How this happened cannot be known; there are no documents to illuminate Hugh's great rise in the king's affections after Edward had disliked him, or at the very least had been indifferent to him, for many years (the two men must have known each other most of their lives). Hugh was immensely ambitious and greedy for power and money, and perhaps deliberately set out to seduce his wife's uncle to achieve his goals.

In February 1312, Hugh the Elder had sent men to abduct the child heiress Elizabeth Hertrigg from the custody of her guardian George Percy, and the kidnap was not the end of Elizabeth's woes at his hands. She married George's son John, and in or shortly before July 1318, several Despenser men broke into the Percys' home and stole their goods. John Berenger, 14-year-old son of the loyal Despenser adherent Sir Ingelram, was accused of raping the unfortunate Elizabeth during this robbery and was taken into custody. [9] Elizabeth's second ordeal at the hands of Despenser followers demonstrates that Hugh the Elder had continued his feud against George Percy. The Percys' home which Despenser ordered his men to attack was in the village of Great Chalfield in Wiltshire, just a few miles from some of Despenser's own extensive properties in the same county, so this may have been a local feud. Despenser's efforts over many years to increase his landholdings in Wiltshire by fair means or foul argue that he wished to make himself a powerful force in the county and its greatest landowner, and that he brooked no opposition.

Sometime before 20 November 1318, Hugh the Elder's second daughter Isabella Hastings, who lost her second husband John in February 1313, married her third, Ralph Monthermer. Ralph had been widowed from Edward II's sister Joan of Acre for eleven years and was the father of the youngest four of her eight children, and was the stepfather of Hugh the Younger's wife Eleanor, Joan's eldest daughter. Like her previous husband, Ralph Monthermer was decades Isabella's senior: he was born *c.* 1262, so was John Hastings' age and just slightly younger than Isabella's father. [10] Isabella and Ralph married without a licence from Edward II, and he temporarily seized their lands, the usual punishment. He pardoned them and restored their lands in August 1319 after they promised to pay a fine of 1,000 marks. They never did pay the fine, and in May 1321 Edward revoked it. [11] Isabella and Ralph had no children together although she was only about 26 or 28 when they married, and perhaps Isabella's granddaughter Maud de la Mare was correct when she stated that Isabella's womb was damaged when she gave birth to her son Thomas Hastings in or before 1313. Isabella continued to use her second husband's name throughout her third marriage, and in his will, Monthermer called her 'Isabella Hastings, my dearest wife'. [12]

Isabella's father Hugh the Elder went to Spain on Edward II's service in early 1319. He appointed Hugh the Younger and Ingelram Berenger as his attorneys while he was away, and among the men he took with him were his son-in-law John St Amand and John Haudlo. [13] Ralph Camoys, another son-in-law, also went to northern Spain in early 1319, on pilgrimage to Santiago de Compostela. Perhaps his wife Elizabeth travelled there with him. [14] In September 1319, Hugh the Younger was one of the many English noblemen who went with the king to besiege the port of Berwick-on-Tweed, captured by Robert Bruce the year before, but the English failed to take Berwick back. One of the men in Hugh's retinue was his cousin Thomas Furnival the younger, son of Hugh the Elder's sister Joan. [15]

Hugh the Elder prepared to go overseas on royal business again in 1320: Edward II appointed him and the Kent baron Bartholomew Badlesmere to travel to Gascony 'to reform its state and to correct the excesses of his [Edward's] ministers there'. The two men were given 'full power to inquire into inadequate ministers, and to remove those that they find insufficient'. In the end, however, their mission was cancelled, though both Hugh and his son Hugh the Younger travelled to France with Edward in June 1320 when the king paid homage for his French lands to his brother-in-law Philip V, brother and successor of Louis X. Hugh the Younger appointed Ralph Camoys, now returned from Santiago, as one of his attorneys while he was away. [16]

Bartholomew Badlesmere was closely associated with Hugh the Younger as well as with Hugh the Elder in 1319/20. Not only did Hugh the Younger rescue Badlesmere's wife Margaret when she was besieged inside a house by a large armed crowd demanding a ransom from her in the Hertfordshire town of Cheshunt sometime in 1319, Hugh and Bartholomew were jointly involved in some deeply shady business concerning one John Lashley of Essex. [17] Lashley was imprisoned for theft in Colchester, and Hugh removed him from there, imprisoned him in his own prison (presumably on one of his Essex manors) and forced him to hand over his manor of Lindsell to Hugh. Hugh then granted the manor to Badlesmere. [18] This is an early sign of his penchant for imprisoning men and women until they gave him lands or money, and far worse was to come when Hugh reached the zenith of his power.

Chapter 13

In 1319, Hugh Despenser the Younger began his meteoric rise in the king's affections. Somehow Hugh turned the king's dislike or indifference to him into what appears to be infatuation, and soon Edward would do whatever Hugh wished him to do. The *Anonimalle* chronicle wrote that Edward 'loved [Hugh] dearly, with all his heart and mind, above all others', and Geoffrey le Baker, in the early 1350s, stated that Hugh had enchanted Edward's mind. [1] This probably reveals that Hugh the Younger was an excellent manipulator; it is remarkable that Edward, entirely indifferent towards his nephew-in-law for many years, became dependent on Hugh mere months after they began spending time together. By 1326, the two men were so close that one abbey annalist called them 'the king and his husband'. [2] Unlike Piers Gaveston, who enjoyed the wealth that came from being the king's beloved but had little if any interest in governing through Edward, Hugh the Younger parlayed his new-found status into considerable political influence.

Edward's excessive favouritism towards Hugh caused much grumbling, and in October 1320 the two men pushed some of the English magnates over the edge. Hugh yearned to own the Gower Peninsula in South Wales, which belonged to a baron called William Braose. Braose's son-in-law John, Lord Mowbray took possession of Gower, and Edward confiscated it, presumably with the intention of giving it to Hugh. This proved the final straw. The king travelled to Gloucester in early 1321 to attempt to reconcile the disaffected lords, spending two nights with Hugh the Elder at Vastern on his way, but to no avail. On 4 May 1321, the rebel lords, whom Edward began calling the 'Contrariants', began a massive assault on Hugh the Younger's lands in South Wales, an event known to posterity as the Despenser War. The assault was led by Edward's brother-in-law Humphrey Bohun, earl of Hereford, Roger Mortimer of Chirk and his nephew Roger Mortimer of Wigmore, Lords Mowbray and Clifford, and

Hugh Audley and Roger Damory, husbands of Hugh the Younger's sisters-in-law Margaret and Elizabeth. At least seventeen of Hugh the Younger's adherents were killed, and others were badly wounded or imprisoned. Hugh's ten castles and twenty-three manors in South Wales, including Cardiff, Caerphilly, Neath, Llanbethian and Dinefwr, were attacked, and the Marchers moved into England and attacked his lands there as well, even in distant Essex, Suffolk and Lincolnshire. The constable of Hugh's castle of Neath, John Iweyn, and one of Iweyn's servants, were beheaded without a trial in Swansea and their goods were stolen. [3]

The Contrariants' spite and lust for plunder were nowhere near sated after nearly six weeks of destruction, and they aimed their rage at Hugh the Elder as well. They met at Vastern, presumably because they knew it was his favourite residence, on 11 June 1321. They sacked it, and subsequently travelled through the elder Hugh's sixty-seven manors across England, vandalising and robbing them. [4] His daughter Alina Burnell also saw four of her manors in Warwickshire, Worcestershire and Shropshire attacked and robbed, and Ingelram Berenger and John Haudlo complained that their own manors had been plundered. [5] The Contrariants' spiteful destructiveness is almost beyond imagining; they killed fish in the two Hughs' fishponds, tore down hedges, smashed doors and windows, burned down houses and barns, destroyed or stole whatever goods they found, either carried away or burned the Despensers' crops, and stole their livestock and horses. It was the Despensers' innocent tenants who suffered the most, who saw their homes destroyed, their animals taken or killed, their food supplies stolen or burned, and their livelihoods taken from them, and who were imprisoned and forced to pay ransoms to the Contrariants for their release. The 'poor people' of Hugh the Elder's manor of Loughborough in Leicestershire were chased away from their homes for three months, and the residents of Hugh the Younger's manor of Swansea and the priory of Brecon begged the king to help them. [6] The Despenser War, far from being a heroic enterprise of brave men battling a tyrannical king and his favourite for their rights, involved many weeks of astonishing destruction, mayhem and murder across much of Wales and England. The Marchers, carried away with their own brutal vindictiveness and lust for plunder, attacked manors which did not belong to the Despensers, and even went so far as to steal from a Yorkshire church. [7]

The long list of Hugh the Elder's belongings stolen by Contrariants reveals that he was a great fan of chess: they stole several of his sets 'made partly of nut and partly of ginger-root', and another three sets made of crystal. Hugh had stored about £1,000 in cash – several million in modern terms – at Stanley Abbey near Chippenham in Wiltshire, which was stolen, along with his charters and other documents, gold and silver cups and other silver vessels. He kept many more items at the royal castle of Marlborough, of which he was constable, including books – which books were not specified – and a gold cup, a gold cross, an ebony and ivory cross and gold cloths for his chapel.

At a parliament held in London in August 1321, the Contrariants forced Edward II to consent to the perpetual exile and disinheritance of both Hugh Despensers, and the two men were given a deadline of 29 August to leave their homeland for good. Hugh the Elder went abroad, though where exactly is not known; Hugh the Younger became a pirate in the English Channel with the knowledge and connivance of the king, who placed him under the protection of the sailors of the Cinque Ports. Hugh the Younger departed from England about a month after the assigned deadline, and returned at least once to meet the king and to plot the downfall of his enemies. He made a fortune attacking ships and seizing their cargo in the English Channel, and one chronicler refers to him as a 'sea-monster' and 'master of the seas'. He may even have attacked the port of Southampton at the beginning of October 1321 in the company of a baron of Winchelsea called Robert Batail. [8]

Edward II, who could always be stirred to action when someone he loved was threatened, began a campaign against the Contrariants at the end of 1321, with most of the English earls in his company. A royal army led by Sir Andrew Harclay, sheriff of Cumberland, defeated the Contrariant force at the battle of Boroughbridge in Yorkshire on 16 March 1322. The earl of Hereford was killed fighting for the Contrariants, and the earl of Lancaster was captured. Roger Mortimer of Wigmore and Roger Mortimer of Chirk were among the Contrariants who submitted to the king before Boroughbridge and were imprisoned in the Tower of London; Roger Damory was killed during a skirmish at Burton-on-Trent before the battle of Boroughbridge; and Hugh Audley was captured at Boroughbridge and imprisoned.

Ralph, Lord Camoys certainly stood on the side of his Despenser father-in-law and brother-in-law in 1321/2, but his eldest son Thomas, Elizabeth Despenser's stepson, fought against the royal army at Boroughbridge. [9] In March/April 1322 in the aftermath of the Contrariants' defeat, about twenty-two noblemen and knights were executed, including Lords Mowbray and Clifford and the royal and extraordinarily wealthy earl of Lancaster, whom the king ordered to be beheaded just outside Lancaster's own Yorkshire castle of Pontefract in a deliberate parody of Piers Gaveston's execution a decade before. According to one chronicler, Hugh Despenser the Younger hurled malicious and contemptuous words in Lancaster's face when the defeated earl arrived at Pontefract. [10] Hugh and his father, the king, seven earls and several royal justices were the men who sentenced Lancaster to death, though in later years it served the Despensers' enemies well to pretend that the two Hughs had imposed the death sentence on him alone. Dozens of other Contrariants were imprisoned and a handful fled to the Continent, and on 1 August 1323 Roger Mortimer of Wigmore escaped from the Tower of London and joined them there.

The two Hugh Despensers returned to England in or before early March 1322. Edward II officially pardoned them at the parliament held in York in May, and created Hugh the Elder earl of Winchester. Despenser was now 61, and despite his widespread unpopularity, few if any contemporary chroniclers grumbled about his appointment, perhaps because he was a high-ranking nobleman and his elevation did not seem undeserved. Of the twenty manors forfeited by the executed and imprisoned Contrariants which the king bestowed on Despenser in May/June 1322 to support his new title, sixteen were in Wiltshire, including Warminster, Heytesbury and Castle Combe, and three were in neighbouring Gloucestershire. [11] Hugh the Elder had already held seventeen manors in Wiltshire, and now the number was doubled.

Hugh built himself a large power base in his favourite county, and by 1325, his son controlled almost all of South Wales as well as owning numerous manors across the south of England. Between 1322 and 1326, Hugh the Younger would be the real ruler of the kingdom, and made himself astonishingly rich, with an income even higher than his late brother-in-law the earl of Gloucester had ever received. The king's infatuation with Despenser the Younger was as strong as ever, and Edward allowed Hugh to extort manors and lands from various men and women, including Elizabeth Comyn, Alice Lacy, countess of Lincoln (Thomas of Lancaster's widow), John Botetourt, John Sutton and even the king's own half-brother Thomas of Brotherton, earl of Norfolk. Elizabeth Comyn was held captive at two of Hugh the Elder's manors in

Surrey until she released some of her lands to him and his son. People further down the social scale also became victims of Hugh the Younger's greed, such as Thomas Bishopstone, William Cockerell, John Deyville, Alice Danvers and untold others, who were imprisoned or deprived of their lands until they agreed to pay a fine, usually £100, the equivalent of several hundred thousand pounds in today's money. [12]

Even Hugh the Younger's loyal ally Sir John Inge, sheriff of Glamorgan, angered the royal favourite in some way. Despites his years of faithful and industrious service to him, Hugh imprisoned Inge and members of his council and forced them to acknowledge a debt of £300 to him to secure Inge's release, of which they had paid £200 by the time of Hugh's downfall and death. Inge's councillor Thomas Langdon died in Hugh's prison. [13] Hugh victimised his own sister-in-law Elizabeth Burgh, Eleanor Despenser's widowed sister: he forced her to exchange her valuable lordship of Usk for his much less valuable lordship of Gower, and later took Gower from her as well. Edward II permitted Hugh's appalling treatment of his own niece and even facilitated it. Hugh the Elder enthusiastically joined in his son's land grabs, and after his downfall was accused of imprisoning men and women until they handed over manors to him. Alice Lacy, countess of Lincoln, was forced to grant her great North Wales lordship of Denbigh to Hugh the Elder, and she and Elizabeth Comyn were the highest-ranking of the men's many victims.

Chapter 14

Hugh the Younger's eldest son, Hugh or 'Huchon', was 13 or 14 when his father and grandfather returned to England and were restored to their lands in 1322. Huchon's great-uncle the king sent him to 'take fat venison' in twenty-four counties across England in July 1322, in the company of nine expert huntsmen. These hunts lasted until 25 October. [1] Huchon appears on record as 'Hugh Despenser, son of Hugh Despenser the son' or 'Huchon Despenser, son of the son' or 'Hugh Despenser the youngest son'; there were now three Hugh Despensers active in England. Huchon spent much time at court in the 1320s with his parents and his great-uncle, and Edward bought cloth for him in 1325/6 to make aketons (padded defensive jerkins) and coat-armour (jackets embroidered with heraldic devices). The aketon was made of checked vermilion and gold velvet and the coat-armour of vermilion, yellow and white camoca (a kind of heavy and expensive silk), the colours of the Despenser coat of arms. Edward also bought thirteen ells of expensive samite fabric to make matching caparisons for Huchon's horses. [2]

In May 1323, Edward II made a truce with the king of Scotland, Robert Bruce, to last for thirteen years. Bruce sent his relative and adherent Thomas Randolph to England to negotiate the truce, and Edward sent several high-born men to Scotland as hostages to assure Bruce of Randolph's safe return. One of them was Huchon Despenser. [3] In July 1324 and probably at other times as well, Huchon spent time with his mother's first cousin Edward of Windsor, the king's elder son and heir to the throne, who was about four years his junior. Edward II sent letters to the boys, staying together at Shoreham, under his secret seal that month. [4] Edward II's younger son John of Eltham (b. August 1316) was in the care of Eleanor, Lady Despenser in and after 1322, at least sometimes. Hugh the Younger's second sister Isabella Hastings took charge of the household of the king's daughters Eleanor of Woodstock and Joan of the Tower, and also looked after Hugh's third daughter, Eleanor Despenser. In July 1322 Edward II expressed his affection for Hugh's third son Gilbert, and in November 1324 Hugh's fourth son John appears in the king's accounts, so perhaps the younger Despenser boys lived at court. [5]

Edward's brother-in-law Philip V of France died at the start of 1322. Charles IV, third and youngest son of Philip IV, and Queen Isabella's last brother, now became king of France. Edward owed homage again for Gascony and Ponthieu to the new king, but made repeated excuses and failed to travel to France. The annoyed Charles invaded Gascony in the summer of 1324 and suddenly England and France were at war, a conflict known as the War of St-Sardos. The abundant surviving correspondence sent between Hugh Despenser the Younger and men in Gascony make it all too apparent that he, not Edward, was the man directing the war and was in charge of foreign policy. Not a man given to modesty, Hugh told several of his correspondents that no one was capable of organising the English response to the French invasion of Gascony better than he, and he was not shy about coupling himself with Edward, as many of his letters make clear: he often referred to 'the king and ourselves' or 'it seems to our lord the king and to us that...'. A typical example of his haughty self-importance is his comment to one man that 'as a result of your good conduct, the king and ourselves might discuss continuing our goodwill towards you'. [6]

Elizabeth Camoys sent her harper Nicholas to her brother Hugh the Younger and Edward II at Portchester in Hampshire on 16 September 1324, so evidently the Despenser siblings kept in touch. [7] The king and Hugh were in Hampshire again the following spring, and on 3 April 1325 passed through the village of Eling near Southampton, on their way to Beaulieu Abbey where they stayed for three weeks. Eling belonged to Elizabeth and Ralph Camoys jointly – their youngest son Hugh Camoys later held the manor – so presumably Hugh the Younger saw his sister and brother-in-law there. [8] Edward II's clerk recorded Eling as 'the place where the king frightened Sir Hugh' and 'where the king and Sir Hugh were frightened'. [9] This presumably means they played practical jokes or pranks on each other, as the word used can also mean 'startled'.

It is possible that Hugh and Elizabeth's sister Margaret St Amand was already dead, and her husband John had perhaps fallen out with his powerful brother-in-law. John St Amand rarely appears on record during

Hugh's regime in the 1320s, but became far more active in and after 1327, after Hugh's downfall and in the new king's reign. [10] Hugh seems to have had more contact with his sisters Alina Burnell and Isabella Hastings in the 1320s than with Elizabeth Camoys, perhaps because Alina and Isabella were much closer to his own age than Elizabeth, who is likely to have been about a dozen years younger than he. Isabella Hastings was at court with the king and her father and brother on 26 January 1325, when Edward pardoned two former sheriffs of London for allowing prisoners to escape, at Isabella's request. [11]

The queen, Isabella of France, travelled to her homeland in March 1325 to negotiate a peace settlement between her husband and her brother Charles IV to end the war. She would return at the head of an invasion force eighteen months later, determined to destroy Hugh Despenser the Younger. The *Vita Edwardi Secundi* stated how glad she was to 'leave behind some people whom she did not like,' meaning Hugh the Younger and his father. The chronicler added that many people believed she would not return to England unless Hugh the Younger was 'wholly removed from the king's side'. [12] Edward II had confiscated his wife's lands in September 1324 and treated her as an enemy alien, and Isabella blamed Hugh. It is beyond all doubt that the queen of England loathed and feared Hugh, and a few months later, safe at her brother's court and with her elder son the heir to the throne in her custody, she felt confident enough to make her long-hidden hatred of him public.

Hugh the Elder was often at court with his son and the king in the first few months of 1325: he witnessed Edward II's charters on 26 January, 12 and 14 February, 2 April and 14 May, and the king gave his barber Willecok (a nickname for men called William) a gift of a pound on 25 March. [13] His daughter Isabella Hastings, still only in her mid-thirties, was widowed for the third time on 5 April 1325 when Ralph Monthermer died. Ralph left his two daughters and two sons from his first marriage to Edward II's sister Joan of Acre; his elder son Thomas, born 1301, was Ralph's heir. Hugh the Younger lent his widowed sister Isabella one hundred marks a few weeks after Ralph's death, on 3 May 1325. She and her damsel Margaret Costantyn had the care of his third daughter Eleanor, and the king gave Margaret a gift of 50 shillings in April 1325 for taking good care of the girl. [14] On 9 April, four days after the death of his former brother-in-law Monthermer, Edward gave his niece, the elder Eleanor Despenser, a gift of one hundred marks. [15]

Eleanor was then about a month pregnant for at least the ninth or tenth time, and the gift was probably the king's reaction to the news.

The young nobleman Richard Foliot died in late May 1325, and the heirs to the Foliot family's lands in Norfolk, Nottinghamshire and Yorkshire were his sisters Margery and Margaret, then aged about 12 and 11. Edward II sold the girls' wardships and marriage rights for £200 each to the recently-widowed Isabella Hastings and her brother-in-law Ralph Camoys. Margery Foliot married Isabella's son Hugh Hastings, and her younger sister Margaret married Hugh's first cousin John Camoys, Elizabeth Despenser's son. [16] Margery stayed at Elsing in Norfolk, a Hastings manor, shortly before 22 July 1325, when she was taken from there to London and then on to Hadleigh Castle in Essex to see the king. The journey lasted a week, and Margery was attended by a damsel and two squires. [17] This may reveal when her wedding to Hugh Hastings was arranged, or perhaps when it took place. Hugh was 14 or 15 in July 1325, about two years older than Margery. His brother Thomas, who died in early 1333, never married. It is curious that Thomas's brother married an heiress while no match was arranged for Thomas himself, so there must have been some reason why he was deemed unable to marry, perhaps a disability caused by his difficult birth.

Edward still owed homage for his lands in France to his brother-in-law Charles IV, but Hugh Despenser the Younger was desperate to prevent the king leaving England. Hugh was certain, probably correctly, that he and his father the earl of Winchester would be assassinated in Edward's absence, and indeed in November 1325 rumours swept the country that Hugh the Younger had been murdered. One chronicler stated that Hugh the Elder was 'hated by everyone'. [18] Edward II, after much uncertainty and changing his mind on an almost daily basis, sent his elder son Edward of Windsor, not yet 13 years old, to France in his place on 12 September 1325. A few weeks later, under the protection of her brother Charles IV and with her son the king's heir in her custody, Queen Isabella felt confident enough to make her loathing of Hugh the Younger public. In front of the French court, she refused to return to England or to permit her son to do so unless Edward sent Hugh away. [19] Edward, dependent on Hugh personally or politically or both, ignored his wife's ultimatum and left her with no choice but to stay in France. At the end of 1325 or in early 1326, she allied with the remnant of the Contrariant faction who had fled from England in 1322/3, including their leader Roger Mortimer of Wigmore, the Despensers' nemesis. Isabella threatened to destroy Hugh the Younger, and Mortimer and his allies, who also loathed him, would be able to help her achieve it. The greed and despotism of Hugh the Younger in particular, and his father's as well, had made them countless enemies.

Hugh the Younger and Eleanor Despenser's youngest child, their ninth who survived infancy, was born at Sheen in December 1325 and named Elizabeth. Hugh spent that Christmas and New Year, the last of his life, in Suffolk with the king, while Eleanor remained at Sheen. Hugh the Elder apparently did not spend the festive season of 1325/6 with the king, as he witnessed no charters Edward issued from late October 1325 until late February 1326; perhaps he spent the time at Vastern, as he so often did. [20] Hugh the Younger visited South Wales several times in 1325/6, and had the great hall at his castle of Caerphilly, his wife's birthplace in 1292, rebuilt; what exists there now is mostly his work. A carved stone corbel in the great hall which may depict Hugh has an oval, perhaps rather plump face, fashionably long hair and a goatee beard.

On 30 January 1326, Edward appointed Alina Burnell as constable of the mighty Conwy Castle in North Wales, built by his father. [21] Alina was only the second female castle constable of the fourteenth century after Isabella Vescy at Bamburgh in Northumberland, and her appointment almost certainly came as a result of her brother's great influence with the king. Edward replaced Isabella Hastings as his daughters' governess in early 1326 with Joan Jermy, sister of his half-brother the earl of Norfolk's wife Alice Hales. This represents the king's need to gain the support of his half-brother Norfolk – his other half-brother the earl of Kent was in Paris with the queen, refusing to return to England – rather than his dissatisfaction with Isabella Hastings, and Lady Hastings spent much time with the king throughout 1326. In February, ten years almost to the day since he assaulted Sir John Ros in Lincoln, Hugh Despenser the Younger 'made a small affray' in the Northamptonshire town of Rothwell, and Edward II hastily sent Hugh's squire Thomelyn Bradeston to deal with the situation. [22]

Isabella Hastings' only daughter Margaret, who was in her early teens, was widowed from her first husband William, Lord Martin (b. *c.* 1294) shortly before 4 April 1326. The marriage may never have been consummated and certainly it produced no children, and William's heirs were his sister and his nephew. [23] On 19 May 1326, Margaret married her second husband Sir Robert Wateville in Marlborough, Wiltshire, in the presence of her mother, her uncle Hugh the Younger and aunt-in-law Eleanor Despenser, her grandfather the earl of Winchester, and the king of England himself. [24] Wateville was a Contrariant of 1321/2 who had pragmatically switched sides after their defeat at the battle of Boroughbridge in 1322 and joined the Despensers; events were soon to show that, despite the great favour shown to him by the king and Hugh the Younger, he had retained his former loyalties.

The royal party left Marlborough the day after the wedding and travelled to Kent via Hungerford, Caversham and Bisham; on 25 May, the king and Hugh the Younger sent a messenger back to Marlborough with letters to Lady Hastings from them both. Edward met Isabella Hastings again on or shortly before 8 August and dined with her, and on 21 August the king granted a pardon to a prisoner called Stephen Pulton at Isabella's request, so she must have been in his company or in contact with him on or soon before that date. She also spent time with him when he was in Marlborough on 8 May a few days before her daughter Margaret's wedding. [25] Her father Hugh the Elder had turned 65 at the start of March 1326, and late May marked the twentieth anniversary of his wife Isabella Beauchamp's death. It also marked the twentieth wedding anniversary of Eleanor and Hugh the Younger.

Queen Isabella, meanwhile, continued to refuse to return to Edward or allow her 13-year-old son Edward of Windsor to return to England unless the king sent Hugh the Younger away from him, and carried on with her plans to bring Hugh down. In or before August 1326 she moved from her brother's court in Paris to the county of Hainault on France's northern border, ruled by her first cousin Jeanne de Valois's husband Willem. In exchange for ships and mercenaries, Isabella betrothed Edward of Windsor to one of Jeanne and Willem's daughters, and he later married Philippa, their third daughter. The queen's campaign to destroy Hugh Despenser the Younger had become deadly serious.

Chapter 15

The summer of 1326, the last on earth for the two Hugh Despensers, was one of the hottest and driest of the Middle Ages; chroniclers noted how rivers, wells and lakes dried up and fires burst out spontaneously in the dryness. [1] Hugh the Younger made a quick visit to Wales at the end of July and early August, and just before he departed, received a gift from the king of a manuscript containing the tragic love story of Tristan and Isolde. His wife Eleanor was almost always at court with her uncle the king in 1326 and remained with Edward while Hugh was away in Wales, and their eldest son Huchon was often there as well. Eleanor and Hugh, still only 33 and about 37 years old respectively, became grandparents in 1326 when their eldest daughter Isabella gave birth to her son Edmund Arundel. Isabella and her husband Richard, son and heir of the earl of Arundel, were only at the start of their teens, and Richard later claimed they had been forced to consummate their marriage by violence (at the hands of whom was not stated) even though they had repudiated the vows taken when they were children in 1321 once they reached puberty. Edmund Arundel was 18 in late 1344 and 20 in early 1347, so was born at or before the end of 1326. [2]

Edward II wrote to Alina Burnell at Conwy Castle under his secret seal on 2 September, and told his messenger, a Franciscan friar of Oxford called Adam Freford, to bring her reply to him 'wherever the king may be'. [3] It must have been an important letter, perhaps relating to the queen's impending invasion. In October after the queen and her forces arrived, Edward replaced Alina as constable of Conwy with Sir William Ercalewe (b. December 1284), sheriff of Staffordshire and Shropshire and an experienced military man. This was almost certainly at Alina's own suggestion, as Ercalewe was one of her adherents. Alina, called 'Lady Burnell, sister of Sir Hugh' in the king's accounts, sent Freford back to the king with her reply, and he reached Edward at Wallingford on 6 October. [4]

Isabella Hastings may have been at the Tower of London with the king, her father Hugh the Elder, brother Hugh the Younger and sister-in-law Eleanor Despenser, on 25 September, when Edward II gave her custody of the manor of Alvington. [5] Although they did not yet know it, the queen's invasion force had landed at the River Orwell in Suffolk the day before. Queen Isabella had the king's half-brother the earl of Kent with her, and his other half-brother the earl of Norfolk immediately went to join them after their arrival. So did Edward's cousin Henry of Lancaster, earl of Leicester, who took the northern lords with him, several English bishops, and the archbishop of Dublin. One London chronicler states that 'the mariners of England were not minded to prevent' the invasion force arriving, 'by reason of the great anger they entertained against Sir Hugh Despenser [the Younger]'. [6]

The king, Hugh the Elder and Younger, and Eleanor were all still at the Tower of London on 28 September when news reached them that Isabella and her allies had arrived. Edward and the two Hugh Despensers left London at the beginning of October 1326 and headed west towards South Wales, where they hoped to find more aid and support. It did not come. Their support, and the king's, simply collapsed, and within a few weeks the king and Hugh the Younger, and their sole remaining important ally Edmund, earl of Arundel, were little more than fugitives.

Hugh Despenser the Elder, earl of Winchester, was left behind in Bristol to hold the city against the queen, but on 27 October it fell to her. Despenser was given a mock trial which consisted of a list of charges being read out by Sir William Trussell, a Contrariant of 1321/2 and a lawyer, and was denied any right of response because Thomas, earl of Lancaster had not been allowed a defence before his execution in 1322. 'You are a robber and have robbed the land by your cruelty, wherefore all people cry out and demand vengeance,' declared Trussell, who did at least show a modicum of respect to the 65-year-old by addressing him as 'Hugh, sire'. Hugh was condemned to be drawn through the streets for his treason, hanged for his robberies, and finally beheaded for his offences against the Holy Church. His headless body was dangled by the arms on the gallows for four days after death, then, horribly, was cut to pieces and fed to dogs. His head was carried to Winchester, the town which was his earldom, and publicly displayed there on the point of a spear. [7] In 1265 Roger Mortimer of Wigmore (d. 1282) and Edward I desecrated and hacked apart the body of Hugh Despenser the justiciar's ally and friend Simon Montfort, and sixty-one years later Mortimer's grandson and Edward's daughter-in-law desecrated and hacked apart the body of the justiciar's son, the only high-ranking English nobleman who remained loyal to Edward I's son from the beginning to the end of his reign.

Margaret Hastings' husband Sir Robert Wateville most probably watched her grandfather's execution: Wateville was named as one of Queen Isabella's chief allies present with her and her son in Bristol the day before Despenser's execution. [8] Edward of Windsor, not yet 14 years old, may also have witnessed his godfather's death. Another man who saw Hugh the Elder die was Henry of Lancaster, earl of Leicester and now calling himself earl of Lancaster as well, the widower of Hugh's stepdaughter Maud Chaworth (d. 1322). Despenser left twenty or so grandchildren: in October 1326, Hugh the Younger's nine surviving children were aged between 18 and under a year old, Philip Despenser II was 13, Amaury St Amand was 11 and his sister Isabel somewhat younger, the Hastings boys Hugh and Thomas and their sister Margaret Wateville were in their early to mid-teens, and the Camoys children were all under 10. Hugh the Elder was also a great-grandfather to the infant Edmund Arundel.

By mid-November 1326, the king and Despenser the Younger appear to have given up completely – most of the armed men they summoned simply ignored the orders or joined the queen instead – and wandered hopelessly around South Wales, leaving the safety of Hugh's great stronghold at Caerphilly at the beginning of November for reasons which remain unclear. Hugh's son Huchon was left behind at Caerphilly, and the king left most of his remaining household servants there as well, though many of them had already slipped away and abandoned him. Their last important ally, the earl of Arundel, was captured and put to death without a trial in Hereford on 17 November, with two other men, and the king and Hugh were found near Llantrisant on 16 November by a search party which included William Zouche, lord of Ashby in Leicestershire. Edward II was treated with all respect and placed in the custody of his cousin Henry of Lancaster.

Hugh the Younger was led slowly to Hereford and pelted with rubbish and filth all the way by the local populace, a crown of sharp nettles was placed on his head and verses from the Bible were scrawled over his skin, and squires riding alongside him blew bugle-horns in his ears. He refused to eat or drink anything after his capture, and although Isabella and his other enemies wished to take him to London to be executed, they had to abandon this idea as Hugh was 'almost dead for fasting' and they did not want him to slip away quietly and cheat them of their revenge and the grand showpiece of his execution. [9] At Hereford, in front of the queen, Roger Mortimer, Henry of Lancaster and the earls of Norfolk and Kent, Hugh was given a show trial. It consisted of Sir William Trussell reading out a list of accusations in French, as he had also done to Hugh the Elder less than four weeks before, though now Trussell addressed the younger man by his first name without the 'Sir' to which he was entitled. Many of the accusations were simply ludicrous, propaganda which piled all the woes of Edward's reign on Hugh's head because the queen and her allies did not yet dare to blame the king himself, at least in public. [10] Hugh was tied to four horses which dragged him through Hereford, partially strangled on a gallows fifty feet high, disembowelled, possibly castrated, and finally beheaded. He was 37 or 38 years old when he died. His head was placed on a spike on London Bridge ten days later and his body was cut into four pieces and displayed publicly in York, Carlisle, Bristol and Dover.

Within a month, the two Hugh Despensers had been destroyed. Their regime collapsed, all their lands and goods were forfeit to the Crown, Hugh the Younger's widow and children were imprisoned, and their misdeeds were soon to bring down a king. They came close to destroying their own family as well.

Part 3

Regaining Lost Ground: Huchon and Edward the Elder, 1326–1349

Dramatis Personae

Hugh Despenser the Elder (b. 1261), earl of Winchester, and his son **Hugh Despenser the Younger** (b. *c.* 1288/9), lord of Glamorgan, both executed 1326

Eleanor Despenser, née Clare (b. 1292): widow of Hugh the Younger; niece of Edward II and first cousin of Edward III; inherits a third of the earldom of Gloucester, including the lordship of Glamorgan, from her brother Gilbert Clare (1291–1314)

Hugh Despenser, called 'Huchon' (b. 1308/9), lord of Glamorgan: eldest son of Hugh the Younger and Eleanor, and heir to his mother; eldest great-grandchild of King Edward I; marries Elizabeth Montacute in or before 1341 but has no children

Edward Despenser the Elder (b. *c.* 1310): second son of Hugh the Younger and Eleanor; marries Anne Ferrers in 1335; father of Edward the Younger, Hugh, Thomas and Henry Despenser

Gilbert Despenser (b. *c.* mid or late 1310s): third son of Hugh the Younger

John Despenser (b. *c.* late 1310s/early 1320s): fourth and youngest son of Hugh the Younger

Isabella Despenser, countess of Arundel (b. *c.* 1312): eldest daughter of Hugh the Younger; marries Richard, later earl of Arundel, in 1321; mother of **Edmund Arundel**, b. *c.* 1326; her marriage is annulled 1344

75

Joan (b. *c.* mid-1310s), **Eleanor** (b. *c.* late 1310s/early 1320s) and **Margaret Despenser** (b. 1323): middle three daughters of Hugh the Younger; all nuns

Elizabeth Berkeley, née Despenser (probably b. December 1325): fifth daughter and youngest child of Hugh the Younger; marries Maurice Berkeley (b. *c.* 1330), heir to his father Lord Berkeley, in 1338

Alina Burnell (b. *c.* 1286/7), widow of Edward Burnell, and **Isabella Hastings** (b. *c.* 1290/92), widow of Gilbert Clare of Thomond, John Hastings and Ralph Monthermer: daughters of Hugh Despenser the Elder and sisters of Hugh the Younger; their sisters **Margaret St Amand** and **Elizabeth Camoys** probably die before 1330 and before 1335 respectively

Hugh Hastings I (b. 1310/11): son of Isabella Hastings; grandson of Hugh Despenser the Elder; marries Margery Foliot *c.* 1325; half-brother of John, Lord Hastings (1286–1325) and uncle of Laurence Hastings, earl of Pembroke (1321–48); has children John Hastings (b. *c.* 1329/31), Hugh Hastings II and Maud de la Mare

Philip Despenser II (b. 1313): son of Philip Despenser I (*c.* 1292/4–1313); grandson of Hugh Despenser the Elder; father of Philip Despenser III (b. 1342), Hawise, later Luttrell (b. 1344/5) and Hugh Despenser (b. 1346/7)

Amaury St Amand (b. 1315) and **Ralph, John** (b. *c.* 1320) and **Hugh Camoys** (b. *c.* 1322/4): other grandsons of Hugh Despenser the Elder

William Zouche (b. *c.* 1270s), lord of Ashby in Leicestershire: captures Hugh Despenser the Younger in November 1326; abducts and forcibly marries Hugh's widow Eleanor in January 1329; stepfather of Huchon and his siblings

Edward II (b. 1284), king of England from 1307, forced to abdicate in January 1327

Edward III (b. 1312), king of England from January 1327; eldest child of Edward II and Isabella of France; marries **Philippa of Hainault** (b. *c.* 1314) in 1328

Edward of Woodstock, prince of Wales (b. 1330): eldest child of Edward III and Queen Philippa; heir to the English throne

Isabella of France (b. *c.* 1295), dowager queen of England: wife of Edward II, mother of Edward III, grandmother of Edward of Woodstock

Chapter 16

The extensive lands of the two executed Hugh Despensers were distributed to others in 1327, while Queen Isabella took personal possession of the many valuable items Hugh the Younger had stored in his wardrobe at the Tower of London. Edward II's half-brothers the earls of Norfolk and Kent each received a generous portion of Despenser lands, as did Roger Swynnerton, a knight of Staffordshire, who was given all Hugh the Elder's lands in Staffordshire and Cheshire. Many Despenser manors eventually passed into the possession of the Holland family via the marriage of the earl of Kent's daughter and ultimate heir, Joan of Kent, later princess of Wales, to Sir Thomas Holland. As late as 1398, Hugh the Younger's great-grandson Thomas Despenser quit-claimed all his rights to his family's former manors to Joan and Holland's grandson. Some of the lands in Wales which Hugh the Elder and Younger grabbed in the 1320s, including the lordships of Denbigh and Usk, passed to the Mortimers, and Thomas Despenser quit-claimed all rights to these in 1398 as well. [1] Hugh the Elder's earldom of Winchester remained dormant until Edward IV granted it to his friend Louis of Bruges, lord of Gruuthuse, a century and a half later in 1472.

Both Hugh Despensers had taken the opportunity to enrich themselves hugely during the years of Hugh the Younger's dominance of Edward II's government. In August 1337, the staggeringly large sum of £10,000 was discovered at Malmesbury Abbey in Wiltshire (ten miles from Vastern), where the two men had stored it. So wealthy had they made themselves that this sum of money, tens of millions in modern terms, was not missed or even known about until eleven years after their deaths. [2] The chancery rolls from 1327 onwards are full of references to money and goods of the two Despensers being sought, found and handed to royal officials all over the country. In 1368, forty-two years after their deaths, a clerk called Robert Despenser, presumably a relative, was charged with having 'hidden in the ground ... goods of Hugh Despenser, knight, a convicted felon' at Kessingland in Suffolk (this probably means Hugh the Younger). [3] Petitions poured into Chancery by the dozen in and after late 1326 as the many victims of the Despensers' extortion and land grabs sought restitution.

Ralph Camoys, son-in-law of Hugh the Elder and long-term supporter of the Despensers, did well to avoid their fate: he was pardoned for adherence to Hugh the Younger in February 1327, though had to acknowledge a huge debt of 2,000 marks to Queen Isabella. Other adherents of the two men such as Ingelram Berenger and John Inge were pardoned in early 1327 as well. [4] Queen Isabella and Roger Mortimer, to their credit, left the Despenser women – Hugh the Younger's sisters Alina Burnell, Isabella Hastings and Elizabeth Camoys, and Hugh the Elder's only surviving sister Eleanor Courtenay – alone. [5]

Hugh the Younger's middle three daughters Joan, Eleanor and Margaret Despenser were not so fortunate, and on 1 January 1327, Queen Isabella ordered them to be forcibly veiled as nuns in three separate and distant convents. Margaret, the youngest, was only 3 years old and was sent to Watton Priory in Yorkshire, where she would die in 1337, barely into her teens; Eleanor, somewhere between 5 and 8 years old, was sent to Sempringham Priory in Lincolnshire; and Joan, about 10 or 12, went to Shaftesbury Abbey in Dorset. It is possible that Hugh the Younger himself had made the decision to send Joan to Shaftesbury in or before 1326, as the order for her veiling is missing. Edward I sent Gwenllian ferch Llywelyn, daughter of the last native prince of Wales, to Sempringham in 1282, and sent Robert Bruce's daughter Marjorie to Watton in 1306, perhaps the reason why those convents were chosen, and the Despenser girls' aunt Margaret Audley née Clare spent the years 1322 to 1326 in captivity at Sempringham. As noted above, Hugh the Elder had sisters, the girls' great-aunts, living at Sempringham in 1312. It cost just under £40 to veil the young Eleanor Despenser as a nun. She had been betrothed to the future earl of Pembroke in 1325, but Laurence Hastings' marriage was granted to Roger Mortimer in early 1327 and he later wed Mortimer's daughter Agnes instead. [6] Hugh the Younger's widow, the elder Eleanor, was imprisoned in the Tower of London on 17 November 1326, the day after her husband and uncle were captured in distant South Wales. She would remain there for fifteen months. [7]

Hugh the Younger and Eleanor's eldest son Huchon, now probably 18, was besieged inside Caerphilly Castle from November 1326 until

20 March 1327, but the castle garrison refused to surrender him to Queen Isabella for execution. Had they wished to do so, it would have been easy to drag the young Despenser outside and hand him over to the besiegers, and reap the rewards from a grateful Isabella, but they did not. Four hundred footmen, twenty-five knights, twenty-one squires and an uncertain number of men-at-arms besieged Caerphilly, while of the 135 or so men inside, only two were knights (John Felton and Thomas Lovell). The vast majority were carpenters or blacksmiths and Edward II's chamber staff, and had little if any military training. Still, they bravely held out for more than four months, helped considerably by the vast stocks of food and drink inside the castle. Isabella finally gave up when the siege proved too expensive to continue. On 20 March 1327 she agreed to spare Huchon's life, but he would spend the next few years in prison. [8] Where he was held until December 1328 (when he was moved to Bristol Castle) is unknown, but he was officially in the custody of Roger Mortimer, who had executed his father and grandfather, and his imprisonment is unlikely to have been comfortable or pleasant.

Huchon's brother Edward Despenser was probably 16 when their father was executed, and therefore he was, unlike Huchon, lucky to avoid imprisonment by the new regime. It may be that a staunch Despenser adherent such as Ingelram Berenger or John Haudlo, or Edward's uncle-in-law Ralph Camoys, kept him hidden away somewhere out of sight of Roger Mortimer and Queen Isabella. Haudlo and his wife Maud, sister and heir of Edward Despenser's late uncle-in-law Edward Burnell, went on pilgrimage to Santiago de Compostela in October 1327. [9] Although this is only speculation, perhaps they took Edward with them. The two youngest Despenser boys Gilbert and John, the youngest daughter Elizabeth, and the eldest daughter Isabella and Isabella's infant son Edmund Arundel, perhaps remained in the Tower with their mother Eleanor for the time being. Little Elizabeth Despenser was not even a year old when her father was executed, just a few months older than her nephew Edmund, and her extreme youth spared her from her sisters' forced veiling. A 'Gilbert de la Despense' or 'Gilbert del Despens' ('Despens' was the usual abbreviation of the name Despenser as written by fourteenth-century clerks) was named as a King's Scholar at the University of Cambridge in 1328, 1332 and 1333. [10] Although it may be a coincidence that this boy shared Gilbert Despenser's name, it is possible that he was Hugh the Younger and Eleanor's third son. It was not unknown for young noblemen to study at Cambridge or Oxford, as Gilbert's uncle-in-law John St Amand did, and given that the family's prospects in the late 1320s were bleak, perhaps his mother considered a career in the church for Gilbert. He eventually, however, became a knight, and spent his long life in the secular world.

The Despenser siblings' great-uncle Edward II was held in comfortable captivity at Kenilworth Castle in Warwickshire after his capture in South Wales, and in January 1327 was forced to abdicate his throne to his 14-year-old son. Edward III was crowned king of England at Westminster Abbey on 1 February 1327, though the real rulers of the kingdom during the young king's minority were his mother Queen Isabella and her ally Roger Mortimer. Edward II, now merely Sir Edward of Caernarfon, was moved to Berkeley Castle, Gloucestershire in April 1327, and in September that year news of his death was taken to his son in Lincoln. Whether Edward of Caernarfon was truly dead or not is a matter for speculation, and many influential men including his own half-brother the earl of Kent and his great-nephew Huchon Despenser believed years later that he was still alive, but his funeral was held in Gloucester in December 1327. A month later, Edward's son married his second cousin Philippa, daughter of Willem, count of Hainault and Holland, in York. Edward III was 15 and Philippa not quite 14 at the time of their wedding. Unfortunately for the young queen, her mother-in-law Isabella was determined not to lose one inch of her own influence, and Philippa was neither crowned nor received her rightful income until 1330. Isabella and Roger Mortimer – who created the grandiose earldom of March for himself in late 1328 – maintained their grip on power despite never being elected to rule in the young king's name, and treated him in a way he came to find increasingly infantilising and suffocating.

Hugh Despenser the Elder's only surviving sister or half-sister, Eleanor Courtenay, outlived him by two years and finally died on 30 September 1328 when she must have been a ripe old age. She was buried with her husband Hugh Courtenay, who had died in 1292, at the priory of Cowick near Exeter. [11] Her son, also Hugh Courtenay, was 52 years old in 1328 and would be made earl of Devon a few years later. His son and heir Hugh the younger, born 1303, married Edward II's niece Margaret Bohun (b. 1311), sister of the earls of Hereford and Northampton, and they built a large family.

In December 1328, Eleanor Courtenay's great-nephew Huchon Despenser was sent to prison at Bristol Castle. This was surely a deliberate choice: Edward II had appointed Huchon's father constable of Bristol Castle for life in June 1325, but now a quarter of Hugh the Younger's body adorned the castle walls and Huchon must have seen the remains there, and his grandfather the earl of Winchester had been executed outside the castle. His new jailer, replacing Roger Mortimer, was Thomas Gurney, a knight of Somerset. [12] Gurney had ridden to Edward III at Lincoln in September 1327 to inform the king that his father had died at Berkeley Castle. At the parliament of November 1330 after Edward III took control of his own kingdom, Gurney was sentenced to death in absentia for Edward II's murder; he fled the country. [13] Edward III pursued him to Spain then to Italy, and he died in 1333 on his way back to England under guard. Huchon Despenser, evidently a forgiving kind of man, employed Gurney's namesake son Sir Thomas Gurney (b. February 1319) in his retinue in the 1340s. [14]

Huchon's mother Eleanor was released from the Tower of London in late February 1328 and restored to the lands she had inherited from her brother Gilbert Clare; after Hugh the Younger's execution, her lands reverted to her by right, and as she had not committed treason or any other crime there was no legal reason for them to be kept from her. Eleanor was abducted from her home at Hanley Castle in Worcestershire and forcibly married to her second husband William Zouche, lord of Ashby in Leicestershire, in January 1329. Zouche had captured her first husband and her uncle near Llantrisant in November 1326, and subsequently led the siege of her son Huchon at Caerphilly. Eleanor may not have consented to the marriage, but she was a wealthy and fertile widow, the king's first cousin and still only 36 years old, and therefore a very desirable marriage prospect. Whether she wanted to be married to Zouche or not, she had no choice but to make the best of it, and bore him a son, William Zouche the younger, *c.* 1330. This William became a monk of Glastonbury Abbey in Somerset and lived until 1390 or later. [15] Eleanor and Hugh the Younger's grandson Edward Despenser (b. 1336) acknowledged William as his uncle in 1367 when granting him an annual income from one of his manors. [16] Eleanor Despenser was arrested again in 1329 and imprisoned at Devizes Castle in Wiltshire after she and her new husband (for an unexplained reason) besieged her castle of Caerphilly, and in February 1330 her lands were taken from her once more and given to Edward III's young queen, Philippa of Hainault. Philippa was then five months pregnant with the heir to the throne, Edward of Woodstock, born in June 1330.

Chapter 17

By 1329, the regime of the dowager queen Isabella of France was every bit as unpopular and unsuccessful as her husband Edward II and Hugh Despenser's had been. Isabella lost a lot of support by making a permanent peace settlement with Scotland in 1328 and acknowledging Robert Bruce as king, and her uncle Henry of Lancaster rebelled against her rule in late 1328. This failed in early 1329 when the earls of Norfolk and Kent abandoned Lancaster at the last moment. The earl of Kent, Edmund of Woodstock, came to believe in 1328/9 that his half-brother Edward II was still alive and being held in captivity at Corfe Castle in Dorset. He began gathering supporters who shared this belief, including the archbishop of York, the bishop, mayor and sheriff of London, and a large number of noblemen and others down the social scale.

One man involved was Huchon Despenser, who could only offer his great-uncle the earl of Kent moral support as he was in prison at Bristol Castle, another was Huchon's new stepfather William Zouche, lord of Ashby, and a third was his mother Eleanor's half-brother Edward Monthermer (b. 1304). There were hundreds of other supporters of the earl of Kent, and it does appear that many influential men in 1329/30 genuinely believed that the former king was still alive, and that whoever had been buried in Gloucester in December 1327 was not Edward II. [1] The plan to free Edward and take him to the earl of Kent's castle of Arundel in Sussex, and from there perhaps abroad, was well advanced when Kent was dramatically arrested in Winchester on 13 March, and beheaded there six days later. Huchon, already in prison, suffered no punishment, but his half-uncle Monthermer was imprisoned, and the lands and goods of his stepfather Zouche were temporarily confiscated. The Despenser adherent Sir Ingelram Berenger, another person who seemingly believed that Edward II was still alive, was one of the many men who fled abroad after the failure of the earl of Kent's plot and waited for the regime of Queen Isabella and Roger Mortimer to collapse.

They did not have long to wait. On 19 October 1330, Edward III, not quite 18 years old, launched a coup against his mother and her favourite, and arrested Mortimer at Nottingham Castle. Mortimer was hanged on 29 November, and the dowager queen was made to give up her power and the vast income and estates she had appropriated. The king took over control of his own kingdom. It must have been a great relief to Eleanor Despenser, and to a great many other people, to see the back of Queen Isabella and Mortimer, and Eleanor was restored once more to her lands and given permission to bury the remains of her husband Hugh the Younger four years after his execution. [2] She had him interred at Tewkesbury Abbey in Gloucestershire, mausoleum of her family the Clares, where Hugh's tomb still exists (albeit much vandalised after the Reformation). The men who had fled overseas a few months previously returned to England and were pardoned, and things finally went back to normal – except for Huchon Despenser, now about 22 years old, who remained in prison.

Hugh Despenser the Elder's eldest child Alina Burnell was given protection to go on pilgrimage to Santiago de Compostela on 15 November 1329 and still intended to go on 24 April 1330. By 4 June 1331, she had not yet left England and the protection was extended again, though she appointed two attorneys to take care of her affairs in her absence on 10 March. [3] Alina's brother-in-law John St Amand, the Bedfordshire nobleman who was a graduate in law, died shortly before 25 January 1330. One of St Amand's two executors was his sister Eleanor Keynes. [4] John's heir was his and Margaret Despenser's son Amaury St Amand, born in February 1315 and not quite 15 years old when John died. Amaury lived a long life and died in 1381, the year of the Great Uprising in England. He was appointed justiciar of Ireland in 1357. [5]

Hugh 'Huchon' Despenser, who must have wondered why he alone was not released or pardoned at the parliament of November 1330 when Edward III did his utmost to resolve the chaos of the previous few years, sent his kinsman the king a petition in early July 1331 from his prison at Bristol Castle. Huchon pointed out that he had been pardoned in March 1327 for holding Caerphilly Castle against Queen Isabella, and included a copy of the pardon with his petition to prove it. Though he did not say so, Huchon had been held in prison unlawfully for well over four years, as he had never been convicted – indeed, had never even been accused – of any crime. He had been punished and held in captivity for years simply for being Hugh Despenser the Younger's son and heir. (His father and great-uncle Edward II had done the same thing to some of the Contrariants' sons in the early 1320s, but that was hardly Huchon's fault.) There was perhaps a measure of defiance in the young man calling himself 'Hugh son of Hugh Despenser' in his petition, and his mother Eleanor also kept her first husband's name throughout her second marriage rather than using William Zouche's. Twelve knights acted as Huchon's mainpernors or guarantors and promised to produce him before the September 1331 parliament; he was therefore released from prison on 5 July 1331. Several of the knights had, or their wives had, been victims of Hugh the Younger's greed and extortion, but they did not blame the young man for his father's actions and were willing to allow him to prove himself. [6]

Huchon duly appeared before the parliament held at Westminster beginning on 30 September 1331. His mother's first cousin the king pardoned him for any 'homicides, robberies, felonies and transgressions' committed in Edward II's reign – it is hard to see how or when Huchon might have committed any – as well as for his 'transgression' in holding Caerphilly against Isabella. Evidently some of the English bishops took an interest in Huchon's case: the records of this parliament mention 'the prelates who prayed most especially on his behalf'. [7] Huchon, although personally innocent of wrongdoing, had much to do to clear his family's reviled name. His grandfather Hugh the Elder's favourite residence of Vastern, meanwhile, was given to his cousin Edward Bohun, younger brother of the earl of Hereford and a nephew of Edward II, in 1331. Edward's twin William, later earl of Northampton, received a grant of former Despenser lands in 1332, including Wix in Essex and High Wycombe in Buckinghamshire. [8]

Chapter 18

Huchon, his mother Eleanor and his stepfather William Zouche were part of the retinue who accompanied Edward III's sister Eleanor of Woodstock to her wedding in Nijmegen (in the modern-day Netherlands) in May 1332. Eleanor married Reynald II, count and later duke of Guelders, the month before her fourteenth birthday. Apparently Huchon had not yet been knighted, as his name was not followed by the word 'knight' in the list of men accompanying Zouche, unlike those of several other men who went. [1] Huchon's uncle Hugh Audley, husband of Eleanor Despenser's sister Margaret and imprisoned for years by Huchon's father and great-uncle after the Contrariant rebellion of 1321/2, also went to Nijmegen, and the party left London on 1 May, sailed from Dover on 5 May and returned to London on 11 June after attending the wedding. [2]

Edward III promised to give Huchon 200 marks of lands and rents a year in 1332. This was a small income for such a high-ranking nobleman, but it was at least a first step on Despenser's long journey to prove himself and to restore his reputation, as was Edward's courteously acknowledging him as 'the king's kinsman'. Perhaps the king remembered that he had spent time with Huchon years before when he was the heir to the throne, and in later years and decades, Edward III also called Huchon's brother Edward Despenser and Edward's sons 'the king's kinsmen'. To provide Huchon with the promised income, the king granted him three manors, Freeby in Lincolnshire and Mapledurwell and Ashley in Hampshire, all of which had once belonged to his grandfather Hugh the Elder. [3] The young Despenser was said in late April 1332 to be going on pilgrimage to Santiago de Compostela in Spain, a journey he presumably undertook after the visit to Nijmegen; perhaps his aunt Alina Burnell's pilgrimage there inspired him. [4] He had certainly been knighted when he participated in a jousting tournament in Dunstable probably in January 1334, when he appears as *Monsire* [Sir] *Hugh le Despenser* in the list of participants, carrying the Despenser coat of arms. Huchon fought for the king at the battle of Halidon Hill in July 1333, and acquitted himself well during Edward III's victory over the Scots. He went on campaign to Scotland in 1334, 1335 and 1337 as well. Some of the men who accompanied him in 1333 had previously served in his father's retinue, including Peter Ovedale, Alan Tesdale and John Botiller. [5]

In the 1330s Huchon joined the retinue of John of Eltham, earl of Cornwall, his mother's decades-younger first cousin whom Eleanor had looked after for part of the early and mid-1320s. Huchon and his cousin Sir Philip Despenser II both decided to make a career in the following of the king's younger brother. [6] At an uncertain date before January 1349, Huchon received a gift of a palfrey horse from John of Eltham's nephew Edward of Woodstock (b. June 1330), Edward III and Queen Philippa's eldest son and the heir to the throne. The palfrey was called Veiron Petitwatte. *Veiron* meant a skewbald horse, *Petit* meant 'little' and Watte was a pet form of the name Walter. [7]

On 4 or 5 December 1334, Huchon's aunt Isabella, Lady Hastings died in her early or mid-forties. Isabella's son Thomas had died on 11 January 1333, and her heir was her other son Sir Hugh Hastings, aged 24. [8] She was already a grandmother: Hugh and his wife Margery Foliot had children John, Hugh II and Maud, possibly all born by the end of 1334 when Isabella died. John Hastings, born sometime between 1329 and 1331, was Hugh and Margery's elder son, and was Hugh's heir when he died in 1347. John lived until 1393 but had no children, though his younger brother Hugh II (b. *c.* early or mid-1330s) did. [9] Isabella's death may have left her older sister Alina Burnell as the only surviving child of Hugh Despenser the Elder; their youngest sister Elizabeth Camoys seems to have predeceased her husband Ralph, who died in September 1335, despite being decades his junior. [10]

Not long before she died, sometime in the early 1330s at her Hampshire manor of East Tytherley, Isabella Hastings received a visit from her namesake niece Isabella of Lancaster, second of the six daughters of her late half-sister Maud Chaworth and Henry, earl of Lancaster. Isabella of Lancaster was veiled as a nun of Amesbury Priory in Wiltshire in 1327 and later became its prioress, but spent much time outside the convent visiting her father, siblings and aunt. Lady Hastings lent her niece a palfrey to ride on her return journey to the priory. A 'Hastings child' is mentioned several times in Isabella of Lancaster's accounts of the early 1330s and was in her care at Amesbury, and on one occasion is named as 'Isabel'. Presumably this girl was a daughter of Isabella Hastings' son Hugh, perhaps illegitimate as he does not seem to have had a legitimate daughter with this name, or perhaps Isabel was legitimate but died young. Henry of Grosmont, Maud Chaworth's only son and Isabella of Lancaster's younger brother, was given custody of his aunt Lady Hastings' dower lands a few days after her death. [11]

Chapter 19

Hugh Despenser the Younger's second son Edward (possibly born in October 1310) married Anne Ferrers in 1335. Anne was the daughter of William, Lord Ferrers (1271–1325) of Groby in Leicestershire, whose heir was her brother Henry, and she had two other brothers, Thomas and Ralph Ferrers. Her paternal grandmother Anne may have been an older half-sister of Hugh Despenser the Elder, and if so, Anne Ferrers was her husband's second cousin. Her father William was a household knight of Hugh the Elder in 1298. [1] Edward Despenser and Anne's wedding took place at her brother Henry Ferrers' chief manor of Groby on 20 April 1335. [2] They did not have long to enjoy being newlyweds: on 2 July 1335, Edward and Henry were both given letters of protection to fight together in Scotland until 1 November. [3]

Edward Despenser the Younger, eldest of Edward and Anne's four sons, was born on 24 March 1336, eleven months after their wedding (and thus was conceived not long before his father headed off to Scotland with his uncle), at Essendine in Rutland forty miles from Groby. Essendine was one of the manors Edward the Elder had recently inherited from his grandmother Isabella Beauchamp's childless cousin Idonea Leyburne, and lay only a mile from Ryhall, a manor formerly held by Edward's father, grandfather and great-grandfather Hugh the justiciar. Rather astonishingly, given his later career of grabbing all the lands he could by whatever illegal or quasi-legal means necessary, Hugh the Younger had carried out a perfectly legitimate deal with Idonea in November 1315, and his second son Edward duly inherited Idonea's lands after she and her husband John Cromwell died. Idonea and John tried to backtrack on the arrangement in the early 1330s, claiming that Hugh confessed shortly before death to Lord Wake and other peers that he had used 'force, duress and threats' to induce them to agree to his son inheriting their properties. This is unlikely; in November 1315, Hugh was still years away from becoming an over-mighty royal favourite able to do whatever he wished. Given that he refused to eat or even drink for a week or more before his execution in 1326 and must have been almost insensible, and given that he knew what horrors were about to be inflicted on him, it is most improbable that his land deal with Idonea and John of eleven years previously was uppermost in his mind, as they claimed. An inquisition was held, but the couple's petition failed and Edward Despenser the Elder received their lands after they died. [4] Essendine had a watermill, a grange, a bakehouse, an orchard with a pond, stables, a gatehouse, twenty acres of meadow including two meadows called *Holmet* and *Roweseke*, 200 acres of wood, a close called *Parlond*, and pasture called *Halleendes*. It also had a small moated castle where the Despensers lived. The castle has long since vanished, though its chapel and extensive earthworks still survive. [5]

Edward and Anne's eldest son was baptised in the castle chapel, later the village church of Essendine, in mid-afternoon on the day of his birth, and had a godmother and two godfathers. One of the godfathers gave little Edward a gold ring worth twenty shillings and another gave twenty shillings in cash as christening gifts, and the ceremony was conducted by the abbot of Bourne, six miles away. The godparents' names were unfortunately not recorded, but Edward's godmother may have been the Despensers' cousin Blanche of Lancaster (b. *c.* 1302/5), whose husband Lord Wake owned the manor of Bourne; a few years later, a Despenser wedding took place in Blanche's castle at Bourne. A resident of Essendine called Maud West, perhaps the little boy's nurse, carried him to the chapel, and Ranulf of Paris, 'a lawful man of good condition and gentle estate', William Huntingfield, Robert Crauden, Walter Lamberd and Thomas Neville were among the other inhabitants of Essendine present during the christening. After the ceremony, Edward was laid on the altar, and John Gretford held a basin and towels for his three godparents to wash their hands. The young Edward Despenser was already knighted by October 1349 when he was only 13, and his future marriage to Elizabeth Burghersh seems to have been under discussion by July 1346 when he was 10 and she only about 4. [6] Edward was his childless uncle Huchon's successor as lord of Glamorgan.

The second of Edward Despenser the Elder and Anne's four sons was Hugh, who was born in 1337 or 1338, married the heiress Alice Hotham in 1352, and died in Italy in 1374 leaving two children. The third Despenser son was Thomas, born in 1339 or 1340 and named after his mother's brother Sir Thomas Ferrers. Thomas Despenser was knighted in France in 1360, seems never to have married, and died childless in 1381. The fourth and youngest son was Henry, who was 19 years old in February 1361 and hence was born in 1341 or the beginning of 1342. Edward and Anne named him after Anne's eldest brother Lord Ferrers of Groby. [7] In 1354, it was already planned to give Henry Despenser to the church, and his eldest brother Edward asked Pope Innocent VI to appoint him as a canon of York. [8] After an early career as a soldier in Italy, Henry became bishop of Norwich in his late twenties and held the position for thirty-six years until his death in 1406. He has been described by a modern historian as 'a proud, arrogant man', and a chronicler of his own era called him insolent, arrogant, immature, undisciplined and indiscreet. Another called him 'dissolute rather with military light-mindedness than weighty with pontifical maturity'. [9] Henry Despenser seems to have had something of his grandfather Hugh the Younger about him.

Eleanor Despenser née Clare, widow of Hugh the Younger, died on 30 June 1337 at the age of 44, fifteen months after the birth of her grandson Edward the Younger. She was buried at Tewkesbury Abbey in Gloucestershire, where she had buried Hugh the Younger in late 1330 and her second husband William Zouche just months before her own death. Eleanor's youngest child William Zouche, future monk of Glastonbury, was only about 6 or 7 when she died, and her fourth daughter Margaret Despenser, forcibly veiled as a nun by Queen Isabella in early 1327 when she was 3 years old, died also in 1337. Eleanor's sister Elizabeth Burgh, who treated her Despenser nieces and nephews with affection and kindness despite their father's appalling behaviour towards her in the 1320s, sent wax images and a painting of the four evangelists for Margaret's sepulchre. [10] Just four days before Eleanor's death, her cousin Edward III granted her second and third daughters, the nuns Joan and Eleanor Despenser, an annuity of £20 for the rest of their lives. [11]

Eleanor's eldest son Hugh 'Huchon' Despenser, 28 or 29 years old in the summer of 1337, was sole heir to her vast landholdings in South Wales and the south of England. Edward III ordered his officials on 21 July 1337 to give all Eleanor's lands to Huchon even before her inquisition post mortem officially returned him as his mother's heir, and he had already done homage to the king for them. [12] A few weeks before Eleanor's death, in April 1337, the king had granted Huchon various lands and manors in ten counties, almost all of which had once belonged to his grandfather Hugh the Elder or his father Hugh the Younger, and some of which were in the hands of Margaret, widow of Huchon's cousin Edward Bohun (d. 1334). Edward III politely referred to Huchon as 'the king's kinsman' in this grant. [13]

Huchon had already taken possession of Cardiff Castle on 17 August 1337 when he issued a charter there granting three acres of arable land in Llantrisant to the abbey church of Tewkesbury, where both his parents and his stepfather (and his maternal uncle, grandfather and other Clare ancestors) were now buried. [14] As Huchon was surely all too aware, his father and his great-uncle Edward II had been captured near Llantrisant in November 1326. Huchon seems to have spent much of his time at Cardiff and rarely if ever stayed at Caerphilly Castle which he also now owned; as he had been besieged there for four months as a teenager and threatened with execution, this is hardly surprising. On 12 November 1337, Huchon was given protection to go to Scotland on the king's service, and appointed two attorneys to act for him during his absence. [15] The letters of protection Huchon received in December 1337 and March 1338 for another campaign in Scotland referred to him as 'son and heir of Alianore [Eleanor] Despenser'. [16]

In 1337, King Edward III officially claimed the throne of France, declaring that as the grandson of King Philip IV he had a better right to it than the present incumbent, Philip IV's nephew Philip VI of the house of Valois. All four Despenser brothers, Huchon, Edward the Elder, Gilbert and John, fought in the early years of the Hundred Years War, as it is known to posterity. Huchon, lord of Glamorgan, sent a letter to Edward III around Easter 1338 with three other men: his uncle-in-law Hugh Audley, made earl of Gloucester the year before; his brother-in-law Richard Fitzalan, earl of Arundel; and his father's first cousin Thomas Beauchamp, earl of Warwick, then 24 and at least five years younger than Huchon himself. [17] The letter survives as a draft and there are several crossings-out and alterations, perhaps indicating that the four men were not initially able to agree on the wording. Addressing Edward as 'the very noble, very high and very puissant prince and their very dread lord, Lord Edward, by the grace of God king of England, lord of Ireland and duke of Aquitaine', the four men mentioned the two envoys, Sir John Molyns and Master John Charnels, whom the king had sent to them bearing messages 'touching the estate of your kingdom.' Molyns had been an adherent of Huchon's father and grandfather, and Edward III pardoned him for this in 1331. [18]

The letter indicates that Huchon may have been on close terms with Hugh Audley, despite the conflicts between Audley, a Contrariant of 1321/2, and Huchon's father in the late 1310s and 1320s. If Huchon resented Audley's appointment as earl of Gloucester in 1337, when he himself was the eldest nephew of the previous earl and might have been thought to have a superior claim, he kept it to himself. A man who witnessed a quit-claim of Huchon's in 1336 was Henry, Lord Ferrers of Groby, brother-in-law of Huchon's brother Edward, and another was Sir Maurice Berkeley, whose elder brother Thomas, Lord Berkeley had been imprisoned by Huchon's father and great-uncle from 1322 to 1326. Henry Ferrers witnessed another grant by Huchon in November 1337, as did William Montacute, earl of Salisbury, whose eldest daughter later married Huchon. [19] There is much evidence of a general willingness among the English nobility in the 1330s to allow Huchon Despenser to prove himself and not to blame him for his father's many crimes and misdeeds. He was, after all, the eldest great-grandson of Edward I and grandson of an earl of Gloucester, hence was deemed worthy of respect despite bearing the reviled name of his father and his other grandfather.

Sir Maurice Berkeley's nephew Maurice Berkeley the younger, heir to his father Lord Berkeley, was betrothed to, or perhaps married to, Huchon's youngest sister Elizabeth Despenser in August 1338, and Huchon paid 1,000 marks for the marriage. [20] Assuming that Elizabeth was the child born to Eleanor Despenser at the royal manor of Sheen in December 1325, she was now 12 years old. The seventeenth-century biographer of the Berkeley family believed that her husband Maurice was born late in Edward III's fourth regnal year, i.e. at the end of 1330 or beginning of 1331, around the time that his maternal grandfather Roger Mortimer, first earl of March, was executed on 29 November 1330. [21] If this is correct, Maurice was five years younger than Elizabeth, and only seven in August 1338.

The Berkeleys were wealthy and influential landowners in Gloucestershire and Somerset, and Elizabeth and Maurice's marriage was intended to heal the wounds of Edward II's reign when the Berkeleys and Despensers took different sides during the Despenser War and the Contrariant rebellion. Elizabeth's father Hugh the Younger controlled the Berkeley lands in and after 1322 while Thomas Berkeley languished in prison and his wife Margaret Mortimer was incarcerated in a convent. Young Maurice Berkeley's sister Joan was betrothed to Thomas, son of the Despenser adherent John Haudlo, in early 1337, and their marriage was intended to 'put an end to the strife' between the families owing to their differing allegiances in the 1320s. [22] It would be a few years before Maurice Berkeley was old enough to consummate his marriage, so Elizabeth stayed for about a year and a half with her aunt Elizabeth Burgh and Maurice spent a couple of years in southern Spain between 1342 and 1344. [23] Elizabeth Despenser had previously lived for a time at Wix Priory in Essex, which stood in a manor that had once belonged to her father and grandfather. Her first son was not born until January 1353.

Chapter 20

Huchon Despenser was at his castle of Cardiff on 9 October 1338 after returning from the latest English military campaign in Scotland, when he inspected and confirmed various ancient charters relating to Margam Abbey (founded 1147) which stood on his lands. One of the witnesses was his younger brother Gilbert Despenser. The list of witnesses reveals that Gilbert had not yet been knighted in October 1338, though he had been by December 1344. [1] John Despenser, the youngest brother of Huchon, Edward and Gilbert, is oddly obscure and difficult to find on record. He took part in the king's military campaign to France in 1346 and had been knighted then, Huchon gave him his Lincolnshire manor of Carlton, Edward III granted him an income of £20 a year in 1363, and he was murdered in 1366, but otherwise it is difficult to learn much about John Despenser's life, even whether he married and had children. Edward III restored Carlton to John in August 1359, having taken the manor into his own hands for 'certain causes', unstated. [2]

Huchon turned 30 in 1338 or early 1339, and sometime after June 1338 and before April 1341 made an excellent marriage to Elizabeth, eldest daughter of William and Katherine Montacute, earl and countess of Salisbury. Elizabeth Montacute was a good twenty years Huchon's junior and born *c.* 1330: her parents married in or shortly before 1327, and her brother William, their father's heir, was born in June 1328. [3] Despite her extreme youth, Elizabeth was already the widow of Giles Badlesmere (b. October 1314), son and heir of Bartholomew, a baron of Kent who was a close ally of Hugh Despenser the Elder and Younger in 1319/20 but switched sides and was executed as a Contrariant in 1322. Giles died in June 1338, and as he was Huchon's second cousin, Huchon and Elizabeth required a papal dispensation to wed. This was granted on 27 April 1341, after they had already married. [4] Elizabeth's sister Sybil married Huchon's nephew Edmund Arundel sometime in the early to mid-1340s, and another Montacute sister, Philippa, married Roger Mortimer's namesake grandson and heir (b. 1328), later the second earl of March. Huchon settled eight of his manors in six counties on himself and Elizabeth jointly on 12 June 1344. One of the manors was Shipton-under-Wychwood in Oxfordshire, where Eustace 'Stacy' Rokele, father of the great poet William Langland, was Huchon's tenant. [5] This grant may indicate that Elizabeth had recently turned 14, and was now of age and legally able to hold lands. Her extreme youth meant that she would be unable to be Huchon's wife in more than name only until a few years after their wedding.

Huchon's aunt Alina Burnell held the manor of Compton Dando in Somerset, and sometime before November 1338 complained that a group of people led by Joan Ryvere had broken into her houses there, stolen her goods and assaulted her servants. In early 1327 shortly after the downfall of Alina's protectors, her father Hugh the Elder and brother Hugh the Younger, Richard Ryvere had complained that Alina and others assaulted his servants and cut down his trees at Wick Fokeram in Somerset, so presumably this was a retaliatory attack by Ryvere's wife. [6] A commission to investigate the break-in at Compton Dando was granted to Alina's nephew Huchon and three other men, one of them Sir John Inge. Inge had in the late 1310s and early 1320s been a loyal supporter of Alina's brother Hugh the Younger in his capacity as sheriff of Glamorgan, but Hugh took against him *c.* 1323 and imprisoned him and members of his council. Possibly working with Hugh's son and heir proved slightly awkward for John Inge, though Huchon was nothing like his father (or at least, Edward III, a very different man to his own father Edward II, gave him no opportunity to be anything like Hugh the Younger).

In February 1339, Huchon gave Alina his Gloucestershire manor of Sodbury for the rest of her life, when it would revert to him and his heirs, though in the end, Alina outlived her nephew by fourteen years. In May 1341 Huchon was in possession of Martley in Worcestershire, a manor given to Alina for life by her father Hugh the Elder in or before 1321, so perhaps they had exchanged manors. [7] Alina granted some acres of land in her Worcestershire manor of Suckley to two chaplains in return for daily prayers for the souls of herself, Huchon, her brother Hugh the Younger, her late husband Edward Burnell and Sir William Ercalewe when they were all dead. [8] Ercalewe was one of the men accused with Alina of attacking the Ryveres' Somerset manor in 1327, was a long-term

Despenser adherent who had replaced Alina as constable of Conwy Castle in October 1326, and served as sheriff of Staffordshire that same year. On 5 February 1328, Ercalewe witnessed one of Alina's grants issued at the Shropshire manor of Ercall Magna which she held from him. [9] When Huchon Despenser went to Scotland on the king's service in 1337 and 1341, he appointed William Ercalewe as his attorney on both occasions, and by October 1338 Ercalewe was his steward. Huchon was at his Berkshire manor of Caversham on 12 May 1340 when he granted his valet Richard Bloundell all his lands and tenements in his Lincolnshire manor of Carlton for life; one of the witnesses to the grant was William Ercalewe. [10] Ercalewe served both Alina and Huchon, further proof that aunt and nephew kept in touch for many years. Huchon also often visited and sent letters to another aunt, his mother Eleanor's sister Elizabeth Burgh. [11]

Chapter 21

Huchon fought in Scotland again, as he had so often in the 1330s, in 1341, this time in the company of his first cousin Henry of Grosmont, earl of Derby, who was heir to his elderly father the earl of Lancaster. [1] That year, Duke John III of Brittany died without children, and the duchy of Brittany was contested by two claimants: the duke's niece Jeanne de Penthièvre, daughter of his late full brother Guy, and his younger half-brother John Montfort. England took the Montfort side, France Jeanne's side, during the War of the Breton Succession. Edward Despenser the Elder fought in Brittany in August and September 1342, under his brother Huchon's banner. Before Edward left England, he wisely took the precaution of regranting all but one of his manors to himself and his wife Anne Ferrers jointly, and made his will on 18 February 1342. [2] In case he died fighting, this would keep his lands together until his eldest son came of age, and it also demonstrates his trust in his wife. As it happened, Edward Despenser did die in Brittany: he was killed at the battle of Morlaix on 30 September 1342, fighting alongside Huchon. If Edward was born in October 1310, he was not quite 32 years old when he died, and his eldest son Edward the Younger was 6 and his fourth and youngest, Henry, just a baby. [3] Edward's widow Anne outlived him by twenty-five years, but never remarried.

Philip Despenser II, only child of Hugh the Elder's second son Philip I who died in 1313 when his son was five months old, married Joan Cobham around June 1339. [4] Their first son, inevitably also called Philip, was born on 18 October 1342 in Gedney, Lincolnshire, a manor which passed to this branch of the Despenser family from Philip II's mother Margaret Goushill. When Philip Despenser III proved that he had turned 21 years old in 1363, four of the jurors remembered his birth because they were in charge of the sea-wall near Gedney and the year previously there had been 'a great inundation of the sea' which broke the wall. Philip II was at

Newsham Abbey sixty-five miles away on the day of his son's birth and received the news by letter from a William Hode. [5]

Philip II and Joan Cobham also had a daughter, Hawise, born sometime in 1344/5, and a younger son, Hugh, born 1346/7; Hawise was 14 and Hugh was 12 in mid-February 1359, when a canon of Lincoln was instructed to appoint guardians for them. [6] This Hugh Despenser is probably the *donsel* – a boy or young man of noble birth not yet knighted – of this name in the diocese of Lincoln granted papal permission to choose a confessor in April 1357. [7] Other than these two references, Hugh is obscure, and probably died young. His sister Hawise married the widower Andrew, Lord Luttrell, who was born in 1313 and was exactly the same age as her father, in a castle at Bourne, Lincolnshire belonging to the Despensers' cousin Blanche of Lancaster, Lady Wake, in 1363. Andrew's father Geoffrey (d. 1345) commissioned the famous and gorgeous Luttrell Psalter, now in the British Library, and attacked Sempringham Priory in 1312 supposedly with the support of Hugh Despenser the Elder's sisters there. Hawise and Andrew Luttrell had a son also named Andrew who was born the year after their wedding, and grandchildren Geoffrey Luttrell (*c.* 1383–1419) and Hawise Beelsby, the Luttrell heir after Geoffrey died. When the elder Andrew made his will on 10 November 1389, he appointed 'my brother Philip Despenser [III]' as its supervisor. Andrew died on 6 September 1390 at age 77, and Hawise née Despenser on 10 April 1414 at 70. [8]

Huchon Despenser, lord of Glamorgan, did not forget his sisters Joan and Eleanor the nuns. In January 1343, he granted ten marks annually out of the rents of his Wiltshire manor of Broad Town (which had belonged to his ancestor Philip Basset and lay four miles from Vastern) for Joan's upkeep at Shaftesbury. At an unknown date he granted Broad Town to his brother Gilbert, who continued to pay the money to their sister, and another ten marks for Joan came out of Huchon's Gloucestershire manor of Fairford. Eleanor, the third Despenser sister, seems to have died in early 1351. [9] Huchon was at his castle of Cardiff on 22 May 1344, when he gave the church in his manor of Llantrisant to the abbey church of Tewkesbury, and a few weeks later settled eight manors on himself and his young wife Elizabeth jointly. [10] His father-in-law William Montacute, earl of Salisbury, had died in January 1344 while jousting, and his brother-in-law William the younger, heir to the earldom, turned 16 in June 1344.

Richard Fitzalan, earl of Arundel, had his marriage to Huchon's sister Isabella annulled in December 1344 on the grounds that they were underage when it took place in early 1321, did not consent to being married, consummated the marriage only because they were forced to by violence, and renounced their vows when they reached puberty. Isabella's reaction to and feelings about the annulment are unrecorded. In early February 1345 in the presence of Edward III and Queen Philippa, Arundel married his second wife Eleanor, fifth of the six daughters of Henry, earl of Lancaster and the late Maud Chaworth, and widow of John, Lord Beaumont (d. 1342).

Arundel gave Isabella Despenser six manors in Essex for her sustenance, and the annulment made their 18-year-old son Edmund illegitimate and ineligible to succeed his father as earl. Two years later, Pope Clement VI's response to Edmund's petition protesting against his treatment reveals that Arundel and Eleanor of Lancaster had lied to the pope and deliberately disguised Eleanor's real identity, in order to evade the problem of Eleanor's close family relationship to Isabella Despenser (they were first cousins). They pretended that Eleanor was called 'Joan Beaumont' and that she was related to Isabella via her father, rather than via her mother Maud Chaworth, older half-sister of Hugh Despenser the Younger. [11] The earl of Arundel and Eleanor of Lancaster's first child was born in late 1345 or early 1346, and they had five children together: the next earl of Arundel, the countesses of Hereford and Kent, the marshal of England, and the archbishop of Canterbury. Their eldest child Joan, countess of Hereford, was the grandmother of King Henry V, and their fourth child, John, had a son who married into the Despenser family in 1380.

Isabella Despenser, as far as is known, never remarried, and is difficult to trace after the annulment. She was still alive in 1356 and apparently dead by 1369. It may be significant that her brother Sir Gilbert Despenser was arrested and imprisoned in the Tower of London 'by reason of certain excesses' in December 1344, the month of the annulment. Perhaps Gilbert had forcefully made his feelings about the earl of Arundel's shabby treatment of his sister and nephew known to Arundel. Gilbert was released on the mainprise of his eldest brother Huchon and their cousin William Bohun, earl of Northampton. [12] The unfortunate Edmund Arundel, as well as being made illegitimate by the annulment, also saw his relationship with his father destroyed forever.

Cruelly and callously, the earl sneered at him as 'that certain Edmund who claims to be my son' and left 5,000 marks in his will for his heirs from his second marriage to fight any claim Edmund might make to his earldom. [13] Edmund Arundel and his wife Sybil Montacute had three daughters, Elizabeth, Philippa and Katherine, and grandchildren from all three, but Edmund lost any entitlement to his father's earldoms and vast wealth, and they passed to his much younger half-brother Richard (b. 1346/7).

Chapter 22

On 2 July 1346, Bartholomew, Lord Burghersh was one of a number of men who acknowledged that they owed 400 marks to Anne Ferrers, widow of Edward Despenser the Elder. This probably indicates that a marriage between Anne's eldest son Edward the Younger, then 10 years old, and Burghersh's granddaughter and ultimate heir Elizabeth Burghersh, about 4, was under discussion. The marriage was certainly on the table by 6 February 1350, and they were married by early August 1354. [1] Elizabeth was born *c.* 1342, and her grandfather Lord Burghersh was a nephew of Bartholomew, Lord Badlesmere, executed by Edward II as a Contrariant in 1322, and named after him. Burghersh was imprisoned at the Tower of London from October 1321 until October 1326, and Elizabeth's father Bartholomew the younger was probably born while his parents were prisoners. Bartholomew Burghersh the younger's remains in Walsingham, Norfolk were examined in 1961, and he was found to have stood five feet ten inches tall, to have twisted an ankle and broken several ribs at some point, and to have had a full set of rather worn teeth. [2]

Elizabeth was the younger Bartholomew's only child from his first marriage to Cecily Weyland, and as his second marriage remained childless, Elizabeth was the Burghersh heir. Her grandmother Elizabeth, Lady Burghersh, was one of the four co-heirs of her father Theobald Verdon (d. 1316), and her quarter of the large Verdon inheritance as well as the Burghersh lands ultimately passed to Elizabeth. [3] The marriage of Edward Despenser and Elizabeth Burghersh appears to have been a resounding success, and Elizabeth was a formidable character who did much to keep the Despenser patrimony intact after her husband's early death.

King Edward III left England in July 1346 with a large force including his sixteen-year-old eldest son Edward of Woodstock, now prince of Wales, and his Despenser cousins Huchon, Gilbert and John. John Despenser had now been knighted, and both he and Gilbert fought in the king's own division during that summer's French campaign. The Despenser brothers' first cousins Philip Despenser II, Hugh Hastings, Amaury St Amand and the Camoys brothers also took part in the campaign, as did an unidentified 'Sir Hugh Despenser the younger'. This was not Huchon, lord of Glamorgan, as Huchon appears elsewhere in the list of knights summoned to the French campaign and is named as a knight banneret. [4] The king inflicted a massive defeat on the forces of Philip VI of France at the battle of Crécy on 26 August 1346. Huchon Despenser played a vital role in the Crécy campaign just days before the battle by leading a small force of men across a ford of the River Somme. A large French force led by Godemar Fay shot at them from the other side with crossbows and longbows, and it took Huchon and his men forty-five minutes to wade through a mile and a half of waist-deep water, under fire the whole time. This remarkably brave, even foolhardy action prevented the English army becoming trapped and destroyed between the Seine and Somme rivers. [5]

Huchon was pardoned on 30 October 1346, in consideration of his good service in the wars against France, of 'all homicides, felonies, robberies and trespasses in England'. [6] He and his younger brothers had done their utmost to restore their family's name over the previous fifteen years, and Huchon's courageous deeds in France earned him accolades. Huchon was back in England and staying at his castle of Hanley in Worcestershire, where his stepfather William Zouche had abducted his mother Eleanor in 1329, on Easter Sunday, 1 April 1347. He granted his chamberlain Walter Bacheler £10 a year from his manor of Fairford. [7]

Huchon's cousin Sir Hugh Hastings was appointed as the steward of Queen Philippa's household in or before January 1345, acted as her attorney in December 1343 and surely on other occasions, and died in July 1347, still only thirty-seven years old. [8] In his will, Hugh appointed his 'lord and cousin' Henry of Grosmont, earl of Lancaster, Leicester and Derby, and his wife Margery Foliot as two of his four executors. To Henry Hastings, obviously a relative, Hugh left a horse called Morel de Tyrweyn, to Sir William Redenesse another one called Lyard de Ebor ('dapple-grey horse of York'), and to John of Bury he bequeathed his best set of clothes. [9] Hugh and Margery's elder son John Hastings, aged either 16, 17 or 18 in 1347, was his heir and lived until 1393, but had no children. Hugh also left his daughter Maud, later de la Mare, and his younger son Hugh Hastings II, and this Hugh had a son, Hugh III, who was born in 1354 and would marry back into the Despenser family in the 1370s.

Hugh Hastings I was buried in a church in Elsing, Norfolk which he himself had founded. His remains were examined in 1978 and it was found that he had stood five feet ten inches tall, suffered from osteoarthritis in the shoulder and elbow joints, and had at one point taken a severe blow to the mouth, presumably during a military engagement, which damaged his incisors. [10] A magnificent brass image of him can still be seen in Elsing, with eight figures depicted as 'weepers', who were members of his family and his comrades-in-arms: King Edward III; Hugh's first cousins Huchon Despenser, Amaury St Amand, John Grey of Ruthin and Henry of Grosmont; his half-nephew Laurence Hastings, earl of Pembroke; his mother Isabella Despenser's first cousin Thomas Beauchamp, earl of Warwick; and Ralph Stafford, made first earl of Stafford in 1351.

Hugh 'Huchon' Despenser, lord of Glamorgan, outlived his Hastings cousin by nineteen months, and died on 8 February 1349 at the age of 40. His kinsman Edward III, at Langley in Hertfordshire, heard of his death the next day. [11] This indicates that Huchon died somewhere not far from Langley, perhaps at one of the manors he owned in Buckinghamshire or Berkshire; if he had died in Gloucestershire, Worcestershire or at one of his many castles in South Wales, the news would have taken much longer to reach the king. The cause of his death is not known, but as the Black Death swept through England in 1348 and 1349 and killed a huge percentage of the population, he may well have died of bubonic plague. At the time of Huchon's death, Edward III owed him £2,770 in war wages, though Huchon's executors pardoned the king £1,170 of it. [12] His marriage to Elizabeth Montacute remained childless, so his heir to Glamorgan and all his other landholdings was his nephew Edward Despenser the Younger, eldest son of his deceased next eldest brother, Edward the Elder. Elizabeth Montacute married her third husband Sir Guy Bryan or Brien in 1350 and had children with him, so probably Huchon was infertile. Bryan was one of the two men appointed by Edward III in February 1349 as the official keeper of Elizabeth's jointure lands from her Despenser marriage, which surely reveals how she came to know him. [13]

Huchon was buried in Tewkesbury Abbey on the opposite side of the high altar from his father Hugh the Younger, and his magnificent alabaster effigy can still be seen there. If it is true to life, Huchon Despenser was a handsome, clean-shaven man with a short nose and a full, rather pouty mouth, and is depicted wearing a round basinet (helmet) and a tight-fitting leather jupon over chainmail and armour. Elizabeth was buried next to him ten years later, and her effigy depicts her with a square head-dress which was surely the height of contemporary fashion. Guy Bryan outlived her by more than thirty years, and was buried a few yards away from Elizabeth and Huchon. [14]

Edward the Younger was not quite 13 years old when his uncle died. On 6 February 1350, Edward and his soon-to-be grandfather-in-law Bartholomew Burghersh were made custodians of Huchon's lands in England and Wales, minus the large dower and jointure lands held by Huchon's widow Elizabeth, in exchange for £1,000 annually. Somewhat curiously, this grant talks about the need for Burghersh and Despenser to 'maintain the heir', as though the heir was not Edward himself. In September 1353, these lands were given into the custody of Edward's mother Anne Ferrers. [15] Huchon's cousin Philip Despenser II survived him by only a few months and died at the age of 36 on 22 August 1349, just weeks after his mother Margaret Goushill passed away. [16] Philip left his 6-year-old son Philip III as his heir, and his daughter Hawise and younger son Hugh as well. Perhaps Philip and his mother were also victims of the Black Death.

Hugh 'Huchon' Despenser was not chosen as a Knight of the Garter when his kinsman Edward III instituted the prestigious order in April 1348, though might have been had he not died in February 1349, and his nephew and heir Edward Despenser became a member of the order a few years later. Perhaps Huchon was disappointed that he did not receive the earldom of Gloucester after the death of his uncle-in-law Hugh Audley in November 1347; Audley left a daughter but no sons, and the earldom previously held by the Despensers' Clare ancestors lay dormant until revived as a dukedom for Edward III's youngest son in 1385. Neither was Huchon's grandfather's earldom of Winchester awarded to him. Huchon and his brothers had, however, done a great deal to restore the Despenser family's pride and reputation after the catastrophic downfall of his father and grandfather in 1326, and his nephews were to continue the good work.

Part 4

A Great and Worthy Knight: Edward the Younger, 1349–1375

Dramatis Personae

Edward Despenser the Younger (b. 1336), lord of Glamorgan: eldest son of Edward Despenser the Elder (d. 1342) and Anne Ferrers (d. 1367); heir to his childless uncle Hugh 'Huchon' Despenser, lord of Glamorgan; great-great-grandson of King Edward I

Elizabeth Despenser, née Burghersh (b. *c.* 1342): heir of her father Bartholomew (d. 1369) and grandparents Bartholomew Burghersh (d. 1355) and Elizabeth Verdon (d. 1360); marries Edward Despenser *c.* 1350

Hugh Despenser (b. *c.* 1337/8): second son of Edward the Elder and Anne Ferrers; marries Alice Hotham in 1352; father of Hugh (b. *c.* 1355) and Anne Despenser

Alice Despenser, née Hotham (b. *c.* 1335): daughter of John Hotham and heir of the Hotham family; abducted by Sir John Trussell in 1374 as a widow and forcibly married

Thomas Despenser (b. c. 1339/40): third son of Edward and Anne; never marries and has no children

Henry Despenser (b. 1341/2): fourth and youngest son of Edward and Anne; elected bishop of Norwich 1370

Hugh Despenser (b. *c.* 1355): only son and heir of Hugh Despenser (b. 1337/8) and Alice Hotham; nephew of Edward the Younger, lord of Glamorgan; marries Sybil, parentage unknown; has a daughter, Elizabeth, who dies young

Anne Botiller, née Despenser (b. late 1350s or 1360s): only daughter of Hugh Despenser (b. 1337/8) and Alice Hotham, and sister of Hugh (b. *c.*

1355); marries Edward Botiller (b. 1337); has a son, name unknown, who dies young

Anne (b. *c.* early 1360s), **Elizabeth** (b. *c.* late 1360s), **Margaret** (b. late 1360s or early 1370s) and **Thomas Despenser** (b. 1373): children of Edward the Younger and Elizabeth Burghersh; Thomas is the Despenser and Burghersh heir

Edward, **Hugh** and **Cecily Despenser**: children of Edward the Younger and Elizabeth who die young

Isabella Despenser (b. *c.* 1312): eldest daughter of Hugh the Younger (d. 1326); aunt of Edward the Younger and his three brothers; her marriage to Richard Fitzalan, earl of Arundel (b. *c.* 1313), was annulled in 1344 and he married her cousin Eleanor of Lancaster

Elizabeth Berkeley, née Despenser (b. 1325): youngest child of Hugh the Younger; marries Maurice (b. *c.* 1330), later Lord Berkeley, in 1338; mother of Thomas (b. 1353) and James (b. *c.* 1354/5) Berkeley

Gilbert Despenser (b. *c.* mid or late 1310s): third son of Hugh the Younger; marries Ela Calveley in or before 1360; father of John Despenser the Younger (b. 1361)

John Despenser the Elder (b. *c.* late 1310s/early 1320s): fourth and youngest son of Hugh the Younger; no known record of his wife and children, if any

Philip Despenser III (b. 1342): son of Philip Despenser II (1313–49) and grandson of Philip I (*c.* 1292/4–1313); second cousin of Edward the Younger; his son and heir is Philip Despenser IV (b. *c.* 1365) and his sister is Hawise Luttrell (b. 1344/5)

Edmund Arundel (b. *c.* 1326): only child of Richard Fitzalan, earl of Arundel, and Isabella Despenser; grandson of Hugh the Younger; made illegitimate on the annulment of his parents' marriage in 1344; married to Sybil, sister of William Montacute (b. 1328), earl of Salisbury, and father of Elizabeth, Philippa and Katherine

Richard Fitzalan, later earl of Arundel (b. 1346/7): eldest son of Richard Fitzalan and his second wife Eleanor of Lancaster; half-brother of Edmund Arundel; their father's heir

John Arundel I (b. *c.* 1350): second son of Richard Fitzalan and Eleanor of Lancaster; half-brother of Edmund Arundel; marries Eleanor Maltravers (b. 1344/5) and their son and heir is John Arundel II (b. 1364)

Hugh Hastings I (1310/11–47), grandson of Hugh Despenser the Elder, earl of Winchester; his second son **Hugh Hastings II** (*c.* early or mid-1330s–69); and his grandson **Hugh Hastings III** (b. *c.* 1354), who marries Anne, eldest daughter of Edward Despenser the Younger, in 1376

Edward III (b. 1312), king of England since 1327; married to Philippa of Hainault (b. *c.* 1314)

Edward of Woodstock, prince of Wales (b. 1330): eldest child of Edward III and Queen Philippa, heir to the English throne; marries his cousin Joan of Kent in 1361

Lionel of Antwerp, duke of Clarence (b. 1338), **John of Gaunt**, duke of Lancaster (b. 1340), **Edmund of Langley**, later duke of York (b. 1341) and **Thomas of Woodstock**, later duke of Gloucester (b. 1355): the younger sons of Edward III and Queen Philippa

Chapter 23

Edward Despenser the Younger was given into the custody of Edward III's chamberlain Bartholomew, Lord Burghersh in or before May 1349. The king, however, kept Despenser's wardship officially in his own hands – Edward was one of the most important heirs in the country – and granted Burghersh £100 a year for the young man's sustenance. [1] The young Edward married Bartholomew's granddaughter and ultimate heir Elizabeth Burghersh in 1350 or a little later. They were both far too young for the marriage to be consummated yet, though as Edward was in the custody of Elizabeth's grandfather, the young couple probably came to know each other very well long before they lived together as husband and wife.

Henry of Lancaster, earl of Lancaster and Leicester, brother-in-law of Hugh Despenser the Younger, had died in September 1345 at the age of about 65. His heir was his only son Henry of Grosmont (b. *c.* 1310/12), and he also left his six daughters Blanche, Isabella, Maud, Joan, Eleanor and Mary from his marriage to the long-dead Maud Chaworth. Henry of Grosmont was one of the greatest of all fourteenth-century English noblemen, a mighty warrior, widely considered the absolute epitome of chivalry, and a thoughtful, intelligent man who in 1354 wrote a treatise in French about the seven deadly sins called the *Book of Holy Medicines*. Edward III upgraded his kinsman Grosmont's title in 1351 and made him duke of Lancaster rather than merely earl (Henry was also earl of Leicester, Derby and Lincoln). On 8 October 1350, Henry of Grosmont and his wife Isabella Beaumont gave their Hampshire manor of Longstock to Sir Hugh Camoys for life. Hugh was the youngest son of Elizabeth Despenser, the much younger half-sister of Grosmont's mother, and hence was Grosmont's first cousin. [2] Grosmont's heirs were his daughters Maud (b. 1340) and Blanche (b. 1342). Maud married Queen Philippa's nephew Wilhelm of Bavaria in early 1352 but was destined to die in her early twenties without any surviving children, and Blanche married Edward III and Queen Philippa's third son John of Gaunt in 1359. Blanche became her father's sole heir when Maud died at 22, and her vast inheritance made her husband one of the richest men in England in the entire fourteenth century.

Around 24 February 1352, Hugh Despenser, second of the four sons of the late Edward the Elder and Anne Ferrers, married Alice Hotham. Hugh was about 14 at the time of his wedding, and Alice was a little older; the inquisition post mortem of her brother John Hotham says she was 16 in late 1351, so she was apparently born in 1335. Alice's father John Hotham the elder and Hugh's mother Anne and uncle Sir Thomas Ferrers arranged the marriage on or just before 9 February 1352. [3] The Despenser-Hotham match made good sense, as Alice inherited the manor of Collyweston, which lay just eight miles from Essendine. This was where Hugh's elder brother Edward the Younger was born in 1336, and perhaps he himself was born there too, as it was his late father's chief manor. The Despensers also held Burley, ten miles from Collyweston.

Alice's brother John Hotham the younger died on 27 September 1351 and left Alice and her 19-year-old older sister Katherine as the Hotham heirs, and within months of her brother's death, Alice married Hugh. [4] Whether Hugh Despenser ever met his wife's brother is unknown, but John Hotham was a bad lot: in January 1350 he was said to have committed 'notorious contempts' against the king by cutting off the left hand of a royal servant called Robert Basset. [5] Sometime before June 1336 when still underage, Hotham had married Ivetta, daughter of Sir Geoffrey Scrope (d. 1340), chief justice of the court of King's Bench and one of the premier judges in fourteenth-century England, but the couple had no children. [6] Alice Despenser née Hotham herself was closely related to John Hotham (d. 1337), bishop of Ely, treasurer and chancellor of England; her father Sir John often appears in the Chancery rolls in association with the bishop, and was called his 'kinsman and heir'. [7]

On 14 October 1351 within weeks of John Hotham the younger's death, Edward III appointed a man to search for John's sisters Katherine and Alice, 'who as the king understands are hidden in private places and taken by night from place to place that he may be excluded from their marriages, which pertain to him'. The young women were to be brought to London, and on 1 May 1352 were ordered to pay homage to the king for the lands they had inherited from their brother. [8] Alice's marriage to the king's cousin Hugh Despenser was, however, recorded on the Close Roll by royal clerks, so Edward must have given permission for it to take place. Katherine Hotham vanishes from history after 1352 and must have died (unless she entered a religious house), and her younger sister Alice carried their family's entire inheritance to the Despensers.

Hugh and Alice's first child, yet another Hugh Despenser, was born in an uncertain year in the 1350s. In October 1374 this Hugh was specifically said to be '22 years on the feast of St Nicholas last', which would mean that he had turned 22 years old on 6 December 1373, hence was born in December 1351. This, however, would predate his parents' wedding, so the year cannot be correct. He was also said to be 18 in October 1374 and 24 in October 1379. [9] This would indicate that Hugh the younger was born c. 1355, probably on or around 6 December, when his father was about 17 or 18 and his mother Alice about 20. He was old enough in 1375 to lead soldiers to the duchy of Brittany, where his grandfather Edward Despenser the Elder was killed fighting in 1342. [10] Hugh and Alice also had a daughter, named Anne after Hugh's mother, who was apparently much younger than her brother: she was said to be between 30 and 36 years old in October 1401, which would place her date of birth around 1365 to 1371. [11] Then again, Inquisitions Post Mortem could often be very vague on adults' ages; to give just one example of many, Henry of Lancaster, earl of Lancaster and Leicester, was said in his brother Thomas's inquisition post mortem of March 1327 to be 'aged 30 years and more', when in fact he was about 46 then. [12] Anne Despenser may therefore have been considerably older than this evidence would seem to indicate.

By the time of Hugh Despenser's death, he and Alice held the Lincolnshire manor of Bonby, the Northamptonshire manor of Collyweston, the Warwickshire manor of Solihull, and various houses, tenements, cottages and land in five Yorkshire manors. Bonby was held from the king 'by service of carrying a white rod before the king at Christmas if he should be in Lincolnshire.' By 1374, Bonby was a 'waste and without buildings' and the meadows and pastures were flooded by the river, so it was only worth £5 annually. Hugh and Alice probably lived mostly at their manor of Collyweston, and their son and heir called himself 'Hugh Despenser of Collyweston' and appears on record as 'Hugh Despenser of the county of Northampton, knight'. Collyweston is three miles from Stamford, just over the border in Lincolnshire, where Hugh, Alice and their son Hugh were all buried. [13]

As well as their English lands, Hugh and Alice Despenser held lands in Ireland: the castle of Kilkenny with five mills, five acres of meadow and sixteen of pasture, the borough of Rosborgan or Rosbergoun, the manors of Dumfret and Kildermay, and lands and rents in another sixteen places. The Irish lands were given to Hugh's mother Anne and passed to Hugh and Alice on her death in 1367, and the grant of them to the Despensers in February 1352 was witnessed by John St Paul, archbishop of Dublin; Henry Scrope, brother of Alice's sister-in-law Ivetta Hotham; and 19-year-old William Ferrers of Groby, the Despenser brothers' first cousin. The grant stated that if Hugh and Alice Despenser had no children, the lands would pass to Hugh's younger brothers Thomas and then Henry. [14] The Despenser/Hotham lands were ultimately inherited by Hugh's great-niece Isabelle Despenser (b. 1400). The Hotham family, though they took their name from a village in Yorkshire, were partly Irish and had strong connections there: John Hotham, bishop of Ely (d. 1337) first appears on record as a baron of the Irish exchequer in 1291, and his uncle William Hotham (d. 1298) was one of John St Paul's predecessors as archbishop of Dublin. [15]

The closeness of the Despenser and Ferrers families is apparent from William Ferrers of Groby witnessing the grant of lands in Ireland to his aunt Anne and her sons, and in later years Sir Ralph Ferrers, uncle of both William Ferrers and the four Despenser brothers, was a member of the council of Anne's eldest son Edward the Younger. [16] Edward left a valuable goblet to his uncle Ralph in his will of November 1375, and another uncle, Sir Thomas Ferrers, was involved in arranging the marriage of Edward's brother Hugh and Alice Hotham. Edward Despenser and his youngest brother Henry were also associated with Nicholas Litlington, prior and later abbot of Westminster, most probably also their uncle, the illegitimate son of their grandfather Hugh Despenser the Younger. Edward appointed Nicholas as his attorney on at least one occasion and left him a valuable goblet in his will, and Henry dined with Nicholas three times in the period from October 1371 to July 1372 (and surely in other years as well). [17]

Chapter 24

The Despenser brothers' aunt Elizabeth Berkeley gave birth to her first son Thomas, future Lord Berkeley, on 4 or 5 January 1353. [1] She was probably 27 years old and her husband Maurice about 22, and their son was named after her father-in-law Thomas, Lord Berkeley, who lived until 1361. Elizabeth and Maurice's second son James Berkeley was born in 1354 or 1355, and was the father of James the younger, born *c.* 1394, his uncle Thomas's successor as Lord Berkeley and the ancestor of the future lords of Berkeley.

Elizabeth's eldest sister Isabella Despenser, the cast-off wife of the earl of Arundel, was still alive in 1356 when she was involved in a legal case, though she seems to have died before November 1369 when some of the six manors Arundel had given to her were apparently back in his hands. [2] Isabella's life is, unfortunately, very obscure after the annulment of her marriage. A survey of London in 1603 states that she was buried in the London house of the Austin Friars with her brother Philip, presumably the little son of Hugh the Younger who died at the end of 1320 or beginning of 1321. [3] Isabella's only child Edmund Arundel, the now illegitimate son of the earl of Arundel and displaced as his father's heir by his two-decades younger half-brother Richard, received gifts of £5 and £20 from Edward of Woodstock, prince of Wales, on 24 November and 21 December 1355. [4] The reason for the gifts is not stated, though it may have been connected to the birth of a child to Edmund's wife Sybil Montacute. Although Edmund had been made illegitimate, he was still the brother-in-law of the earl of Salisbury and a great-great-grandson of Edward I, and therefore was deemed worthy of respect and consideration by his kinsman the prince of Wales. Edward III also courteously acknowledged Edmund Arundel as 'the king's kinsman' in September 1359, and Edmund often accompanied the prince of Wales on his overseas expeditions. [5] In 1368, Edmund was appointed as an envoy of Pope Urban V to Edward III. [6]

The Despenser heir Edward the Younger, now 19, accompanied his father-in-law Bartholomew Burghersh the younger – whose father the elder Bartholomew had recently died – to France in 1355 in a campaign led by the prince of Wales. [7] Edward fought at the battle of Poitiers on 19 September 1356, a great victory for the English side, and King John II of France himself was captured. Edward Despenser's uncle-in-law Maurice Berkeley also fought at Poitiers and was badly wounded and captured; he spent several years as a hostage in France and returned to England as an invalid. Edward of Woodstock returned to England in triumph and led a procession through London to show off his captive, the king of France, who would remain in England until his death in 1364. Woodstock's grandmother, the dowager queen Isabella of France, now 60 or 61, who normally spent most of her time at her favourite residence of Castle Rising in Norfolk, attended the procession. She died in August 1358 and was buried in London. Given her actions against the Despensers in 1326/7, the family surely did not grieve for her loss.

Edward Despenser's proof of age was taken at his birthplace of Essendine on Sunday, 7 August 1356 a few months before he turned 21 in March 1357. He probably returned to England from Gascony in April 1357, was summoned to the parliament held in February 1358, and by July 1359 was referred to as lord of Glamorgan. [8] Edward's aunt-in-law Elizabeth Montacute, Huchon's widow and the sister of the earl of Salisbury and the countess of March, died on 30 or 31 May 1359. Her extensive dower and jointure lands passed to Edward as Huchon's heir. According to the chronicle of Tewkesbury Abbey, Elizabeth died in Ashley, Hampshire, a Despenser manor she held. Another of the manors she had held was Hanley in Worcestershire, with its castle, a favourite residence of her late husband Huchon's mother Eleanor Clare and, in later decades, of Eleanor's great-grandson and heir Thomas and his wife Constance. She also held Tewkesbury, and her inquisition post mortem states that there were vineyards there. [9]

Edward Despenser, lord of Glamorgan, now held the entire Despenser inheritance, or rather, what remained of it. Many of the extensive lands across the midlands and south of England which had passed to Hugh the Elder, earl of Winchester, from his father Hugh the justiciar and mother Aline Basset were held by other people, but Edward had the third of the earldom of Gloucester his grandmother Eleanor inherited from her brother Gilbert in 1317, and some of Hugh the Elder's lands which Edward III had granted to Huchon over the years. He and his wife Elizabeth could also look forward to inheriting the Burghersh lands and the quarter of the Verdon lands held by Elizabeth's grandmother and father.

In the fourth decade of his reign, King Edward III continued to press his claim to the French throne, and in late October 1359 left England on yet another military campaign to France. Edward Despenser's brother Thomas, third son of the late Edward the Elder and aged about twenty or twenty-one, was knighted in France around April 1360 by the king of England personally, on volunteering with several other men to lead a sally towards Paris. [10] Edward and Thomas's youngest brother Henry Despenser was a master of the University of Oxford and had obtained his bachelor's degree by February 1361 when he was 19, and three years later became archdeacon of Llandaff. [11] Henry was, however, a warrior by inclination, like his three older brothers.

Sir Gilbert Despenser, third son of Hugh the Younger and uncle of the four Despenser brothers, married a woman from Norfolk called Ela Calveley in or before 1360. She was a widow, though had no surviving children from her first marriage; there are references in 1352 and 1354 to Ela Wyrham, daughter of John Calveley of Southburgh in Norfolk, and 'Richard of Wyrham and Ela his wife'. Wyrham in modern spelling is the Norfolk village of Wereham, and Gilbert's aunt Elizabeth Burgh (d. November 1360) owned lands there. [12] Elizabeth's son-in-law John Bardolf and his wife Elizabeth Damory, Gilbert's first cousin, held nearby Wormegay. These family connections to the area might indicate how Gilbert and Ela came to know each other. She was perhaps a rather lowly bride for a man who was a great-grandson of King Edward I and grandson of the earls of Gloucester and Winchester, so presumably it was a love-match. Gilbert was rather elderly to be marrying for the first time, so he may have been married before, though if so there is no known record of it and, like Ela, he had no surviving children. In early May 1361, when Gilbert was probably about 45, Ela gave birth to their son, John Despenser, who was named either after Gilbert's younger brother or Ela's brother John Calveley.

The unfortunate Ela died after giving birth, sometime before 6 December 1361 when her son was 30 weeks old. Her brother John Calveley died on 3 September 1361, and William Calveley, either John's son or his and Ela's brother, alive in 1356, had died before him.

The bell tower of Evesham Abbey, Worcestershire. Hugh Despenser the justiciar was buried before the high altar in the abbey church next to Simon Montfort, after falling alongside Montfort at the battle of Evesham on 4 August 1265. The abbey was founded around 700 and was dissolved in 1540, and little of it remains. (*Milo Bostock on Flickr*)

(*Above and below*) Caerphilly Castle, Glamorgan, which passed into the Despenser family in 1317. Hugh 'Huchon' Despenser was besieged here as a teenager between November 1326 and March 1327. His mother Eleanor Clare was born in the castle in 1292, and her father Gilbert built it. (*David on Flickr*)

A stone corbel in the great hall of Caerphilly Castle, perhaps a representation of Hugh Despenser the Younger, who rebuilt the hall in the 1320s. The bearded, crowned man on the right is almost certainly Edward II. (© Crown copyright (2019) Cadw, Welsh Government; used with kind permission)

Tewkesbury Abbey, Gloucestershire, mausoleum of the Despensers and their Clare ancestors. (*Author's Collection; image used with the permission of the Vicar and Churchwardens of Tewkesbury Abbey*)

Inside the abbey church of Tewkesbury: the tomb of Hugh Despenser the Younger, lord of Glamorgan, buried here more than four years after his execution in November 1326. It was much vandalised after the Reformation. (*Author's Collection; image used with the permission of the Vicar and Churchwardens of Tewkesbury Abbey*)

(*Opposite, right and below*) The effigy and tomb of Hugh the Younger's eldest son Hugh 'Huchon' Despenser, lord of Glamorgan (1308/9–49), in Tewkesbury Abbey. His wife Elizabeth Montacute (d. 1359) lies next to him. (*Craig Robinson; image used with the permission of the Vicar and Churchwardens of Tewkesbury Abbey*)

Edward Despenser, lord of Glamorgan (1336–75), grandson of Hugh the Younger, nephew and heir of Huchon; the 'Kneeling Knight' of Tewkesbury. (*Craig Robinson; image used with the permission of the Vicar and Churchwardens of Tewkesbury Abbey*)

(*Right and below*) Plaques on the floor of Tewkesbury Abbey commemorating the Kneeling Knight's son Thomas Despenser, lord of Glamorgan and earl of Gloucester (1373–1400) and Thomas's son Richard (1396–1413). (*Author's Collection; image used with the permission of the Vicar and Churchwardens of Tewkesbury Abbey*)

The chapel of Thomas's posthumous daughter and heir Isabelle Despenser, countess of Worcester and Warwick (1400–39), in Tewkesbury Abbey. She was buried next to her first husband Richard Beauchamp, earl of Worcester (d. 1422). (*Author's Collection; image used with the permission of the Vicar and Churchwardens of Tewkesbury Abbey*)

(*Above*) Stamford, Lincolnshire, where some of the Despensers were buried in the now-vanished Greyfriars church: Hugh in 1374, his widow Alice Hotham in 1379, his brother Thomas in 1381, his son Hugh in 1401, and probably the younger Hugh's widow Sybil in 1415 and their daughter Elizabeth in 1400/01. (*Author's Collection*)

(*Below*) Church of St Mary Magdalene, Essendine, Rutland, where Edward Despenser the Younger, lord of Glamorgan, was baptised in 1336. (*Author's Collection*)

The picturesque village of Kersey, Suffolk, which Hugh Despenser the Elder inherited from his mother Aline Basset in 1281 and gave to his son Hugh the Younger in or after 1310. (*Rob Glover on Flickr*)

Site of Hanley Castle, Worcestershire, where Hugh the Younger's widow Eleanor was abducted in January 1329, and where Isabelle Despenser gave birth to her son and heir Henry Beauchamp, duke of Warwick, in March 1425. Henry died there in June 1446. The castle was derelict by the 1540s and has now vanished. (*Author's Collection*)

The abbey church of Sempringham Priory, Lincolnshire. Queen Isabella forced Hugh Despenser the Younger's third daughter Eleanor to become a nun here at the beginning of 1327, and she died here probably in early 1351. (*Author's Collection*)

Norwich Cathedral. Henry Despenser, bishop of Norwich, was buried before the high altar in 1406. (*Martin Pettitt on Flickr*)

The site of the medieval manor-house at Woking in Surrey, later Woking Palace, almost certainly where Hugh Despenser the Elder and Younger kept Elizabeth Comyn imprisoned in 1324/25 until she handed over several manors to them. (*Author's Collection*)

The baby John Despenser was therefore named as co-heir to his maternal uncle's Norfolk manor of Calveley with Ela's sister Annora Coroner, then aged about 30. [13] Gilbert Despenser held half of his late brother-in-law's manor during his son John's minority, and also held manors in Gloucestershire, Wiltshire, Hampshire and Surrey, some as a gift of his late brother Huchon. He was surprisingly wealthy: among other examples, he lent £40 to John Burdon of Gloucestershire in 1353, and £500 to John Cottelegh of Dorset in 1361. [14] Gilbert was a household knight of Edward III and Queen Philippa, and in February 1368 received a grant of forty marks a year from the king. [15]

Edward III had founded the chivalric Order of the Garter in 1348, and one of the new Knights of the Garter created during the celebrations of 1361, held as always at Edward III's birthplace of Windsor Castle, was Edward Despenser, lord of Glamorgan. The king's middle three sons Lionel of Antwerp, John of Gaunt and Edmund of Langley, born in 1338, 1340 and 1341 respectively, were also made Knights of the Garter that year, so Edward Despenser was in particularly prestigious company. The rehabilitation of the Despensers was complete; Hugh the Younger's sons and grandsons spent decades patiently rebuilding the family's fortunes and demonstrating their loyalty to their kinsman Edward III, and reaped the rewards.

Chapter 25

King Edward celebrated his fiftieth birthday in November 1362 by raising his three middle sons to peerages (Thomas of Woodstock, his fifth and youngest son, was not yet 8 years old). Lionel of Antwerp became duke of Clarence, John of Gaunt became duke of Lancaster, and Edmund of Langley became earl of Cambridge. The Despenser brothers, especially the two eldest, Edward and Hugh, were closely associated with Lionel of Antwerp and John of Gaunt, and Thomas the third Despenser brother was in the company of Edward of Woodstock, prince of Wales, on 27 August 1362 when he received a gift of fifty marks from the prince. [1] Woodstock had recently been appointed prince of Aquitaine by his father, and set off for the south of France to rule the duchy, with his wife Joan, countess of Kent, at his side; both their sons would be born there.

Alina, Lady Burnell, eldest child of Hugh Despenser the Elder, finally died on 16 May 1363, well into her seventies. She had lived as a widow for almost half a century since Edward Burnell died in August 1315, and outlived all her siblings by decades. Alina had no children and her heir was Edward Despenser the Younger, her brother Hugh the Younger's grandson. She had lived so quietly for so many years after her father and brother's downfall in 1326 that in November 1353 she was wrongly believed to be dead. [2] Alina's great-nephews Edward and Thomas Despenser were both in England in September 1363, and Thomas granted several manors to the king. The grant was witnessed by the king's sons John of Gaunt and Edmund of Langley, Edward Despenser, and Humphrey Bohun, earl of Hereford (b. 1342), a great-grandson of Edward I and thus a kinsman of the Despensers. [3]

One of the most obscure Despensers of the fourteenth century was John (b. c. 1320), youngest son of Hugh the Younger and Eleanor Clare, Alina Burnell's nephew, and uncle of the four Despenser brothers. According to the chronicler John of Reading, John Despenser was murdered in London around the feast of St Barnabas, i.e. 11 June, in 1366, and his murderers were subsequently hanged. [4] An entry in the Chancery rolls confirms that John died shortly before 10 June 1366 when the escheator in Hampshire was ordered to take his lands and goods into the king's hands. [5] There is no inquisition post mortem for John and it is not known whether he married and left children, and although the chronicler's account of his murder cannot be confirmed, he did get the date of John Despenser's death correct. John of Reading, unfortunately, gives no details of the murder or why it happened.

In September 1366, John Despenser's 30-year-old nephew Edward Despenser visited Berkeley Castle in Gloucestershire. He travelled there with the chronicler Jean Froissart, a friend and admirer of his who called Edward *li grans sires Espensiers*, 'the great Lord Despenser', and 'the most handsome, the most courteous and the most honourable knight in all England'. Froissart added that noble ladies considered a social function imperfect if Lord Despenser were not present. [6] The two men stayed at Berkeley for three days. The lady of Berkeley Castle at the time, though Froissart fails to mention the fact, was Edward's aunt Elizabeth Despenser. Her husband Maurice had finally succeeded his long-lived father as Lord Berkeley in 1361, but Maurice had been badly wounded at the battle of Poitiers in 1356 which cut short both his career and his life, and he died less than two years after his nephew-in-law's visit. He and Edward Despenser had been appointed two of the six keepers of the peace in Gloucestershire in March 1364, and as they were both wealthy landowners in that part of the country and had a close family connection, they must have known each other well. [7] Jean Froissart was curious about the fate of Edward II at Berkeley Castle in 1327, a curiosity presumably shared by Edward Despenser given that the king was his great-great-uncle and that his grandfather Hugh the Younger was probably the king's lover, but they learned nothing useful about Edward II's death. Either people at Berkeley did not know what had happened there almost forty years previously, or did not wish to tell.

Far away in the south-west of France, the future king of England was born in Bordeaux in the duchy of Aquitaine on 6 January 1367, and Jean Froissart was in the city at the time, having travelled to Gascony not long after his visit to Berkeley Castle with Despenser. Richard of Bordeaux was the second son of Edward of Woodstock, prince of Wales and Aquitaine, and Joan of Kent, and became heir to the English throne after his father when his elder brother Edward of Angoulême (b. January 1365) died in childhood. Richard's first cousin Henry of Lancaster, the future King Henry IV, was born just three months later, at Bolingbroke in Lincolnshire, the only surviving son of Edward III's third son John of Gaunt and his first wife Blanche of Lancaster, daughter and heir of Henry of Grosmont, duke of Lancaster (d. 1361).

On 3 April 1367, Richard of Bordeaux and Henry of Lancaster's fathers Edward of Woodstock and John of Gaunt fought the battle of Najera in Spain in aid of Pedro 'the Cruel', king of Castile (b. 1334), against Pedro's illegitimate half-brother Enrique of Trastamara (also b. 1334). Edward, John and Pedro won the battle, but less than two years later Trastamara returned to Castile, defeated Pedro at another battle, stabbed him to death, and made himself king of Castile. One young English nobleman killed at the battle of Najera in 1367 – in fact, the only high-ranking Englishman who fell there – was John, Lord Ferrers of Chartley, leaving his young son Robert, who would later marry a Despenser bride, as his heir. [8] And Edward of Woodstock, the great prince of Wales, came down with a serious recurring illness in Spain which would kill him nine years later.

Chapter 26

Anne Ferrers, widow of Edward Despenser the Elder, died on 8 August 1367, and her dower lands passed to her eldest son Edward the Younger. [1] Sir Hugh Despenser (b. 1337/8), Anne's second son, was given permission on 21 November 1367 to go to Prussia with three squires, four valets, and eight horses. [2] Almost certainly he took part in a *reyse*, a crusade against the pagans of Lithuania which was hugely popular among fourteenth-century European noblemen until Lithuania completed its process of Christianisation later in the century, and in effect was a kind of 'knightly package tour' with plenty of feasting and hunting organised as side attractions. [3] Hugh may have spent a few months in Prussia and Lithuania, but by late May 1368 he was far to the south, in and around Milan, Italy with his elder brother Edward Despenser and their kinsman Lionel of Antwerp, duke of Clarence. Pope Urban V wrote to Hugh in August 1368, asking him to aid the papal chaplain Robert Stratton whom he had sent to Lionel to inquire after the royal duke's health. Lionel died in October 1368 a few weeks before his thirtieth birthday, and evidently was ill enough two months before his death for the pope to have heard about it, and to be concerned. [4]

Duke Lionel, widowed from the heiress Elizabeth Burgh since December 1363, married his second wife Violante Visconti, daughter of Galeazzo, lord of Milan and Pavia, on 28 May or 5 June 1368. Edward Despenser was the second-highest ranking member of the entire retinue behind Lionel himself. The party, including Edward's brother Hugh, left England in early April 1368 and travelled through Paris and over the Alps into Italy, and arrived in Milan on 27 May. [5] A magnificent banquet of eighteen courses was held after the wedding at which Edward Despenser and other magnates served at table, and Edward and Hugh Despenser were two of the seven men lucky enough to receive splendid gifts from Galeazzo Visconti. Edward received two coursers (horses), two pieces of gold brocade and two of silk brocade, while Hugh was given a courser, cloth of gold and woollen cloth. [6]

Things were soon to go badly wrong, however. Duke Lionel died mere months after his splendid Italian wedding, and the English party accused his in-laws the Viscontis of having poisoned him. This seems extremely unlikely, given that Lionel was already ill in August when Urban V sent his chaplain to see him and sent a letter to Hugh Despenser on the matter. In his will made two weeks before his death, Lionel left his wife Violante his clothes and gold coronets, and appointed her as one of his executors. [7] This would argue against the notion that he thought her family had had him killed, but Edward Despenser seems to have been convinced that his kinsman had been murdered, and in revenge, joined Pope Urban V's ongoing war against Galeazzo Visconti and the city of Milan. His youngest brother Henry Despenser also took part. In the late 1360s, three of the four Despenser brothers, Edward, Hugh and Henry, were in Italy. The remaining brother, Thomas, spent the years 1368 and 1369 in Gascony as part of the standing force of the prince of Wales and Aquitaine, Edward of Woodstock. Their kinsman Philip Depenser III was also in Gascony with the prince. [8]

Lionel of Antwerp's mother Queen Philippa, who had been married to Edward III for over forty years, died on 15 August 1369 at the age of about fifty-five. Sir Gilbert Despenser was one of the knights of the royal household provided with black cloth and fur to make mourning robes. [9] Gilbert's nephew Edward Despenser was in Lombardy, Italy around Easter 1369, and his brother Hugh was with him, but Edward and the youngest Despenser brother Henry were back in England by 17 December 1369 when they were together at Edward's castle of Hanley in Worcestershire. Both men were the godfathers of one Edward Carent, son and heir of Alexander Carent, born and baptised at Hanley on 17 December and named after the lord of Glamorgan. The two men 'raised him from the sacred font' on the day of his birth. [10] A year later, on 12 December 1370, Henry Despenser dated a commission 'at the castle of Henle'. Almost certainly this means Hanley in Worcestershire, so Henry was visiting Edward again though he had been appointed bishop of Norwich on the other side of the country by then. [11] All four Despenser brothers seem to have been very close and to have spent much time together.

As well as being extremely popular in England, especially among ladies, Edward the Younger made an excellent impression in Italy, where he spent much of his career in the 1360s and early 1370s. Pope Urban V wrote to Edward III's third son John of Gaunt, duke of Lancaster, in early 1370, 'commending through him to the king, Edward, Lord Despenser ... who has won a glorious name in the battles of Lombardy.' [12] In the chapel of Santa Maria Novella in Florence, a fresco still exists which depicts Urban V's meeting with the Holy Roman Emperor Karl IV at Viterbo on 17 October 1368. One of the men depicted in the fresco is an English Knight of the Garter, a handsome man apparently in his early to mid-thirties with a thin face and a reddish-brown, short, pointed beard. This man has been identified as Edward, Lord Despenser, the only Knight of the Garter in Italy at this date with the exception of Lionel of Antwerp, who died on the same day as the meeting between the emperor and the pope. Edward Despenser was 32 years old in 1368. If it truly is he, Despenser was the first Englishman depicted in Italian art since St Thomas Becket, the archbishop of Canterbury murdered in 1170; further evidence of his excellent reputation in Italy. [13] Edward's grandfather Hugh the Younger and great-grandfather Hugh the Elder were arguably the most reviled Englishmen of the entire fourteenth century, but Edward, by his own achievements and his force of personality, made himself widely admired, respected and loved.

Chapter 27

Edward Despenser must have returned to England on a few occasions in the 1360s and early 1370s, in addition to his visit in late 1369, in order to father his children, unless his wife Elizabeth accompanied him to Italy. [1] When he was in England, he spent much time at court, as evidenced by his witnessing many of Edward III's charters in the 1360s. [2] If Elizabeth did travel abroad with her husband, it is likely, however, that she returned to England or Wales to give birth to all their children there rather than in Italy. Although Edward III had changed the law in 1351 so that English people born outside the lands he ruled could still inherit lands in England and Wales, the nobility generally liked their offspring to be born in their homeland and preferably in one of their own lordships. Edward returned to his homeland from Italy in the summer of 1372. He passed through the German city of Cologne in late July on his way, and granted an income of £20 a year to a citizen of Cologne from his treasury in England. No sooner had he arrived home, however, when he headed off to France again in September 1372 on Edward III's latest expedition there. [3] Edward and Elizabeth Despenser must have been together at Christmas 1372 to conceive their youngest child, Thomas, born the following September.

Of their seven children, Edward and Elizabeth lost three in childhood: their daughter Cecily and their sons Edward and Hugh. Edward, the first son, died at the age of 12 in Cardiff and Hugh, the second son, died shortly after birth, and all three Despenser children were buried in Tewkesbury Abbey in Gloucestershire, the Despenser mausoleum. [4] The youngest of their seven children, the third and only surviving son and the Despenser/ Burghersh heir was Thomas, and they had three daughters who lived into adulthood. The chronicle of Tewkesbury Abbey lists the daughters as Elizabeth, Anne and Margaret in that order, though Anne married four years before Elizabeth and gave birth to her first child seven years before Elizabeth gave birth to hers, and therefore must have been a few years older than she. The chronicle is not as accurate on its patrons, the Despenser family, as one might expect or hope; for example, it wrongly gives the sons of Edward the Elder and Anne Ferrers as Edward, Thomas, Henry and Gilbert rather than Edward, Hugh, Thomas and Henry. [5]

Anne Despenser was named after her paternal grandmother Anne Ferrers, indirect evidence that she was indeed the eldest daughter. Cecily Despenser, who died young and was named after their maternal grandmother Cecily Weyland, was probably the second daughter. Anne married in 1376 and her first child was born *c.* 1378, so she is unlikely to have been born after 1362/3 and was at least a decade older than her youngest sibling, Thomas. Either Anne or her brother Edward was the eldest Despenser child; the young Edward died before their father, and when Lord Despenser passed away in November 1375, his youngest son Thomas was named as his heir. As young Edward died when he was 12 years old, he must have been born before 1363. Elizabeth, the third Despenser daughter after Anne and Cecily, married in 1380 and gave birth to her first child in 1385, and was probably born in or after *c.* 1367/8; the five-year delay between wedding and eldest child might indicate that the marriage could not be consummated for some years owing to her youth. Margaret was the fourth and youngest daughter, and was probably born around 1369/71, two to four years before her brother Thomas. Her children were born between *c.* 1386 or 1389 and *c.* 1400.

Anne Despenser married Sir Hugh Hastings III of Elsing and Gressenhall in Norfolk around 1 November 1376. [6] As the great-grandson of Isabella Hastings (d. 1334), second daughter of Hugh Despenser the Elder, Hastings was Anne's third cousin. He was born a little before 2 February 1354, so was a few years her senior. [7] Anne and Hugh had two sons before his death in 1386. Their first son, inevitably also called Hugh, was nine years old in April 1387, outlived his father, but died as a teenager in 1396. Their second son and ultimate heir was Edward Hastings, born in May 1382.

Elizabeth Despenser married John Arundel II on or before 1 August 1380. [8] He was born on 30 November 1364 as the eldest son and heir of John Arundel I and the heiress Eleanor Maltravers, and hence was 15 at marriage. Elizabeth's father-in-law John Arundel I, marshal of England, was the second son of Richard, earl of Arundel (b. *c.* 1313) and his second wife Eleanor of Lancaster, and his elder brother Richard succeeded their father as earl of Arundel in 1376; they were the much younger half-brothers of the half-Despenser Edmund Arundel. John Arundel I became a father at a young age. According to an entry in the Chancery rolls, he was the fourth child of his parents, who married in February 1345, and there is no doubt that Elizabeth Despenser's husband John II, eldest of John I and Eleanor Maltravers' seven children, was born in late 1364. John I was probably born around 1350 and therefore was only about 14 when he became a father; his wife Eleanor Maltravers was born *c*. 1344/5 and was a few years his senior. [9]

John Arundel II was raised with Richard of Bordeaux, the future King Richard II, and was knighted with him by Richard's grandfather Edward III on 23 April 1377 when he was 12 years old. Another boy knighted on that date was Henry of Lancaster, also a grandson of Edward III and the future King Henry IV. [10] As grandson and nephew of earls of Arundel, nephew of the earls of Hereford and Kent and the future archbishop of Canterbury, and a companion of the young king of England, John Arundel II was an excellent marital prospect. In 1381 his first cousin Mary Bohun married Henry of Lancaster, a connection which would give his and Elizabeth Despenser's children kinship to the Lancastrian kings of England in and after 1399. John Arundel I arranged his eldest son's marriage to Elizabeth Despenser sometime before he drowned in December 1379, and he and his wife Eleanor granted the Gloucestershire manor of King's Stanley, which Eleanor had inherited from her grandfather John Maltravers, to John II and Elizabeth jointly. [11] John and Elizabeth had three sons born between 1385 and *c*. 1389/90, and their descendants inherited the earldom of Arundel after John's cousin Thomas died childless in 1415.

At an unknown date in or before the mid-1380s, the youngest Despenser daughter Margaret married Robert Ferrers of Chartley, a descendant of the family who had been earls of Derby in the twelfth and thirteenth centuries. Robert's great-great-grandfather Robert Ferrers (*c*. 1239–79) was deprived of his earldom of Derby by Henry III's son the future King Edward I in the late 1260s to benefit Edward's younger brother Edmund of Lancaster. The direct descendants of Robert Ferrers, earl of Derby, were known as the Ferrers of Chartley (in Staffordshire), and there was another branch of the family, the Ferrers of Groby (in Leicestershire), who descended from Earl Robert's younger brother William (*c*. 1240–87). Anne Ferrers, who married Edward Despenser the Elder in 1335, was a Ferrers of Groby.

Chapter 27

Robert Ferrers of Chartley, husband of Margaret Despenser, was a grandson of Ralph Stafford, first earl of Stafford (d. 1372) via his mother Elizabeth, and like his wife was a descendant of Edward I. His father John, Lord Ferrers was killed at the battle of Najera in Spain on 3 April 1367. Robert was said to be 7 years old in John's inquisition post mortem of June 1367, though according to his mother Elizabeth Stafford's inquisition post mortem of 1375, he was born on 31 October 1357. As he proved that he had come of age (i.e. 21) on 23 July 1381 and received his parents' lands that month, however, 1357 seems too early, and a date of birth in 1359/60, perhaps 31 October 1359, is more likely. Edward III gave the rights to Robert's marriage and custody of his parents' lands to his squire John Beverley on 16 September 1376. Margaret Despenser's paternal grandmother Anne Ferrers was the godmother of John Beverley's elder daughter and co-heir Anne, born in London on 3 March 1367 and named after her, and this connection might indicate how Robert and Margaret came to know each other and how their marriage was arranged. [12]

Robert and Margaret, who was a decade or so his junior, had three sons, Edmund, Thomas and Edward Ferrers, and two daughters, Philippa and Elizabeth. Edmund Ferrers the eldest son and his father's heir was born between 1386 and 1389 and died in 1435. [13] It would be unusual and unconventional by the standards of the era if Robert and Margaret had not named one of their sons John after Robert's father, so they may have had another child who died young, perhaps their first son. Their daughter Philippa Ferrers married Sir Thomas Greene, who was born in 1399 or 1400, and gave birth to her son Thomas Greene II in about 1427. Via her daughter Philippa Ferrers and Philippa's grandson Thomas Greene III, born c. 1461, Margaret Despenser was the great-great-great-grandmother of Henry VIII's sixth and last queen Katherine Parr (1512–48). Margaret was also an ancestor of Robert Devereux, earl of Essex, beheaded by Elizabeth I in 1601, via her son Edmund Ferrers, and she and her older sisters Anne and Elizabeth and their younger brother Thomas had and have numerous descendants.

Thomas was the youngest of Edward Despenser and Elizabeth Burghersh's seven children, and the Despenser/Burghersh heir. He was born on 22 September 1373, almost certainly at one of his father's Gloucestershire manors, perhaps Tewkesbury. The Gloucestershire men were the only jurors at Edward's inquisition post mortem in late 1375 who gave a precise date of birth for Thomas rather than merely stating that he was two years old as the jurors of all the other counties did, a good indication that he was born in Gloucestershire. [14] Thomas was perhaps named after his father's brother Sir Thomas Despenser, or after Thomas Chesterton, abbot of Tewkesbury from 1361 to 1389. Although Edward Despenser was in England in May/June 1373, he was appointed as the constable of John of Gaunt's army for the great *chevauchée* (raid) which the king's third son led through France in 1373. If Edward left England with Gaunt rather than joining the army later, he must have sailed in early July and hence missed Thomas's birth, and entries in the chancery rolls reveal that he was going overseas yet again in May 1375, a few months before his death. In or a little before May 1374, Edward captured a ship of Sluys called the *Seinte Anne*, took it to Chichester, and confiscated the 138 tuns (about 35,000 litres) of wine it carried. [15]

Thomas Despenser married when he was still a child, and made a startlingly good match. On 16 April 1379, Thomas's marriage was granted to Edward III's fourth son Edmund of Langley, earl of Cambridge and later duke of York, 'for the purpose of marrying the said heir to his daughter'. [16] Edmund and his Spanish wife Isabel of Castile had one daughter, Constance, named after her aunt Constanza of Castile, duchess of Lancaster, who may have been her godmother. Constance, born sometime between 1374 and 1376, was even younger than her fiancé, but despite their extreme youth the child-couple married on or a little before 7 November 1379. [17] Thomas's great-grandfather Hugh the Younger had married a king's granddaughter, Eleanor Clare, in 1306; Thomas went one better and married a girl who was the granddaughter of two kings, Edward III of England and Pedro 'the Cruel' of Castile. Thomas and Constance would not of course have lived together as husband and wife until they were much older, but Thomas is likely to have spent much time with the York family as he grew up. He lost his father when he was only two years old, and although his mother Elizabeth remained his official guardian, she may well have sent him to live in the York household when he was seven or thereabouts.

Chapter 28

Sir Hugh Despenser, the brother closest in age to Edward Despenser, was in Italy in May 1370 and in the spring of 1371 when he was named as a soldier at the head of thirty lances. *Messer Ugo di Edwardo Despenser*, 'Sir Hugh of Edward Despenser', received a large annual salary of 160 florins, so evidently Hugh was highly regarded as a soldier. He appears to have remained in Italy, as in 1373 he received an advance of 900 florins from the famous English mercenary Sir John Hawkwood (who spent a long and highly successful career in Italy) to pay off his debts so that he could take up papal service against Bernabo Visconti, lord of Milan, brother and co-ruler of Galeazzo. [1] Perhaps his wife Alice Hotham accompanied him, and their children Hugh the younger and Anne too. Hugh the younger was probably born in 1355, so was old enough to fight from the early 1370s onwards and may have done so alongside his father.

Hugh's youngest brother Henry Despenser was elected bishop of Norwich by Pope Urban V on 3 April 1370, a few months before Urban's death. Henry was supposedly elected as a result of the pope's gratitude for his and his eldest brother Edward's excellent military service on Urban V's behalf in Italy, and he was only 28 years old at the time and, for various reasons, not least his predilection for warfare, a rather improbable bishop. Still, he would hold the position for thirty-six years.

Edward of Woodstock, prince of Wales and Aquitaine, returned to England with his wife Joan of Kent and their 4-year-old son Richard of Bordeaux in early 1371; their elder son Edward of Angoulême had died not long before. The heir to the throne was seriously ill, and his father the king was now close to 60 and also ailing. Edward of Woodstock granted Sir Thomas Despenser, younger brother of Edward and Hugh Despenser and older brother of Bishop Henry, an annual income of £100 in February 1372, courteously acknowledging Thomas as his kinsman. [2] Thomas was probably in England in November 1372 and February

1373 when a Yorkshire man named William Grindale acknowledged before the mayor of London that he owed Thomas forty marks (£26). Later that year Thomas returned to France with John of Gaunt, duke of Lancaster and with his brother Edward Despenser, constable of the army, and was captured during a skirmish with French forces at Ochy-les-Soissons. Thomas had to pay a sizeable sum to secure his own release. [3]

John of Gaunt had lost his wife, the great heiress Blanche of Lancaster, in September 1368. Thanks to the custom known as the 'courtesy of England', he was entitled to keep all of Blanche's enormous inheritance for the rest of his life, when it would pass to their son and heir Henry. Three years after Blanche's death, in September 1371, John married Constanza of Castile (b. 1354), elder daughter and co-heir of the late Pedro 'the Cruel', king of Castile. Pedro was murdered by his half-brother Enrique of Trastamara, who took his throne, and John and Constanza would spend many years claiming the throne of Castile. Constanza's younger sister Isabel (b. 1355) married John's younger brother Edmund of Langley, fourth son of Edward III and Queen Philippa, in 1372. Seven years later, Edmund and Isabel became the parents-in-law of the younger Thomas Despenser (b. 1373). Edmund's heir was his and Isabel's elder son Edward, born 1373/4, and they had a younger son, Richard, probably born *c.* 1385, later earl of Cambridge and the grandfather of two kings, Edward IV and Richard III.

Pope Gregory XI, Urban V's successor, sent a letter to Sir Hugh Despenser on 18 January 1374. Hugh was then in or near Bordeaux in the duchy of Aquitaine with John of Gaunt, and Gregory asked Hugh to use his influence with the duke regarding the release of the imprisoned Sir Roger Beaufort. [4] Although Gaunt and Edward Despenser returned to England a few weeks later, Hugh never saw his homeland again. He died in Pavia, Italy on 2 or 11 March 1374, aged about 36; possibly he was killed during a military engagement. His body was returned to England and buried at the Greyfriars' church in Stamford, Lincolnshire, near his and Alice Hotham's manor of Collyweston. It took almost six months for news of Hugh's demise to reach England: the order to hold his inquisition post mortem was issued on 1 September 1374. [5] Hugh's heir was his son Hugh, probably 18 when his father died, and he left his daughter Anne as well.

Hugh's widow Alice was back in England by 18 September 1374 when she appointed attorneys to act on her behalf in Ireland. She was presumably the person who brought the news of Hugh's death to the king and government officials in England, and perhaps travelled home with her late husband's body. The unfortunate Alice was abducted and forcibly married to her second husband, the Northamptonshire knight Sir John Trussell, sometime before 7 November 1374, two months after her return to England. [6] She was the second Despenser widow of the fourteenth century, after Eleanor Clare in 1329, to be abducted by a second husband. John Trussell, born *c.* 1349, was much younger than Alice (b. *c.* 1335), and ironically was the grandson of William Trussell, who in 1326 pronounced the death sentences on Hugh Despenser the Elder and the Younger, great-grandfather and grandfather of Alice's first husband. John was a violent and difficult man, and sometime before June 1378, during his marriage to Alice, was placed in solitary confinement in the Tower of London. His stepson, the younger Hugh Despenser, who was only about six years his junior, and his brother Sir Alvered Trussell recognised a debt of £100 to the king as a guarantee of his future good behaviour. [7] Alice bore a son, John, to John Trussell, and died in Northamptonshire on 5 or 6 October 1379. She was buried with her first husband at the Greyfriars' church in Stamford. [8] Alice's son Hugh, meanwhile, led a contingent of soldiers during a military campaign to the duchy of Brittany in 1375, aged barely 20, and was as active a soldier as his father and uncles. [9]

Fourteen-year-old John Despenser, only child of Sir Gilbert Despenser and the late Ela Calveley, and a grandson of Hugh the Younger, died on 16 August 1375. His heir to the Norfolk manor of Calveley and the fifty acres of land he would have inherited from his maternal uncle John Calveley when he reached 21 was his late mother Ela's sister Annora, wife of John Coroner, aged '40 and more' in 1375. [10] His father Gilbert outlived him by nearly seven years. And less than three months after John's death, on 11, 12 or 13 November 1375, the Despenser family suffered a great loss when John's much older first cousin Edward the Younger, lord of Glamorgan, died at the age of 39. [11] The cause of his death is unknown. Edward wrote his will on 6 November at his castle of Llanblethian in South Wales, so apparently was already seriously ill a few days before he died. He left a hanap (goblet) to his maternal uncle Sir Ralph Ferrers and another to Nicholas Litlington, abbot of Westminster, probably also his uncle, whose name was spelt 'Nicole' in the will. To Tewkesbury Abbey in Gloucestershire, Edward left a chalice once given to him by the king of France, either John II (d. 1364) or his son Charles V (d. 1380). [12] He was buried as he had requested in the abbey church of Tewkesbury, where an unusual, impressive and colourful life-sized memorial statue of him, the famous Kneeling Knight of Tewkesbury, still exists. Edward is depicted in stone kneeling towards the high altar, his hands together in front of his chest in prayer, and has a brown moustache and beard. His request to lie 'near my ancestors' in Tewkesbury reveals how important his family was to him.

The unlucky Despenser family lost their greatest member before he even turned 40, and had Edward lived longer, he might have expected to be rewarded for his loyalty to the king and his sons with an earldom, perhaps Gloucester. On the other hand, Edward was the only important Despenser lord from 1265 to 1400 to die peacefully in his bed, quite an achievement. His heir, his son Thomas, was only 2 years old, which meant a long minority for the family, and another turbulent reign, Richard II's, lay just around the corner.

Part 5

From Grace to Execution: Thomas, 1375–1400

Dramatis Personae

Edward Despenser the Younger, lord of Glamorgan, b. March 1336, d. November 1375

Elizabeth Despenser, née Burghersh (b. *c.* 1342), heir of the Burghersh family; Edward's widow

Thomas Despenser (b. 1373): Edward and Elizabeth's youngest child, only surviving son, and the Despenser heir; marries Constance of York in 1379; father of Richard, Elizabeth and Isabelle Despenser

Constance Despenser (b. *c.* 1374/6): only daughter of Edmund of Langley, earl of Cambridge and later duke of York; granddaughter of Edward III, king of England, and of Pedro 'the Cruel', king of Castile; first cousin of Richard II

Anne Hastings, née Despenser, later Morley (b. *c.* early 1360s): eldest daughter of Edward the Younger; marries Hugh Hastings III (b. *c.* 1354) in 1376 and mother of Hugh Hastings IV (*c.* 1378–96) and Edward Hastings (b. 1382); marries secondly Thomas Morley (b. *c.* 1354) in or before 1390

Elizabeth Arundel, née Despenser, later Zouche (b. *c.* late 1360s): second daughter of Edward; marries John Arundel II (b. 1364) in 1380; mother of John Arundel III (b. 1385), Edward and Thomas Arundel; marries secondly William Zouche (b. *c.* 1342) in 1392/3

Margaret Ferrers, née Despenser (b. *c.* early 1370s): youngest daughter of Edward; marries Robert, Lord Ferrers of Chartley (b. 1357/9); mother of Edmund (b. 1386/9), Thomas, Edward, Philippa and Elizabeth Ferrers

Thomas Despenser (b. *c.* 1339/40): brother of Edward the Younger; not married

Henry Despenser (b. 1341/2): youngest brother of Edward the Younger; bishop of Norwich from 1370

Hugh Despenser (b. *c.* 1355): son and heir of Hugh Despenser (1337/8–74), Edward's other brother, and Alice Hotham (*c.* 1335–79); first cousin of Thomas Despenser (b. 1373) and his sisters

Anne Botiller, née Despenser (b. late 1350s or 1360s): younger sister of Hugh, above; marries Edward Botiller

Elizabeth Berkeley, née Despenser (b. 1325): youngest child of Hugh Despenser the Younger and aunt of Edward the Younger; mother of Thomas, Lord Berkeley (b. 1353), and grandmother of Elizabeth Berkeley (b. 1385/6), countess of Warwick

Gilbert Despenser (b. *c.* mid or late 1310s): third and only surviving son of Hugh the Younger; brother of Elizabeth Berkeley; widower of Ela Calveley

Philip Despenser III (b. 1342): son of Philip Despenser II (1313–49) and grandson of Philip Despenser I (*c.* 1292/4–1313); father of Philip Despenser IV (b. *c.* 1365), John and Robert Despenser, and Joan Ros; second cousin of Edward the Younger

Edward III, king of England (b. 1312), his eldest son **Edward of Woodstock**, prince of Wales (b. 1330), and Edward of Woodstock's son **Richard of Bordeaux** (b. 1367), later King Richard II

John of Gaunt, duke of Lancaster (b. 1340): third son of Edward III; his eldest daughter **Philippa** (b. 1360), queen of Portugal; and his son and heir **Henry** (b. 1367), earl of Derby, duke of Hereford, later King Henry IV

Edmund of Langley, earl of Cambridge, duke of York (b. 1341): fourth son of Edward III; father-in-law of Thomas Despenser; and his sons **Edward** (b. 1373/4) and **Richard of Conisbrough** (b. *c.* 1385)

Isabel of Castile (b. 1355), duchess of York: mother-in-law of Thomas Despenser; daughter of Pedro 'the Cruel', king of Castile (1334–69); younger sister of Constanza of Castile (b. 1354), duchess of Lancaster, second wife of John of Gaunt

Chapter 29

Edward Despenser's widow Elizabeth Burghersh petitioned for custody of her infant son Thomas after Edward's death, and it was, rather unusually, granted to her. She also petitioned to have all her late husband's lands given to her during Thomas's minority, and this was also approved. [1] Elizabeth fought hard and tenaciously to keep the Despenser lands intact for her son and looked after his inheritance, and complained vociferously on his behalf when, for example, the bishop of Worcester and the abbot of Westminster (Nicholas Litlington, probably her late husband's half-uncle) 'outrageously' cut down trees in her son's chases in Malvern and Corse without a licence. [2]

Richard, earl of Arundel, died on 24 January 1376, two months after Lord Despenser. Richard the younger, the late earl's eldest son from his second marriage to Eleanor of Lancaster (d. 1372), then about 29, inherited the earldoms of Arundel and Surrey and his father's enormous wealth. The elder Richard's eldest son was Edmund Arundel, grandson of Hugh Despenser the Younger, and Edmund saw the vast Arundel riches pass to his half-brother Richard, who was two decades younger than he was. Sometime before the end of 1376, Edmund and at least fourteen of his supporters attacked the six manors in Essex which his father had granted to his late mother Isabella for her sustenance in 1344/5 after the annulment of their marriage, and which now were in his half-brother's hands. They broke into houses, fished in Earl Richard's fishery, stole £100, and assaulted and imprisoned Richard's servants. Edmund appointed his cousin Henry Despenser, bishop of Norwich, as his proctor when the matter came to the attention of the authorities, and he and his half-brother met each other before the king in person and agreed to settle the 'quarrel, dissensions, strife and controversy' between them. Edmund appeared again before the king and his council on 16 February 1377 and was imprisoned in the Tower of London, though was released on 5 June that year, sixteen days before Edward III died. He may have encountered John Trussell, second husband of his cousin Hugh Despenser's widow Alice Hotham, in the Tower prison. [3]

Richard, earl of Arundel complained again in November 1377 about Edmund attacking the same six Essex manors; either this was another incident after Edmund's release from captivity at the Tower, or the earl was not happy about the outcome of the first investigation. [4] Little is known of Edmund Arundel after late 1377. In July 1379, he and his son-in-law Sir Richard Sergeaux of Cornwall borrowed £500 from Matthew Gurney, one of the sons of Thomas Gurney, jailer of Huchon Despenser at Bristol Castle in and after late 1328 and accused in 1330 of killing Edward II at Berkeley Castle. By 1390, Sergeaux had still not paid Gurney back. [5] Edmund Arundel was still active in February 1381, now in his mid-fifties, and appointed attorneys to act for him when he went to Gascony on a military expedition. He was dead by February 1382, when his two surviving daughters, Elizabeth Meriet (formerly Carew) and Philippa Sergeaux, and Robert Deincourt, his grandson from his other daughter Katherine, were involved in a legal case. Elizabeth Meriet née Arundel was an ancestor of George Carew, earl of Totnes (d. 1629) from her first marriage, and one of her sister Philippa Sergeaux's four daughters, Alice (d. 1452), married Richard Vere, earl of Oxford (1385–1417) and was the mother of John Vere, earl of Oxford (1408–62). Custody of the underage Robert Deincourt, son of the third Arundel sister Katherine and a great-great-grandson of Hugh Despenser the Younger, passed to John of Gaunt, duke of Lancaster. In January 1375, Lancaster granted Robert's marriage rights to his mistress, Katherine Swynford, for the use of her daughter Blanche Swynford, and also gave Katherine custody of Robert's late father's lands and of the boy himself. [6]

King Edward III died on 21 June 1377 at the age of 64, leaving his ten-year-grandson Richard II, only surviving legitimate son of Edward's eldest son Edward of Woodstock (who had died the year before), as the new king. Edward III had reigned for fifty years and six months, and his funeral took place at Westminster Abbey on 5 July. Just eleven days later, the young Richard II was crowned king. Edward of York, son of Richard's uncle Edmund of Langley, earl of Cambridge, and the future brother-in-law of Thomas Despenser, was knighted at the coronation even though he was only 3 or 4 years old. Henry Percy (b. 1341), from a great northern family, was made earl of Northumberland, and John

Mowbray, not quite 12, was made earl of Nottingham. Perhaps if Edward Despenser had lived two years longer, he might also have received an earldom. [7] No regent or regency council was officially appointed for the child-king, though Richard's mother Joan of Kent and his uncles John of Gaunt, Edmund of Langley and Thomas of Woodstock were among those who wielded power. The first few years of the boy-king Richard's reign were mostly quiet, though a truce with the French ended within days of Edward III's death, and French ships attacked the south coast of England.

Alice Hotham, widow of Sir Hugh Despenser (d. 1374), died in early October 1379. Her son Hugh, born *c.* 1355, received her lands in Yorkshire, Warwickshire and Northamptonshire on 22 November 1379, and in 1400 left money in his will for a marble stone to be placed on his parents' tomb at the Greyfriars' Church in Stamford. [8] Alice also left her daughter Anne Despenser and her son from her forced second marriage, John Trussell the younger, who cannot have been more than 4 or 5 when she died. Alice's widower Sir John Trussell, much her junior, lived until 1424. Shortly after his mother's death, on 4 December 1379, Hugh Despenser was given letters of protection to go to Ireland, and he appointed two attorneys to act for him in England in his absence. [9] He went in the retinue of Edmund Mortimer, third earl of March (1352–81), whose great-grandfather Roger Mortimer had invaded England with Queen Isabella in 1326 and executed Hugh's great-grandfather Hugh Despenser the Younger and great-great-grandfather Hugh the Elder. Hugh was still, or again, in Ireland in June 1382, and owned lands there which he inherited from his mother and her family. [10]

In or before 1379, Richard II retained Hugh's great-uncle Gilbert Despenser as one of his household knights, and paid him forty marks a year. [11] Gilbert was now over 60, and he and his sisters Joan the nun of Shaftesbury and Elizabeth, dowager Lady Berkeley, were the only children of Hugh the Younger still alive. Richard II evinced a deep interest in his great-grandfather Edward II and spent many years trying unsuccessfully to have him canonised, and no doubt Gilbert had personal memories of his long-dead great-uncle which he was able to share with his kinsman the young king. Edward II had spoken in 1322 of his affection for Gilbert and granted him five forfeited manors to hold when he came of age, but the manors were restored to their rightful owners after Edward's downfall, and Gilbert never did hold them. [12]

The 6-year-old Despenser heir, Thomas, married Constance of Cambridge (later called Constance of York when her father the earl of Cambridge became duke of York) in or before early November 1379, when their wedding was recorded in the register of her uncle John of Gaunt, duke of Lancaster. [13] Constance, granddaughter of two kings and first cousin of Richard II, made a remarkably impressive bride for Thomas Despenser. Presumably both Constance and Thomas were aware of her mother Isabel of Castile's intriguing upbringing: Isabel and her older sister Constanza were born in the mid-1350s to King Pedro the Cruel's mistress María Padilla, and probably grew up in the Alcázar, the royal palace in the Spanish city of Seville built by Pedro himself, while his rightful queen Blanche Bourbon languished in prison. Freshwater baths which can still be seen today in the Alcázar are known as *Los Baños de Doña María de Padilla*, and Doña Maria, Constance's grandmother, was a Castilian noblewoman who caught the eye of King Pedro. The unfortunate Blanche Bourbon, queen of Castile in name only, died in 1361 after eight years of captivity and Constanza and Isabel were legitimised, but in 1369 their father was stabbed to death by his illegitimate half-brother Enrique of Trastamara. An English chronicler called Isabel of Castile a 'pampered and voluptuous lady', but she was only about 14 when her father was killed by her uncle and her situation suddenly became precarious and impoverished. Things improved dramatically when Isabel moved to England and married Edward III's fourth son in 1372, although the couple seem to have been mismatched on a personal level.

Constance was about 4 or 5 at the time of her wedding to Thomas, and the child-couple - who, as descendants of Edward I, were distantly related – would not be able to consummate their marriage and live together as husband and wife for at least a decade. On 14 January 1384, Constance was granted an annuity of eighty marks 'for her maintenance', payable by her mother-in-law Elizabeth out of the lands Thomas Despenser would hold when he came of age. Thomas himself, aged 4, had been awarded an annual income of one hundred marks on 30 May 1378 to be paid from the issues of Cardiff Castle, which one day he would own, in line with a grant made to him by his father Edward. [14] In modern terms, eighty and one hundred marks are both in excess of £100,000, exceedingly generous annual amounts for small children, so evidently both Thomas and Constance lived in some style (as she was the granddaughter of two kings, both Constance herself and everyone else would have considered this only right and proper). Constance Despenser may well have lived in her mother-in-law's household and may have been raised with her husband from the earliest childhood, though perhaps she stayed with her parents Edmund and Isabel. By 1 January 1381, Edmund, earl of Cambridge, was in possession of the Wiltshire manor of Vastern, the favourite residence of Thomas's great-great-grandfather Hugh the Elder and possibly the birthplace of his great-grandfather Hugh the Younger. [15] Perhaps Thomas had the opportunity to stay there on occasion.

Thomas's second eldest sister Elizabeth, born c. late 1360s, was already betrothed to Sir John Arundel II (b. 1364) when her father-in-law John Arundel I, marshal of England, drowned in the Irish Sea on 15 or 16 December 1379. Elizabeth and John II married on or before 1 August 1380, and in early 1381 John was granted an annuity of forty marks a year during his minority, payable by his uncle the earl of Arundel. [16] Elizabeth must have been aware of her father-in-law's notoriety. John Arundel I, sent to aid the duke of Brittany against his internal enemies in late 1379, was said by several contemporary chroniclers to have allowed his men to pillage the countryside on their way to the coast and to steal from the poor, and allegedly John and his men abducted and raped a group of nuns and subsequently threw the women overboard when trying to prevent their ships capsizing during a terrible storm. He 'piled sin upon sin and added atrocity to atrocity,' says chronicler Thomas Walsingham. How much truth there is to this story is not completely clear, but as several chroniclers narrate a version of it, it seems unlikely to have been entirely invented. Walsingham states that as well as losing his life in the Irish Sea, John lost his entire wardrobe 'which in its splendour was fit to be ranked above that of a king,' containing fifty-two new outfits either of gold or with gold thread. [17] The Despenser and Arundel families had intermarried in 1321, when Elizabeth's great-aunt Isabella Despenser married John Arundel II's grandfather Richard, later earl of Arundel, as his first wife. Had that marriage not been annulled in 1344, Elizabeth's husband, his siblings, his father and his aunts and uncles would never have been born.

Elizabeth's uncle Sir Thomas Despenser (b. c. 1339/40), who, like his brothers Edward, Hugh and Henry, spent much of his career fighting in Italy and France, was in England for once in March 1380. He arranged for his manor of Burley in Rutland to be given to 'any secular person or persons', and his feoffees included his younger brother Bishop Henry, his nephew Hugh Despenser (b. *c.* 1355), and his second cousin Philip Despenser III. [18] The manor of Burley must have passed to Thomas's nephew Hugh, as Hugh sold it in 1381 a few months after his uncle's death, and Thomas's brother Bishop Henry was staying at Burley in June 1381 when the Great Uprising broke out. [19] Possibly Thomas was glad to be rid of Burley: in September 1374, his tenants and the tenants of the neighbouring villages of Oakham and Langham began a violent feud, and before 20 October 1375 Burley was 'destroyed by fire'. [20]

Sir Thomas Despenser died on 9, 12 or 13 February 1381 in his early forties, and his death left his younger brother the bishop of Norwich as the only surviving child of Edward Despenser the Elder and Anne Ferrers. Thomas seems never to have married and therefore left no legitimate children, and his heir was his namesake nephew, 7-year-old Thomas. [21] The 1400 will of Hugh Despenser, another of the late Sir Thomas's nephews, states that an uncle of his was buried in a chapel at the Greyfriars' (Franciscans') church in Stamford with Hugh's parents Hugh and Alice, and this must mean Thomas. [22] In 1366, Thomas and his brother Henry had granted land in Stamford to the warden of the Franciscan order and his fellows, so it makes sense that Thomas would have been buried there fifteen years later, and Stamford lay only ten miles from the Despenser manor of Burley. [23] Edward Despenser the Younger had given his brother Thomas land in his manors of Essendine and Skellingthorpe to hold during his lifetime, and Edward's son Thomas (b. 1373), to whom they passed after his uncle's death, later gave the manors to his much older first cousin Hugh Despenser. [24] Edward also gave his brother Thomas the manors of Buckland and Singleborough in Buckinghamshire and an income of one hundred marks (£66) a year from his manor of Cardiff, generous gifts which reveal his great affection for his brother. [25]

Chapter 30

The Great Uprising, once known as the Peasants' Revolt, broke out in England in June 1381. The reasons for this mass outbreak of rage and violence are complex but have much to do with the harsh social conditions the bulk of the English population suffered after the first great outbreak of the Black Death in 1348/9, and the imposition of an absurdly unfair poll tax which taxed everyone, rich and poor, at the same rate. Large groups of people gathered in Kent and Essex and marched towards London, where they demanded the abolition of the poll tax and of serfdom altogether. Fourteen-year-old King Richard was forced to seek refuge in the Tower of London, and with him may have been one of his household knights, Gilbert Despenser. Gilbert was probably just about old enough to remember the Despenser War and Contrariant rebellion against his father in 1321/2, and six decades later he witnessed the greatest social convulsion of the fourteenth century in England.

Gilbert's nephew Henry, bishop of Norwich, was staying at Burley in Rutland, a manor which belonged to his own nephew Hugh Despenser since the death of Henry's brother Thomas earlier in the year, when he heard the news of the uprising. Chronicler Thomas Walsingham stated that Bishop Henry was 'a man quite capable of bearing arms, and indeed was armed to the teeth.' On 25 June 1381, Henry encountered a group of rebels who had four knights with them (including Sir Thomas Morley, later Henry's nephew-in-law) whom they had persuaded, by virtue of having murdered another knight in front of them, to act as though they believed in the rebels' demands and to serve their leader John Lister at table on bended knee. Henry dealt with the rebels by beheading two of them and nailed their heads in public at Newmarket, berated the knights for not having overcome the rebels themselves, raised a force of men, and supposedly defeated another large group of rebels in armed combat. Not for nothing had Henry Despenser gained military experience in Italy: the awed Thomas Walsingham states 'the warrior priest, grinding his teeth like a wild boar … did not cease from fierce slaughter'. [1] Richard II met the rebels near London and agreed to their demands, and after a while they dispersed and the immediate danger was over, though not before a mob invaded the Tower of London and killed the treasurer and chancellor of England. Later, the king's advisers forced him to go back on his promises.

Anne of Bohemia, daughter of the Holy Roman Emperor Karl IV and his fourth, Polish wife Elizabeth of Pomerania, arrived in England in early 1382 a few months after the Great Uprising, and married Richard II on 20 January, two weeks after his fifteenth birthday. Born in Prague in May 1366, Queen Anne was eight months the young king's senior, and her older half-brother Wenzel was the king of Germany and Bohemia. Some years later, her younger full brother Zikmund or Sigismund became king of Hungary and Croatia, and a couple of years before his death was elected Holy Roman Emperor as well. Anne of Bohemia was crowned queen of England two days after her wedding. She and Richard would have a very happy and close, albeit childless, marriage.

A future Despenser husband, Richard Beauchamp, heir to the earldom of Warwick, was born in Salwarpe, Worcestershire on 25 January 1382, a few days after the 15-year-old queen's coronation. [2] He was the son of Thomas Beauchamp (b. 1338/9), earl of Warwick, and Margaret Ferrers of Groby, a cousin of the Despensers. Elizabeth Burghersh, dowager Lady Despenser, was Richard's godmother and attended his christening, performed by Henry Wakefield, bishop of Worcester, in Salwarpe. Another godparent was Hugh Stafford, earl of Stafford, who gave the infant a sword, and Richard Beauchamp was named after his chief godfather, Richard II. The newlywed 15-year-old king was not present in person, but sent one of his household knights to the christening 'carrying two cloths of gold with the arms of King Richard'. Walter, prior of Worcester, sent a silver goblet and 100 shillings as christening gifts, and the earl of Warwick gave £10 to Peter Holt for bringing him news of his son and heir's birth.

Sir Gilbert Despenser died on 22 April 1382 probably in his mid-sixties, a few months after his cousin Amaury St Amand, only son of Hugh Despenser the Elder's third daughter Margaret, also passed away at the age of 66. As Gilbert and his late wife Ela Calveley's son John had died in 1375 at age 14, his heir was his 8-year-old great-nephew Thomas

Despenser, grandson of Gilbert's brother Edward the Elder. Gilbert, son of the most notorious and hated Englishman of the entire fourteenth century, had carved out a long and successful career for himself as a royal knight, faithfully serving his kinsmen Edward III and Richard II for many years. Gilbert's sister Joan Despenser, nun of Shaftesbury Abbey and the second eldest daughter of Hugh the Younger, died on 15 November 1384 when she must have been about 70; her date of birth is not known but was probably *c.* 1314/15. She may be the 'Joan daughter of Sir Hugh Spenser' buried in the Greyfriars' church in Ipswich, Suffolk, though Ipswich is a long way from Shaftesbury in Dorset. [3] Perhaps this lady in fact was Hugh Despenser the justiciar's daughter Joan, who married Thomas Furnival (d. 1332). Gilbert and Joan's deaths left their youngest sister Elizabeth Berkeley as the only surviving legitimate child of Hugh the Younger, though Nicholas Litlington, abbot of Westminster, probably their illegitimate half-brother, lived until 1386 when he was over 70, and their other half-brother William Zouche, monk of Glastonbury, lived until 1390 or later. Elizabeth Berkeley, widowed from her first husband in 1368, lost her second, Sir Maurice Wyth of Somerset, in July 1383 as well. The last line of Wyth's will stated: 'It is my final wish that my said wife hold herself contented with all bequeathed to her'. [4]

Anne Despenser (b. late 1350s or 1360s), great-niece of Gilbert, Joan and Elizabeth and the only daughter of Hugh Despenser (d. 1374) and Alice Hotham, married Sir Edward Botiller at an uncertain date. Anne and Edward may have been married by 8 March 1382, when Anne's brother Hugh was associated with Edward on a commission in Bedfordshire. [5] Sir Edward Botiller or Boteler (or Butler in modern spelling) owned lands in eight counties, and was the same age as Anne's parents. He was born on 17 July 1337 in Cockayne Hatley, Bedfordshire, and his father John died in Cologne when Edward was only 6 weeks old. Edward was the heir of his older brother, Ralph. [6] Anne's uncle the bishop of Norwich wrote to her as 'Lady Botillere' and his 'dearest and most entirely well-beloved niece' at an unknown date. He congratulated her on the birth of a 'fair son', *beal fitz* in the French original; Henry Despenser always wrote his letters in French. A servant of Anne's with the curious name of Chef had brought the bishop the good news, which Henry said made him 'very joyous of heart'. He affectionately scolded his niece for not sending him frequent reports of her health, which he said troubled him greatly, and asked her to do so more often in future. [7]

Anne and Edward Botiller's son, whose name is unknown, must have died young; when Edward died in 1412, his heir was not his own son but his cousin's son Philip Botiller. [8] Anne's elder brother, 'Sir Hugh Despenser of Collyweston' as he called himself, married a woman called Sybil sometime before September 1388, and perhaps before the summer of 1386, when he went to Spain with the duke of Lancaster. [9] Sybil Despenser's parentage is uncertain, though sometime in the late 1380s or 1390s she and Hugh presented a petition stating that a group of men had attacked their Bedfordshire manor of Little Barford near St Neots, and had stolen goods from them and destroyed documents. [10] Earlier in the fourteenth century the manor of Little Barford was held by the Dale family, which possibly gives a hint as to Sybil's origins, and Hugh's brother-in-law Edward Botiller held the manor of Higham Gobion in Bedfordshire, just a few miles from Little Barford. [11] Evidently Hugh and Sybil were not very well-off, as in early 1384 Hugh borrowed £52 from two merchants. They had a daughter, Elizabeth Despenser, who was alive in 1400 but who died that year or in 1401. [12] Hugh Despenser (d. 1374) and Alice Hotham's two grandchildren Elizabeth Despenser and the Botiller boy whose name is unknown died young and childless, and thus Hugh and Alice's line ended. Hugh's younger brothers Thomas (d. 1381) and Bishop Henry had no children either, so the children and grandchildren of Edward Despenser the Younger were the only descendants of Edward the Elder and Anne Ferrers.

Anne Hastings, eldest daughter of Edward the Younger, gave birth to her second son on 21 May 1382 in Fenwick near Doncaster, Yorkshire, and named him after her father. [13] When Edward Hastings proved that he had come of age in 1403, one of the jurors, William Dawson, remembered the date because he was in Pontefract twelve miles from Fenwick on the day Edward was born and saw a man arrested for casting the evil eye on his neighbour's horse, then someone told him that Lady Hastings had borne a son a few miles away. Another juror remembered the date because there was an earthquake throughout England on the day Edward was born, and a third because he fell from his horse while riding to Doncaster that day and broke two ribs.

Chapter 31

A period of European history from 1378 to 1417 is known as the 'Great Schism', when two popes existed in strict opposition to each other. One was in Rome, supported by England and its allies, and the other was in Avignon, supported by France and its allies. Henry Despenser, a fierce defender of the church, decided to lead a crusade in 1383 to aid the citizens of Ghent against the supporters of Clement VII, the Avignon pope or, as far as England was concerned, the anti-pope. Bishop Henry was given more than £6,000 to pay for 2,500 men-at-arms and 2,500 archers for his campaign against Clement. During the parliament held at Westminster which narrowly approved Henry's crusade and awarded him the money for it, John of Gaunt, duke of Lancaster, walked out of the session in disgust; he and many other nobles favoured an expedition to the Iberian peninsula rather than to Flanders. Unfortunately, Henry's mission proved an embarrassing and costly failure which led to his being impeached in parliament later in 1383. Richard II tried to comfort his humiliated kinsman by assuring him that he himself 'remained well disposed towards him'. [1]

Henry's nephew Hugh Despenser was appointed as a keeper of the peace in Bedfordshire in April 1385. [2] One of his fellow keepers was Thomas Mowbray, earl of Nottingham and son-in-law of the earl of Arundel, who was only 18 and who, like Hugh, was a descendant of Edward I. Hugh's cousin Elizabeth Arundel, second of the three daughters of Edward Despenser the Younger, gave birth to her eldest son on 1 August 1385 at Ditton in Buckinghamshire, five years (possibly to the day) after her wedding. Inevitably he was named John Arundel after his father and grandfather, and was baptised at St Mary's Church in nearby Datchet, apparently after dark, as a servant called Thomas Neel carried a torch during the ceremony. The attendees drank two bottles of wine afterwards, and another servant was sent the thirty miles to London 'to discover where John the father could be found' and informed of his son's birth. [3]

John Arundel II was 20 when his son was born and Elizabeth was still a teenager. John decided to go to London even though he must have known that his wife was about to give birth, and she did not know where he might be staying there. This perhaps reveals that they had quarrelled or that their marriage, at least at this stage, was not a particularly harmonious one, though evidently things had much improved by the time of Arundel's death some years later. They had younger sons, Thomas and Edward Arundel, as well, born c. 1387 and c. 1389/90. Thomas was probably named after Elizabeth's younger brother Thomas Despenser or after her husband's uncle Thomas Arundel (b. 1352/3), bishop of Ely and later archbishop of York and Canterbury, while Edward must have been named in honour of his Despenser grandfather. Elizabeth's younger sister Margaret, meanwhile, gave birth to her own eldest son, Edmund Ferrers of Chartley, sometime between 1386 and 1389.

The eldest Despenser sister, Anne, was widowed on 6 November 1386 when her husband Sir Hugh Hastings III died at Villanueva de Arosa in Galicia, Spain, a few months after he sailed from England with Richard II's eldest uncle, John of Gaunt. [4] Hugh was probably 32 when he died and Anne was perhaps 24 or a little more. His inquisition post mortem was held in April 1387, and another inquisition held in October 1390 reveals that he gave his Norfolk manor of Gressenhall to his mother-in-law Elizabeth, Lady Despenser on 15 April 1386. Hugh had settled his other three manors in Norfolk and Suffolk on himself and his wife jointly, and Anne held them for the remaining forty years of her life. [5] At an unknown date before 1386, Hugh had gone on pilgrimage to Jerusalem, and visited Rhodes during the journey. [6] Hugh and Anne's elder son Hugh died in his teens, and their second son Edward Hastings was only 4 when his father died in faraway Spain.

John of Gaunt had gone to Spain to attempt to secure the throne of Castile by right of his second wife Constanza of Castile, but ultimately failed in this endeavour and had to settle for marrying his and Constanza's daughter Katherine or Catalina (b. 1372/3) to her cousin, the future King Enrique III of Castile. During his three-year sojourn in Iberia, Duke John also arranged the marriage of his eldest daughter Philippa of Lancaster (b. 1360) and King João of Portugal. By the standards of the day and of her own family, Philippa, who was almost 27, was old at marriage – it was not uncommon for royalty and nobility to wed as children, as Philippa's first cousin Constance and Thomas Despenser did – but her marriage to João proved to be a fruitful one. Six of their nine children lived into adulthood and are known to historians as the Illustrious Generation.

Philippa of Lancaster, the new queen of Portugal, was, perhaps surprisingly, a friend and correspondent of her kinsman Henry Despenser, bishop of Norwich, who was eighteen years older than she. Several of their letters in French to each other survive, and reveal that Philippa addressed Henry as 'Reverend father in God, my dearest and most entirely beloved cousin' and that he addressed her as 'Very excellent and very dread, very gracious, and my sovereign lady'. [7] Henry sent Philippa expensive cloth on two occasions for which she thanked him, and at another time told her that he had been 'a little ill' (*un poy malade*) but that God's mercy and Philippa's lovely letters containing good news of herself had 'cured him completely'.

Henry's nephew Hugh Despenser, as enthusiastic a soldier as his father and uncles had been, also accompanied the duke of Lancaster to Spain in 1386. [8] His father the elder Hugh had been in the south of France with Lancaster in early 1374 shortly before his death. The younger Hugh fought in Flanders in 1386, not long before he travelled to Spain with Lancaster. Hugh fought again in Flanders in 1388, and was captured by the French on this occasion. Richard II immediately paid his ransom of £200, and Hugh was in England in February and early March 1387 and back there by 26 September 1388, a year or so before the duke of Lancaster himself returned to England. In January 1384 and again in 1385/6, Hugh was commissioned to defend the port of Berwick-on-Tweed, and until 6 October 1389 he was the acting captain of the town and castle of Brest in Brittany, 'supplying the place' of the earl of Huntingdon, the king's older half-brother John Holland. Hugh served in Scotland with Henry Percy, earl of Northumberland, in 1384 and 1385, and on 15 February 1389 was again 'preparing with all possible haste to go to Scotland'. He received letters of protection to accompany his uncle Henry on the bishop's crusade to Flanders in 1383, and in 1388 took part in a naval expedition with the earl of Arundel. Somehow he also found time to go on crusade to Prussia, as his father had done, in or shortly before May 1383. [9] Hugh enjoyed a remarkably busy career as a soldier in various parts of Europe in the second half of the 1370s and the whole of the 1380s. In or before September 1391, now in his mid-thirties, he became a knight of Richard II's household, and the king paid him one hundred marks (£66) a year. [10]

Bishop Henry's other nephew, Thomas Despenser, was knighted by Richard, earl of Arundel, off La Rochelle on 28 June 1388, during the naval campaign the earl undertook that year in which Thomas's cousin Hugh also took part. Thomas may also have been elected a Knight of the Garter in the same year, and certainly became one before 1399. His wife Constance, her mother Isabel, and her cousins Philippa, Elizabeth and Catalina of Lancaster and Philippa Coucy were among the women and girls made Ladies of the Garter during Richard II's reign. [11] Born in September 1373, Thomas was still only 14 years old in June 1388, and in March that year his mother Elizabeth was discharged of his custody so that he could go abroad with Arundel. [12]

In 1387/8, the earl of Arundel and four noble allies – Arundel's son-in-law Thomas Mowbray, earl of Nottingham; Thomas Beauchamp, earl of Warwick; the king's cousin Henry of Lancaster, earl of Derby (John of Gaunt's son and heir); and Richard II and Henry of Lancaster's youngest uncle Thomas of Woodstock, duke of Gloucester – formed an alliance against the young king's chief advisers. Calling themselves the Lords Appellant because they wished to appeal the advisers for treason, they summoned a parliament at Westminster in February 1388 which became known as the Merciless Parliament. Richard II's closest friend and perhaps his lover, the young earl of Oxford, Robert Vere, fled abroad before parliament took place and never returned to England, and Michael de la Pole, earl of Suffolk, also never saw his homeland again. Other allies and advisers of the young king were executed, including his chamberlain and former tutor Simon Burley, Robert Tresilian, James Berners, John Salisbury, Thomas Usk and John Blake. Richard II, shocked and distraught, but unable to prevent the executions, secretly vowed to avenge his friends' deaths, and ten years later hit back at the Appellants. Thomas Despenser, still much too young to have played any role in the events of 1388, would – despite his association with the earl of Arundel that year – be one of the king's chief supporters when Richard finally took his revenge.

Chapter 32

Richard II, now 22 years old, took over the governance of his own realm in May 1389. Not everyone was delighted with the king's efforts: a Londoner was arrested in July 1389 for stating that Richard was 'unfit to govern and should stay in his latrine'. [1] He and Anne of Bohemia had now been married for over seven years but had no children, and it seems likely that one of them was infertile.

Elizabeth, Lady Berkeley, youngest and last surviving child of Hugh Despenser the Younger, and a great-granddaughter of King Edward I, died on 13 July 1389. [2] Assuming Elizabeth was the child born to Eleanor Clare at Sheen in December 1325, she was 63 when she died, and had outlived two husbands. The heir to Elizabeth's dower lands was her eldest son Thomas, Lord Berkeley, 36 years old in 1389. None of Elizabeth's accounts or letters survive so it is difficult to say much about her life as a widow, but it is virtually certain that she kept in touch with her natal family, including her great-nephew Thomas Despenser and his three older sisters, and her nephew Henry, bishop of Norwich.

On 14 August 1390 at Missenden in Buckinghamshire, Sir John Arundel II died at the age of 25. Elizabeth Arundel née Despenser was left a widow in her early 20s with three small sons, the eldest of whom had just turned 5. According to the Westminster chronicler, John was one of a number of gallant and illustrious knights who died of 'a great and deadly pestilence' which occurred during a period of intensely hot weather in England from June until the end of August 1390. [3] Arundel had come to have so much trust in his wife – despite his disappearance in the summer of 1385 before she gave birth to their first son – that he appointed Elizabeth as his sole executor and left her all his goods and chattels, for her to distribute among their children and servants as she saw fit. He was buried at Missenden Abbey. [4] Elizabeth received her dower shortly after 23 November 1390, and Richard II granted the remaining two-thirds of John's lands to his (Richard's) half-brother John Holland, earl of Huntingdon, to hold until Elizabeth's eldest son came of age. Huntingdon was also granted the rights to 5-year-old John Arundel III's marriage in exchange for £300. As well as her dower, Elizabeth held the Gloucestershire manors of Kings Stanley and Woodchester, which she and her husband had owned jointly, for the rest of her life. [5] Both of Elizabeth's Gloucestershire manors lay about twenty miles from Tewkesbury, where her mother Elizabeth Burghersh seems to have spent most of her time during her long widowhood.

Elizabeth had married John Arundel around 1 August 1380, and they were married for almost exactly ten years. In 1392 or 1393 she married her second husband, William, Lord Zouche of Harringworth in Northamptonshire, a widower born *c.* 1342 who was the same age as her mother and twice Elizabeth's age. This second marriage produced no children, though William had several with his first wife; his eldest son William the younger was born about 1373, so was the same age as Elizabeth's younger brother Thomas. [6] Back in 1375 when Elizabeth was a child, her second husband had been one of the six men appointed 'to appease the dissensions lately arisen' between the men of Elizabeth's uncle Sir Thomas Despenser (d. 1381) at his Rutland manor of Burley and the men of two neighbouring lordships. [7] Elizabeth's cousin Hugh Despenser witnessed a grant by Zouche in February 1385, another connection between the families. [8] Her marriage to the much older William Zouche lasted for only three or four years, and she was widowed again in 1396. During her widowhood, Elizabeth became notorious for paying her bills tardily and was sued for debt several times. [9] In August 1402, she asked her agent John Bore somewhat plaintively to 'set [her] house in better governance'. [10] For the rest of her life Elizabeth called herself Lady Zouche, but although she maintained affectionate, long-lasting ties with both her natal family and with the Arundels, she was not on such good terms with her second husband's family, and in the early 1400s was involved in a feud with her stepson which became so bitter and violent that it resulted in the death of her daughter-in-law.

King Richard held a famous jousting tournament at Smithfield, London in October 1390, attended by noblemen and knights from all over Europe. The earl of Huntingdon won a prize as the best defender on the first day, as did Hugh Despenser on a later day of the grand event. By October 1390 Hugh's cousin Anne Hastings, Elizabeth Zouche's older sister, had married her second husband. He was Thomas, Lord Morley, born *c.* 1354, whose first wife Joan Hastings, mother of his son and heir Robert, was the sister of Anne's first husband Hugh and was a Despenser descendant. Anne was Morley's third wife: in June 1380 after Joan's death, he was married to a woman called Elizabeth. [11] On 21 October 1390, Pope Boniface IX told the bishop of Ely to lift the ban of excommunication on Anne and Thomas Morley but to order them to separate for a time, as they had married without a papal dispensation. 'Whichever of the two survive the other shall remain perpetually unwed,' Boniface added. Rather oddly, he also stated that 'Thomas and Anne hold Henry [Despenser], bishop of Norwich … for a certain reason (not mentioned) suspect'. [12]

Anne Morley, formerly Hastings, and her second husband's first wife Joan Hastings were third cousins, and perhaps Henry Despenser had failed to inform his niece and nephew-in-law that they needed a dispensation to marry on these grounds. During the Uprising of 1381, Thomas Morley and other knights had been captured by rebels and ordered to go to London to plead their cause with Richard II. Henry Despenser captured the rebels and beheaded them, then berated the knights for their cowardice. Perhaps this humiliation was another reason why Morley deemed him 'suspect'. [13] The pope's letter to the bishop of Ely about Anne and Morley is somewhat odd, as he called Anne by her maiden name, Despenser, not Hastings, and also referred to her as a 'damsel' as though he was unaware of her previous Hastings marriage. Anne and Thomas Morley would be married for twenty-six years but had no children together, and their descendants intermarried: Thomas's great-granddaughter, confusingly named Anne Morley (d. 1471), married his wife's grandson John Hastings (d. 1477).

Anne's brother Thomas Despenser was given custody of the lands of his own inheritance on 6 December 1390, although he was still only 17. [14] His mother Elizabeth held a third of the Despenser lands as dower, and she and Thomas were granted joint custody of the remaining two-thirds. 'Lord Despenser' was given permission on 20 May 1391 to travel to Prussia with a retinue of fifty people; he was going on crusade against the pagans of Lithuania, as numerous other English noblemen of the late fourteenth century did as well. This expedition was led by Thomas Despenser's uncle-in-law Thomas of Woodstock, duke of Gloucester, but it proved a failure: the fleet of ships failed to make landfall in Denmark or Norway, and was driven back to the English coast. The title 'Lord Despenser' would normally seem to refer to Thomas, but as he was only 17 years old in May 1391, it may mean his much older cousin Hugh, whose father Hugh (d. 1374) had received permission to go on crusade in 1367 and who had himself previously travelled to Prussia in 1383. [15] In 1391, Thomas Despenser and Constance of York had been married for a dozen years, and sometime in the late 1380s or early 1390s would finally have begun to live together as husband and wife, depending on when they both reached maturity.

On 23 December 1392, Thomas's Spanish mother-in-law Isabel of Castile, duchess of York, died at the age of about 37. In her will she left her only daughter Constance a 'fret of pearls', i.e. a head-dress of interlaced wire, and to her elder son Edward, made earl of Rutland in 1390, she bequeathed her crown. There is a story that Duchess Isabel had an affair with Richard II's half-brother John Holland, earl of Huntingdon, and that Holland may have been the father of her youngest child Richard of Conisbrough (b. c. 1385). In the absence of any certain evidence to the contrary, however, it is safest to assume that Isabel's husband Edmund of Langley was Richard's father, and certainly Edmund never disavowed his son. Isabel asked King Richard in her will to look after her son Richard, his godson, and to provide him with an income. [16] Edmund of Langley buried Isabel at the priory of Langley in Hertfordshire, founded by his grandfather Edward II in 1308. Duchess Isabel left a 'tablet of jasper' to her brother-in-law John of Gaunt a 'tablet of gold' and a psalter to her sister-in-law the duchess of Gloucester (Eleanor Bohun, wife of Edward III's youngest son Thomas of Woodstock), and she left all her horses, all her beds, her best brooch and her best gold cup to her husband. Ten years later Edmund requested burial next to his 'dearest consort'.

As of July 1393 or earlier, Thomas and Constance Despenser owned an inn called the 'Belle on the Hope' on Friday Street in London, three rooms next to the garden of the inn with a stable below, the garden itself and a hall, six 'little houses', and three shops with cellars on the corner of Friday Street. Thomas also owned a house which backed onto the convent of the Minoresses, a house of Franciscan nuns founded near the Tower of London in 1293 by Edward I's brother Edmund, earl of Lancaster. Thomas received permission from the abbess and the pope to create a doorway straight from his house into the Minoresses' church. [17]

Thomas and Constance lived in some magnificence. One of their favourite residences was Hanley Castle in Worcestershire, from where Thomas's great-grandmother Eleanor Clare had been abducted by her second husband William Zouche in 1329. Hanley had been given to Thomas's mother Elizabeth as dower, but she seems to have spent most of her time at Tewkesbury in Gloucestershire and allowed her son and daughter-in-law possession of Hanley. [18] A list of Thomas's belongings kept at Hanley was made there in 1400. He owned a silken bed embroidered with golden swans, with three red curtains around it and two matching cushions, a white cloak of damask studded with jewels, a red velvet tunic embroidered with silver thread, a short black tunic with grey fur, a white satin doublet embroidered with gold leaves, a red velvet jacket embroidered with gold thread and much else besides. Richard II himself adored and always wore lavish clothes, and Thomas needed to cut a fine figure among the youthful, fashionable set at court. Chroniclers grumbled about the shoes called *cracowes* worn by Richard's young courtiers, who must have included Thomas Despenser: the toes of the shoes were so long they had to be tied to the wearer's knee so that he could walk in them.

The list of possessions also reveals that Thomas rode a white courser (horse) and a chestnut horse called Hobyn Dirland, i.e. 'of Ireland', which he presumably purchased when he accompanied Richard II to Ireland in 1394/5 or 1399. There was also a coach with its own colourful canopy and five horses, all a different colour, to pull it (presumably for Constance to use) and a saddle for Thomas which had 'red velvet studs with brass pineapples'. [19] Constance Despenser also owned several items 'in his [Thomas's] lifetime as her own by his assent and will': seven gold brooches, a small gold goblet, a silver-gilt cross, a censer made of silver and an *agnus dei* made of gold. [20]

Thomas Despenser and his uncle the bishop of Norwich co-operated in December 1393 when they jointly, and successfully, requested pardons from the king for no fewer than eleven of the bishop's servants who had been found guilty of murder and robbery. [21] Thomas was granted all his lands on 7 March 1394, though he was still more than six months away from his twenty-first birthday and thus from attaining his majority. He was addressed as lord of Glamorgan on 10 September that year, a few days before his birthday. [22] Rather unfortunately for posterity, this favour by the king meant that Thomas did not have to prove his age when he turned twenty-one, which would have revealed some interesting details about his birth and baptism and would have confirmed his birthplace.

Thomas's close alliance with Richard II after he came of age, and the king's promotion of Despenser's interests, rather upset the balance of power in Gloucestershire, where both Thomas and his kinsman Lord Berkeley (a grandson of Hugh Despenser the Younger) were wealthy landowners and where they battled for dominance. Although Thomas does not seem to have had the haughty self-importance and arrogance of his great-grandfather Hugh the Younger and uncle Bishop Henry – or at least nowhere near to the same extent – neither did he have his father's social skills and political judgement. In stark contrast to Edward Despenser's reputation as a beloved, courteous and honourable knight, by the late 1390s Thomas had managed to make himself remarkably unpopular.

Richard II passed through Despenser's lands in South Wales in early September 1394, staying in Newport and Cardiff, and doubtless Thomas and Constance were on hand to make sure he was comfortable and lavishly fed and entertained. In early 1396, the king again stayed on Thomas's lands, this time at Burford (Oxfordshire) and Tewkesbury. [23] Thomas was a staunch royalist and one of the closest allies of the young king (who, born in early January 1367, was six years and nine months his senior), along with Richard's half-brother the earl of Huntingdon and half-nephew the earl of Kent, the earl of Salisbury, and Despenser's brother-in-law Edward of York, made earl of Rutland in 1390. Evidence suggests that Thomas's sisters Elizabeth Zouche (formerly Arundel) and Margaret Ferrers, and his first cousin Anne Botiller née Despenser, also shared his loyalties. Margaret and Anne demonstrated hostility to Richard II's first cousin and usurper Henry IV at the start of his reign, and Thomas himself was to die in rebellion against Henry as a result of his diehard loyalty to Richard. Elizabeth's second husband William Zouche was one of the king's councillors whose removal from Richard II's court the Lords Appellant had demanded in 1388.

Thomas's aunt-in-law Constanza of Castile, duchess of Lancaster and heir of her father King Pedro 'the Cruel', died in March 1394 at the age of about forty, leaving her only surviving child, Catalina, queen-consort of Constanza's native Castile. John of Gaunt had his duchess buried at the Newarke in Leicester, a prestigious collegiate foundation of his first wife Blanche of Lancaster's father and grandfather. Three months later, the queen of England, Anne of Bohemia, died at the age of only 28, at Sheen on the Thames west of London (which, eighty years earlier, had belonged to the young nobleman Edward Burnell, Hugh Despenser the Elder's son-in-law). A devastated Richard II ordered the entire Sheen palace complex to be pulled down a few months later. Grieving terribly, Richard assaulted the earl of Arundel when he turned up late for the queen's funeral in Westminster Abbey and asked to leave early, and the king rather morbidly planned the ceremonies he intended to take place after his own death in obsessive detail, revealing his state of mind in the weeks and months after Queen Anne's early demise. [24] He sent a sad letter to Philip, duke of Burgundy (b. 1342), uncle of Charles VI of France (r. 1380–1422), remarking on the 'grievous heaviness' of the loss of his beloved wife and how he could not cease dwelling on it. [25] The royal couple had no children in more than twelve years of marriage and the king's lack of heirs born of his own body was to cause serious problems in England over the coming decades.

Chapter 33

Thomas Despenser accompanied Richard II to Ireland between October 1394 and May 1395, and his father-in-law the duke of York was left behind in England as regent. Richard's aim in 1394/5 was to bring down Art MacMurrough, self-styled king of Leinster, and to bring the other three Irish kings to heel, and he succeeded in this endeavour. Despenser attended a meeting of the royal council at Eltham in Kent in July 1395 a few weeks after the royal party's return to England. The year after he inherited his lands, it is apparent that he had already begun to play a role in the government of his wife's cousin. [1]

John of Gaunt, uncle of the king and uncle-in-law of Thomas Despenser, caused a scandal in early 1396 when he married his third wife Katherine Swynford, who was his long-term mistress and the mother of four of his children, the Beauforts, born in the 1370s. The Beauforts were legitimised soon afterwards, and two of them made excellent marriages: John the eldest married Richard II's half-niece Margaret Holland, and Joan, the only daughter, married Ralph Neville, made earl of Westmorland in 1397. This Beaufort/Neville marriage was to produce fourteen children and numerous grandchildren, and Thomas and Constance Despenser's son and their three grandchildren were all destined to marry into this huge family.

On 13 May 1396, Thomas's sister Elizabeth was widowed from her second husband when William, Lord Zouche of Harringworth died at the age of about 54. Elizabeth was in her late twenties when she was widowed for the second time, and never remarried. Her husband's heir was his son William from his first marriage, then aged about 23, and Elizabeth received her dower promptly on 3 July. [2] William Zouche the elder left his wife a valuable cross, and in his will mentioned plate he had had as a gift from Lady Despenser, his mother-in-law, whom he courteously referred to as his 'mother'. As Elizabeth's first husband John Arundel had also done, William made Elizabeth his executor, though on this occasion she shared duties with three others including her brother-in-law Eudo Zouche and her first cousin Hugh Despenser. [3] Hugh's appointment as one of the executors of Elizabeth's late husband indicates that the two Despenser cousins kept in touch, and although Elizabeth often paid her bills tardily and was sued for debt, her appointment as executor to both her husbands shows that she was intelligent and competent.

Elizabeth's nephew Hugh Hastings, elder of the two sons of her sister Anne Morley, died on 2 November 1396, aged about 18. His 14-year-old brother Edward Hastings was his and their father's heir. Twenty-eight days later, another of Elizabeth's nephews, Richard Despenser, the only son of Thomas and Constance, was born. [4] The boy must have been named in honour of Richard II, and although the king is unlikely to have attended the boy's baptism in person – Richard II had only recently returned to England from France after marrying his second wife, 7-year-old Isabelle de Valois, in her homeland – he may have been his godfather and have sent representatives to the baptism. Richard Despenser's birthplace was not recorded, but possibly he was born in Cardiff: his father was there on 21 October 1396 and 16 February 1397. [5] Constance favoured their castle at Cardiff, and gave birth to her and Thomas's second daughter, Isabelle, there some years later. The couple's first daughter was named Elizabeth after her paternal grandmother, and she died young in Cardiff and was buried there. The Tewkesbury Abbey chronicle gives the three Despenser children as Richard, Elizabeth and Isabelle (who was born in July 1400) in that order, so apparently Elizabeth Despenser was younger than her brother and was perhaps born c. 1398. [6] It is also possible, however, that the chronicler named Richard first because he was the son and heir, and that Elizabeth was older than her brother and born c. 1394/5. Richard Despenser was, from the moment of his birth, heir to his father's lands and his grandmother's Burghersh/Verdon inheritance.

King Richard had left England in late October 1396 leaving Constance's father Edmund, duke of York behind as regent, and married Isabelle de Valois, eldest daughter of Charles VI of France and his queen Isabeau of Bavaria. The little girl was crowned queen of England on 7 January 1397, the day after her husband's thirtieth birthday, and Richard II was slightly older than his new parents-in-law Charles and Isabeau (born 1368 and c. 1370). The king needed children, but would have to wait at least eight years before his little queen would be able to give him any, by which time he would be close to 40. Hugh Despenser, himself now about 40 or a little older, was appointed as one of the knights of Queen Isabelle's household. [7]

At an unknown date before 1400, Hugh's younger sister Anne went through some painful marital difficulties with her husband Edward Botiller, and Botiller attempted to have their marriage annulled. The Despensers stuck together and had a strong sense of family feeling, and Anne's uncle the bishop of Norwich wrote to the elderly Elizabeth, Lady Audley (b. *c*. mid or late 1320s) about it. Henry told Elizabeth that he had been in London just before Pentecost and asked Edward Botiller twice in the politest possible way to come to him so that he could attempt to resolve the couple's marital discord, but Botiller refused. Henry was deeply angry and upset about the 'disloyal and malicious slander' Botiller was imputing to his niece Anne, and asked Lady Audley to intervene and to persuade Edward Botiller to treat his wife 'in a good and amiable manner as law and Holy Church demands'. Somewhat peculiarly, Bishop Henry claimed that 'an old woman' (*une veile femme*) had been placed in Anne's household by her enemies – he did not say who they were – and had treacherously slandered and defamed Anne publicly. The old woman had recently died at Northbury, one of Edward Botiller's manors, and had publicly confessed there to what she had done. Henry asked Lady Audley to send credible officials to Northbury to record the woman's exact words so that they could be presented before 'judges of Holy Church' in Anne's defence if necessary.

Anne Botiller herself also wrote to 'my very honoured, very reverend and very gracious lady', Elizabeth Audley, presumably around the same time, to ask if she might come to stay with her around the feast of St Michael (29 September) for a week or two so that she could inform the lady more fully of the hardships and wrongs she was suffering. Henry and Anne's letters make it apparent that they were on excellent terms with Lady Audley, and they both thanked her for her many kindnesses to them. [8] The outcome of Henry Despenser and Lady Audley's intervention is not known, nor whether Anne and Edward Botiller ever reconciled; perhaps the death of the 'fair son' Anne had borne contributed to their problems. In July 1405 at least, Anne and Edward were apparently on somewhat cordial terms, as they were jointly involved in a feud of some kind against a *wexchaundeler* or 'wax candle-maker' called Alexander Hevede and were bound over to keep the peace. [9] Anne may have been the niece who sent a letter to Bishop Henry Despenser, also at an unrecorded date, as 'my very reverend father in God and my very honourable and very gracious lord and uncle'. The niece told Henry that she was deeply troubled, but that if she heard good news of 'your health and your gladness of heart, it seems to me that I could be in great joy and hope of a good life'. [10]

Chapter 34

In September 1397, Richard II made a move against the three senior Lords Appellant who had convened the Merciless Parliament in 1388 and executed or exiled many of his friends and supporters. He personally arrested his uncle Thomas of Woodstock, duke of Gloucester, at Gloucester's castle of Pleshey in Essex; the royal duke was imprisoned in Calais and was killed there. Elizabeth Zouche's uncle-in-law from her first marriage, the earl of Arundel, was tried before parliament and beheaded on Tower Hill in London, and Arundel's brother Thomas Arundel, archbishop of Canterbury, was banished from England. The elderly Thomas Beauchamp, earl of Warwick, was exiled to the Isle of Man. Warwick's son and heir Richard Beauchamp, godson of Elizabeth Burghersh, Lady Despenser, was 15 years old and already married to Elizabeth Berkeley (b. 1385/6), only child of Thomas, Lord Berkeley and a great-granddaughter of Hugh Despenser the Younger. Custody of the young couple was given to the king's half-nephew Thomas Holland, earl of Kent on 5 October 1397, and they were to be 'treated duly and honourably by him as their estate demands.' [1]

Thomas Despenser was, with Richard II's half-brother Huntingdon and their nephew Kent, one of the king's most faithful supporters during his campaign against the Appellants. On 29 September 1397, Richard rewarded Thomas for his loyalty to him and created him earl of Gloucester, the title once held by Thomas's great-grandmother Eleanor's brother Gilbert and his Clare ancestors. [2] Most probably, Thomas's father Edward and great-uncle Huchon had desired this earldom; now finally the Despensers had it. Other allies of the king were also promoted to higher titles, including Thomas's brother-in-law Edward of York. Despenser petitioned for the sentences of perpetual disinheritance, exile and treason imposed on his great-grandfather and great-great-grandfather at the parliaments of 1321 and 1327 to be revoked, and this was granted.

Thomas was also given custody of St Briavels Castle and the Forest of Dean in Gloucestershire at a rent of £80 annually. [3] He and Constance hosted the king at Hanley Castle in early March 1398, and charter witness lists reveal that Despenser was often at court at the end of the 1390s. [4] Hugh the Younger's rise in Edward II's affections is easily visible from the increasing frequency with which Hugh witnessed royal charters, from none before 1316 to almost all of them by 1326. Likewise, Thomas's favour with Richard II can be seen in the number of royal charters he witnessed, although there is no reason to suppose that Thomas had a sexual relationship with the king or that Richard was infatuated with him in the way his great-grandfather seems to have been with Thomas's own great-grandfather.

All was not well, however, at Richard II's court. In and after 1397, the king allowed intense factionalism and rivalry to flourish, and no-one, however close he seemed to the king, could feel safe. Thomas Mowbray, although created duke of Norfolk in 1397 and seemingly trusted by Richard II, especially as he had taken charge of the murder of the king's uncle the duke of Gloucester in Calais, had been one of the Lords Appellant of 1388. So had Richard's cousin Henry of Lancaster, John of Gaunt's son and heir. In October 1398 the king exiled both Mowbray and Lancaster after they mutually accused each other of treason. Mowbray died in Venice less than a year later; Henry went to Paris and was joined there by Thomas Arundel, the exiled archbishop of Canterbury. Richard II seems to have become paranoid and frightened in and after 1397, and turned himself into a remote figure sitting on a high throne and forcing everyone who caught his eye or who wished to approach him to kneel three times. He surrounded himself with a private army of archers from Cheshire, and in and after 1397 was widely detested and feared.

Sometime in the late 1390s, Constance Despenser's brother Edward of York married. His surprising choice of bride was Philippa Mohun, a first cousin of Thomas Despenser's mother Elizabeth Burghersh. [5] Philippa was much older than Edward and twice a widow. They were to have no children together and it may be that Philippa was past childbearing age when she wed Edward, though she had no offspring from her previous two marriages either. Edward was one of the greatest noblemen in England, and the king had considered marrying him to one of Charles VI of France's daughters; his marriage to Philippa, who brought him no lands, income or powerful in-laws, must have been a love-match.

In early February 1399, Richard II and Edward of York's uncle John of Gaunt, duke of Lancaster, died in his late fifties. The king made the momentous decision to exile Gaunt's son and heir Henry of Lancaster from England permanently, and confiscated his enormous inheritance, the duchy of Lancaster and the earldoms of Richmond, Lincoln, Derby and Leicester, plus half of the earldoms of Hereford, Essex and Northampton which Henry held by right of his late wife Mary Bohun (d. 1394).

Some months after confiscating his cousin's inheritance, Richard II decided to visit Ireland again, an expedition notably less successful than the one of 1394/5. With hindsight, it seems rather astonishing that the king thought it was a good idea to leave England while his exiled enemies Henry of Lancaster, Thomas Arundel and their allies were at large on the Continent. The king's party reached Waterford on 1 June 1399, and a month later were in Dublin. Richard sent Thomas Despenser to treat with Art MacMurrough, king of Leinster, and the two men met in a glen in Wicklow, but on this occasion Thomas failed to persuade Art to submit to Richard. [6] Thomas's brothers-in-law Thomas Morley and Edward of York also went to Ireland with the king. Despenser appointed his father-in-law the duke of York, now the only surviving child of Edward III, and Roger Walden, the new archbishop of Canterbury, as two of his six attorneys to act for him during his absence. [7] The duke of York was also appointed as regent of England during Richard II's absence. The king had, however, made a terrible mistake in deciding to leave his kingdom, and by the time he returned, he barely had a kingdom left.

Chapter 35

During the king's absence in Ireland, Henry of Lancaster returned to England claiming his rightful inheritance, and was soon joined by a large crowd of followers including Henry Percy, earl of Northumberland, with his son Henry 'Hotspur' and brother the earl of Worcester, and Lancaster's brother-in-law the earl of Westmorland. Thomas Fitzalan, the executed earl of Arundel's teenage son who had escaped abroad, and his uncle the exiled archbishop of Canterbury, returned to England with Henry. Chroniclers claimed that within weeks of his arrival, Henry's army reached 100,000 men, and although this is surely an exaggeration, there is little doubt that Henry was immensely popular while the king was detested. Richard II's uncle Edmund of Langley, duke of York, who was also Henry of Lancaster's uncle, made little attempt to repel Henry; in fairness, there was little he could have done given the massive support Henry enjoyed, and he surely sympathised with his nephew over his recent disinheritance. At some point, exactly when is not clear, Henry also decided to claim the English throne. Whether he was truly the heir to the throne after his childless cousin Richard is a matter for debate. Richard had no brothers or sisters, nieces or nephews, and his kinsman Roger Mortimer, earl of March, great-grandson and heir of Lionel of Antwerp, duke of Clarence, was killed in Ireland in 1398 leaving two young sons. The earl of March and his children were descendants of Edward III's second son in the female line, while Henry of Lancaster was the son of Edward's third son.

Henry of Lancaster met his uncle York at Berkeley Castle in Gloucestershire on 27 July and the duke tamely surrendered to him. At Berkeley, Lancaster arrested Henry Despenser, bishop of Norwich, who, like his nephew Thomas, was a staunch supporter of King Richard. Thomas, Lord Berkeley, owner of Berkeley Castle, was a close kinsman of the Despensers – he was a first cousin of Bishop Henry – but his nose had well and truly been put out of joint by Richard II's promotion of Thomas Despenser and Despenser's subsequent prominence in a part of the country where Berkeley was the largest landowner and where he had previously been highly influential. [1] He therefore supported Henry of Lancaster.

Thomas Despenser himself returned to Wales with Richard II around 24 July. History repeated itself: as Edward II ended his reign in 1326 wandering hopelessly around Wales with Hugh Despenser the Younger, his great-grandson Richard II ended his reign wandering hopelessly around Wales with Hugh's great-grandson Thomas Despenser. Chronicler Adam Usk says that the king sent Thomas to rally the men of Glamorgan, but that the men refused their lord's summons. [2] Richard was taken captive by Henry of Lancaster at Flint Castle in North Wales on 20 August 1399, and was subsequently taken south and imprisoned in the Tower of London. He was forced to give up his throne to his cousin, whose reign as Henry IV began on 30 September 1399, in a coup supported by most of the great magnates of the realm. Richard II, now merely Sir Richard of Bordeaux, was sent to Pontefract Castle in Yorkshire, where his great-grandfather Edward had had his own troublesome Lancastrian cousin Thomas of Lancaster beheaded in 1322.

Sometime in 1399, Philippa of Lancaster, queen of Portugal, wrote to Archbishop Thomas Arundel, asking him to intercede with her brother Henry of Lancaster on behalf of the bishop of Norwich. [3] Philippa referred to her brother Henry as duke of Hereford and Lancaster, so she must have written it after the death of their father John of Gaunt in early February 1399 and before Henry of Lancaster became king of England at the end of September 1399. Presumably the letter was sent in the few weeks between Lancaster and Archbishop Arundel's return to England in July 1399 and the revolution that made Lancaster king of England, and after Philippa heard of her brother's arrest of Henry Despenser at Berkeley Castle. Philippa wrote that her brother was displeased with Despenser because the bishop had wronged Lancaster, and that she was upset about it because Despenser had been so kind to her. She therefore asked Arundel to intervene with Henry of Lancaster and beg him to pardon Despenser for the wrong he had done him, and to be a good lord and friend to Despenser. Bishop Henry Despenser was something of a contradictory personality: violent and fierce, he was also capable of great kindness and courtesy towards ladies, and had made such an excellent impression on Queen Philippa that she interceded on his behalf from distant Portugal.

Henry IV's coronation took place at Westminster Abbey on 13 October 1399, and one of the several dozen young men knighted to mark the occasion was the teenaged Richard Beauchamp, heir to the earldom of Warwick. His father Thomas, now 60 years old, was recalled from exile on the Isle of Man, and restored to his title and lands. The new king was hugely popular, although there remained the thorny issue of the Mortimers, Edmund (b. 1391), his younger brother Roger, and their elder sister Anne (b. 1390), children of the late earl of March. Henry IV's usurpation of the throne from his cousin Richard II, the only legitimate descendant of Edward III's first son, and his setting aside the descendants of the second son, was to bring about the battles for the English throne known as the Wars of the Roses in the next century.

Sir Hugh Despenser joined the new king's household on 12 November 1399 and was promised an income of £100 a year. Henry IV trusted Hugh, and in April 1400 sent him on a mission to Aquitaine in southern France. [4] The king also appointed Hugh justice of South Wales and called him 'our dearest cousin' in a letter to his eldest son Henry of Monmouth (b. September 1386), whom he made prince of Wales at the time of his coronation. The greatest sign of favour came when Hugh was appointed as Monmouth's *maistre* or tutor and a member of the prince's council; Monmouth also acknowledged Hugh as 'our dearest cousin'. [5] Hugh had been retained by Richard II in 1391 and later was a household knight of Richard's child-wife Isabelle, but unlike his cousin Thomas and his uncle Henry had never been particularly wedded to the Ricardian regime, and seamlessly switched sides in 1399. Another close ally of the new king was Thomas Despenser's brother-in-law Lord Morley, his eldest sister Anne's second husband. ,

On 20 October 1399 during his first parliament, Henry IV sent Thomas Despenser and the former king's half-brother and half-nephew John and Thomas Holland to temporary imprisonment in the Tower of London. Eight days later, he ordered the three men to be brought before him and his council. [6] Despenser had his earldom of Gloucester taken from him during this parliament, and became merely lord of Glamorgan once more. He had held his Clare ancestors' earldom for only two years. Henry IV also demoted Richard II's other promotions of 1397, with the exception of Thomas Percy, brother of the earl of Northumberland, who kept his earldom of Worcester. Despenser was ordered to explain his role in the murder of Henry IV's uncle Thomas of Woodstock, duke of Gloucester, two years previously. He explained how he had dined with Richard II at Nottingham Castle on 5 August 1397, when Richard told him to leave the castle and 'do as other lords would do'. Realising that he was being ordered to arrest someone, Despenser put on his habergeon (chainmail) and strapped on his sword, and told six attendants to accompany him wherever the king might order. Standing outside the castle with the other lords whom the king had ordered there, he heard part of the charges against the duke of Gloucester being read out. Despenser's narrative lamely tailed off at this point, no doubt because he was unwilling to incriminate himself too far in the murder of a king's son and uncle, and he claimed that 'through fear and terror of his life, he did not dare to resist the order of the said former king' to arrest Thomas of Woodstock. He added that he knew nothing of the duke's death until it 'was known to the whole realm.' Despenser, his brother-in-law Edward of York, Henry IV's half-brother John Beaufort, and Thomas Holland, earl of Kent, who were all close to Despenser's own age, asked Henry IV 'to take into consideration their youth' in 1397 (the other defendants, John Montacute, earl of Salisbury and John Holland, earl of Huntingdon, were born in the 1350s). [7]

Thomas Despenser's unpopularity at the end of the 1390s is revealed by the chronicler Adam Usk's statement that Thomas poisoned Humphrey of Gloucester, the only son and heir of the late Thomas of Woodstock, duke of Gloucester. Humphrey did die on 2 September 1399 at the age of 17, but there is no reason whatsoever to give credence to Usk's story, and every reason to deem it merely malicious gossip. [8] Henry IV does seem to have tried to reconcile Thomas Despenser by inviting him to a council meeting on 4 December, while Thomas's uncle the bishop of Norwich was released and allowed to attend the new king's first parliament. [9] Henry IV's attempted reconciliation failed to work, however, and Despenser and various discontented allies began to plot his downfall.

Chapter 36

At the end of 1399 and beginning of 1400, Thomas Despenser and his allies the earls of Huntingdon, Kent and Salisbury, Thomas Merk, bishop of Carlisle, and other loyal Ricardians, hatched a plot to free the former king from Pontefract Castle and to kill Henry IV. This rebellion, known as the Epiphany Rising – the feast of Epiphany is 6 January, and in 1400 was Richard of Bordeaux's thirty-third birthday – failed completely. It may have been Thomas's brother-in-law Edward of York, earl of Rutland, who betrayed them to the king, though this is not certain. Henry IV ordered the plotters' arrest on 5 January. [1] The earls of Kent and Salisbury were captured at Cirencester in Gloucestershire and summarily beheaded by a mob who suspected, probably rightly, that a fire which broke out in the town was a diversion intended to cover the men's escape. Their heads were sent to Henry IV in a basket. John Holland, earl of Huntingdon, was captured in Essex by the king's mother-in-law Joan Bohun, dowager countess of Hereford. She had him executed in the presence of her teenage nephew Thomas, son and heir of the earl of Arundel beheaded in 1397, supposedly on the same spot where Richard II had had her other son-in-law the duke of Gloucester arrested in 1397.

The French writer of a chronicle called the *Traison et Mort de Richart Deux* claims that Thomas Despenser was with his allies in Cirencester and escaped by climbing out of a window, but this seems unlikely. [2] More probably, he waited at Tewkesbury (twenty-four miles from Cirencester) or at Cardiff to see what was happening. On hearing of his allies' failure to capture Henry IV or to take London, Thomas and several attendants boarded a ship at Cardiff in his lordship of Glamorgan, intending to flee abroad. The crew, loyal to King Henry, overcame his men and took Thomas to Bristol instead. He sought refuge in the house of the mayor, Thomas Knappe, and although Knappe tried to save him and Thomas managed to send messengers to Henry IV pleading for a chance to speak to him, he was captured by a mob. Thomas was dragged to the marketplace and summarily beheaded there, probably on 13 January 1400, though an inquisition held at the request of his daughter in 1414 gives 5 January as the date of his death. [3] He was wearing a furred gown of motley velvet and damask and a *hanselyn* (short jacket) with silver-gilt spangles when he was executed, which the king gave to his servants, Ralph Ramsey and William Flaxman.

When he was captured by the mob in Bristol, Thomas had the large sum of £30 (tens of thousands of pounds in modern terms) in gold and silver on his person. Rather remarkably, this was not stolen but was handed over to the mayor, and on 3 March 1400 Henry IV allowed Thomas's widow Constance, his first cousin, to have it. He also allowed Constance to keep some other items which had belonged to her late husband and which were worth £200: two dozen dishes, twelve silver saucers and four silver dishes, twelve silver spoons, a pair of silver-gilt basins, two silver-gilt pots and four silver cups with gilt covers. [4] On 21 January, however, the king granted the inn which Thomas and Constance owned in London, the 'Belle on the Hope', along with the tenements that went with it on Friday Street and Watling Street, to his household knight Sir Walter Blount. In December 1403, they passed to John Blount, though Constance was given a third of the inn and its garden and houses in dower, and when she died they passed to her and Thomas's daughter. [5]

Henry IV ordered the mayor and sheriff of Bristol on 24 January 1400 to send Thomas Despenser's head to London for public display, though allowed Thomas's mother Elizabeth to bury the rest of her son's body honourably with his father Edward and numerous other Despenser and Clare ancestors at Tewkesbury Abbey. [6] The city of Bristol was not a happy place for the Despenser family. Hugh the Elder, earl of Winchester, was hanged there in October 1326, and a few weeks later one quarter of his son Hugh the Younger's body was publicly displayed in the city and would remain there for four years. Hugh the Younger's son Huchon was imprisoned at Bristol Castle from December 1328 until July 1331. And now Thomas Despenser had been executed there too, at the age of only 26. He emulated Hugh the Younger's fate in another way: his head was paraded down Cheapside and placed on a spike on London Bridge, exactly as Hugh's had been in 1326. [7]

Thomas left his 3-year-old son Richard and his daughter Elizabeth, probably a year or two old (or possibly 5 or so). Whether Thomas ever knew it or not, Constance was pregnant; she gave birth to his second daughter six and a half months after his death. Depending when Constance found out that she was expecting, and when the couple last saw each other or had the chance to correspond during the frantic last weeks of Thomas's life, he may never have known of his wife's pregnancy. On 25 January, the day after ordering Thomas's severed head to be sent from Bristol to London, Henry IV sent William Beauchamp, Lord Abergavenny, to seize the toddler Richard Despenser and 'all the other sons and daughters of Thomas Despenser'. [8] The wording implies that Henry IV and his clerks had no idea how many children Thomas had. William Beauchamp of Abergavenny was the younger brother of the earl of Warwick whom Richard II exiled to the Isle of Man in 1397, and the son-in-law of the earl of Arundel executed at the same time, so was hardly disposed to look favourably on the former king's allies and their families. Somewhat ironically, though, Beauchamp's son and heir Richard (aged about 2 or 3 in early 1400) would marry Despenser's posthumous daughter a few years later.

Meanwhile, other members of the Epiphany Rising were tried and executed or imprisoned, and the failed plot sealed the former king's fate. Sir Richard of Bordeaux died at Pontefract Castle on or around 14 February 1400, perhaps – as a few contemporary chroniclers believed – by being starved to death. Richard's body was taken south and buried at Langley Priory in Hertfordshire, though in 1413 after Henry IV's death, Henry's son Henry V moved Richard's body to Westminster Abbey and laid him to rest next to his beloved first queen, Anne of Bohemia. Their tomb and effigies can still be seen there. Richard's second queen Isabelle de Valois, meanwhile, only 10 years old when she was widowed in early 1400, was sent back to France in 1401, and in 1406 married her cousin Charles of Angoulême.

Other family members of the Epiphany Rising plotters came under suspicion in 1400. Sometime after Thomas Despenser's summary execution, King Henry demanded that the three sons of Thomas's sister Margaret Ferrers be sent to stay with him at court, presumably so that he could keep them under his eye with their Despenser cousins. The boys' father, Robert Ferrers of Chartley, had been one of the few English noblemen who declared his support for Richard II and opposition to Henry in the summer of 1399, and thus sided with his Despenser brother-in-law, though played no known role in the Epiphany Rising a few months later. The eldest Ferrers boy, Edmund, was somewhere between 10 and 13 years old. Margaret was strongly opposed to her sons being sent to the king, and her cousin Anne Botiller sent a letter to their uncle the bishop of Norwich on Margaret's behalf. She asked Henry to help her 'dearest cousin Lady Ferrers of Chartley' by keeping Margaret's youngest son Edward with him at one of his manors in East Anglia. Meanwhile, Anne wrote, she had arranged for the eldest Ferrers boy to stay with the bishop of Exeter (Edmund Stafford), and for the second, Thomas, to stay with 'my very honoured lady, the Lady Despenser', Bishop Henry's sister-in-law and the Ferrers boys' grandmother, Elizabeth Burghersh. [9]

Anne Botiller clearly took the well-being of her cousin Margaret and Margaret's sons very seriously: she begged her uncle to send his clerk to collect Edward Ferrers and bring him to him as soon as it could possibly be arranged, 'to the very great joy, satisfaction and comfort of my heart'. Anne's letter strongly implies that she and Margaret Ferrers followed the political lead of Margaret's late brother and opposed Henry IV, even though Anne's brother Hugh Despenser was a knight in the king's household and staunchly loyal to him. Both women were absolutely determined to keep Margaret's sons out of the king's grasp, and Anne's letter is a typical example of the Despenser family's support of each other.

Margaret Ferrers was not Thomas Despenser's only family member who came under suspicion. The bishop of Norwich sent a letter in early 1400 to one of his nephews, and this must have been Hugh, unless he meant his nephew-in-law Thomas Morley, who was also in Henry IV's favour. Addressing his correspondent as 'dearest and most entirely beloved nephew', Henry declared that he had had no prior knowledge of the Epiphany Rising and took no part in it nor had any contact with the rebels, with the sole exception of receiving greetings from the earl of Huntingdon via a messenger. A 'well-wisher' told Henry, however, that it was commonly reported at the royal court that he had indeed been involved in the plot. He insisted that he had never left his manor of South Elmham in Suffolk and was unaware of what was going on until mid-afternoon on 8 January, when Lord Scales told him. Stating his case with a vehemence that perhaps rather gives the lie to his words, the bishop declared that he had not mounted or even so much as touched a horse since well before Christmas 1399, and had not left South Elmham on foot either except to conduct a funeral for one of his servants. Henry asked his nephew to defend him from any rumours he might hear claiming that he had been involved. He also asked him not to show his letter to anyone, as 'we do not wish to wake the sleeping dog,' *nous ne vouldrons esveiller le chien qui dort* in the French original, or in modern idiom that Henry wished to let sleeping dogs lie. Relations between bishop and king did not improve much over the coming years: Henry IV wrote to Despenser on 14 July 1404, expressing his amazement that the bishop had failed to obey his orders to cease his feud with the mayor and commons of King's Lynn. The king addressed Despenser rather abruptly as 'Reverend father in God' without adding 'our dearest cousin' as would have been polite and conventional. [10]

On the other hand, Henry IV showed considerable trust in Bishop Henry's nephew Hugh, even appointing him as his eldest son's tutor, so did not lash out at all the Despenser family. Hugh was high in the new king's favour and perhaps was able to put in a good word for his uncle, and the bishop was pardoned in February 1401, having spent a year in the custody of Thomas Arundel, archbishop of Canterbury. [11] Hugh Despenser also helped his cousin Thomas Despenser's widow Constance by standing as one of the guarantors of the king's grant to her of several of her late husband's manors on 20 February 1400, to the value of 1,000 marks a year. [12] And Thomas Despenser's teenage nephews Edward Hastings (b. May 1382) and John Arundel III (b. August 1385) were among the young noblemen knighted on 17 March 1400 only two months after Thomas's execution, so they were not punished either. [13]

Despite his woes, Henry Despenser found time to send a comforting letter to his 'dearest and most entirely beloved with all my heart niece[-in-law]' Constance not long after the Epiphany Rising. [14] He promised to be like a 'father, uncle, husband and brother' all in one to her, called her his 'very dear and very sweet best loved niece', and wrote 'Like myself, who make reason sovereign over the foolishness of my flesh, you should so make your reason also … to grieve, sigh, languish, weep and groan over an irrecoverable thing is often the greatest folly that can be'. He reminded her that it was a great sin and an offence to God to 'murmur against his will'. From a modern perspective, his words might not come across as terribly comforting, but this was of course a very different society, and Henry clearly intended to show kindness and compassion to the grieving and pregnant Constance.

Thomas Despenser, lord of Glamorgan and briefly earl of Gloucester, was dead at the age of 26, and another chapter in the turbulent history of the Despenser family closed. Again, a Despenser had been executed and all his lands and goods forfeited. Again, a child was the Despenser heir. And although Thomas could not possibly have known it, it would be his posthumous daughter who would take the Despensers forward into the fifteenth century.

Part 6

The Last Despenser: Isabelle, 1400–1439

Dramatis Personae

Thomas Despenser, lord of Glamorgan, b. September 1373, summarily executed January 1400

Constance Despenser (b. *c.* 1374/6), Thomas's widow, granddaughter of Edward III, daughter and sister of dukes of York, first cousin of Richard II (d. 1400) and Henry IV

Elizabeth Despenser, née Burghersh (b. *c.* 1342): Thomas's mother, widow of Edward the Younger (1336–75)

Richard Despenser (b. 1396): only son of Thomas and Constance; the Despenser and Burghersh heir; marries Eleanor Neville in 1411 but has no children

Eleanor Despenser, née Neville, later Percy (b. *c.* 1397/8): eldest daughter of Ralph Neville, earl of Westmorland, and his second wife Joan Beaufort; marries secondly Henry Percy (b. 1392/3), earl of Northumberland

Elizabeth Despenser (b. *c.* 1398 or perhaps *c.* 1394/5): elder daughter of Thomas and Constance; dies *c.* 1405

Isabelle Despenser (b. 27 July 1400): Thomas's posthumous daughter; the Despenser heir after her brother Richard dies; marries 1) Richard Beauchamp, Lord Abergavenny, later earl of Worcester, in 1411, and 2) Richard Beauchamp, earl of Warwick, in 1423; mother of Elizabeth Beauchamp by her first marriage, Henry and Anne Beauchamp by her second

Richard Beauchamp, Lord Abergavenny, earl of Worcester (b. *c.* 1397): nephew of Thomas Beauchamp, earl of Warwick (d. 1401) and grandson

171

of Richard Fitzalan, earl of Arundel (d. 1397); his heir is his and Isabelle's daughter Elizabeth (b. *c.* 1418)

Joan Beauchamp, Lady Abergavenny (b. *c.* 1368/75): Isabelle's mother-in-law; sister of Elizabeth Mowbray, duchess of Norfolk, and Thomas Fitzalan, earl of Arundel

Richard Beauchamp, earl of Warwick (b. 1382): son and heir of Thomas, earl of Warwick; marries 1) Elizabeth Berkeley (b. 1385/6), daughter of Thomas, Lord Berkeley and granddaughter of Elizabeth Despenser (1325–89); marries 2) Isabelle Despenser; father of Margaret Talbot, Eleanor Beaufort and Elizabeth Neville by his first marriage

Anne Morley, married to Thomas Morley and widow of Hugh Hastings; **Elizabeth Zouche**, widow of John Arundel II and William Zouche; and **Margaret Ferrers**, married to Robert Ferrers of Chartley: elder sisters of the late Thomas Despenser; Isabelle's aunts

Henry Despenser, bishop of Norwich (b. 1341/2): youngest son of Edward the Elder (*c.* 1310–42) and brother of Edward the Younger; uncle of Thomas Despenser and his sisters

Hugh Despenser (b. *c.* 1355): only son of Hugh Despenser (d. 1374) and Alice Hotham (d. 1379); married to Sybil (parentage unknown) and has a daughter Elizabeth; nephew of Henry, bishop of Norwich, and first cousin of Thomas Despenser

Anne Botiller, née Despenser (b. late 1350s or 1360s): sister of Hugh, above; married to Edward Botiller (b. 1337)

Edward Hastings (b. 1382), **John Arundel III** (b. 1385) and **Edmund Ferrers of Chartley** (b. 1386/9): sons of Thomas Despenser's sisters, heirs of their fathers

Philip Despenser III (b. 1342), great-grandson of Hugh the Elder; his son and heir **Philip IV** (b. *c.* 1365); and Philip IV's daughter and heir **Margery** (b. *c.* 1398/1400), who marries 1) John, Lord Ros and 2) Roger Wentworth

Edmund of Langley, first duke of York (b. 1341), fourth son of Edward III, uncle of Richard II and Henry IV; father of Constance Despenser and grandfather of Richard and Isabelle Despenser

Edward of York (b. *c.* 1373/4), earl of Rutland, second duke of York; Edmund's son and heir, Constance's brother; married to Philippa Mohun

(b. *c.* 1350s), a first cousin of Elizabeth Despenser née Burghersh; has no children

Richard of Conisbrough (b. *c.* 1385), earl of Cambridge; Constance's other brother; marries Anne (b. 1390), daughter of Roger Mortimer, earl of March (1374–98) and sister of Edmund Mortimer, earl of March (1391–1425)

Richard of York (b. 1411), third duke of York; son of Richard of Conisbrough and Anne Mortimer; nephew of Constance Despenser; heir to his childless uncles Edward, second duke of York and Edmund Mortimer, earl of March; marries Cecily Neville (b. 1415) and father of Edward IV (b. 1442) and Richard III (b. 1452)

Henry IV, king of England (b. 1367): usurps the throne of his cousin Richard II in 1399; son of Edward III's third son John of Gaunt (1340–99); widower of Mary Bohun (d. 1394) and marries Juana of Navarre in 1403

Henry V, king of England (b. 1386), known as Henry of Monmouth: eldest son of Henry IV and Mary Bohun; marries Katherine de Valois (b. 1401), youngest daughter of Charles VI of France, in 1420

Henry VI, king of England (b. 1421): only child of Henry V and Katherine; also king of France on the death of his grandfather Charles VI

Thomas, duke of Clarence (b. 1387); **John**, duke of Bedford (b. 1389); and **Humphrey**, duke of Gloucester (b. 1390): younger sons of Henry IV and Mary Bohun, brothers of Henry V, uncles of Henry VI

Edmund Holland, earl of Kent (b. 1383): brother and heir of Thomas Holland, earl of Kent (*c.* 1371/4–1400); has an affair with the widowed Constance Despenser in the early 1400s; marries Lucia Visconti of Milan in 1407

Alianore Holland (b. early 1400s): illegitimate daughter of Constance Despenser and the earl of Kent; half-sister of Isabelle Despenser; marries James Tuchet, Lord Audley

Thomas Fitzalan, earl of Arundel (b. 1381): first cousin of Edmund Holland, earl of Kent, and uncle of Richard Beauchamp, Lord Abergavenny (b. *c.* 1397); his male heir is John Arundel III (b. 1385), Thomas Despenser's nephew

Henry Beauchamp, earl and later duke of Warwick (b. 1425): Isabelle Despenser's son from her second marriage; the Despenser heir, and heir to his father; marries Cecily Neville, daughter of the earl of Salisbury; father of Anne Beauchamp (b. 1444)

Elizabeth Neville, née Beauchamp (b. *c.* 1418): Isabelle's only child from her first marriage; heir to her father; half-sister of Henry Beauchamp; marries Edward Neville, son of the earl of Westmorland

Anne Neville, née Beauchamp (b. 1426): Isabelle's daughter from her second marriage, sister of Henry and half-sister of Elizabeth; marries Richard Neville (b. 1428), eldest son of the earl of Salisbury; mother of Isabel (b. 1451) and Anne (b. 1456); mother-in-law of George, duke of Clarence and King Richard III; the Despenser/Warwick heir after the deaths of her brother Henry and his daughter Anne

Chapter 37

Thomas Despenser's widow Constance gave birth to their daughter in Cardiff on the feast of the Seven Sleepers, 27 July 1400, six months and fourteen days (or possibly twenty-two days) after Thomas's death. Constance named the infant Isabelle after her late Spanish mother, Isabel of Castile, duchess of York. Little Isabelle Despenser was baptised at St Mary's Church in Cardiff by Thomas, bishop of Llandaff, on the day of her birth. Fourteen years later when she proved that she had come of age, several of the jurors claimed that the Welsh nobleman and rebel Owain Glyn Dŵr 'came with his large army to the gates of Cardiff' on the day of her birth and that the bishop of Llandaff had to re-consecrate the church and graveyard of St Mary's because they had become polluted with blood, shortly before he baptised Isabelle. [1] The 27th of July 1400 seems much too early for Glyn Dŵr to have taken a large army to Cardiff, as he raised his standard and began his rebellion outside Ruthin in North Wales, 140 miles from Cardiff, on 16 September 1400. The rebellion did not spread to the south of Wales until 1403, so it seems that the jurors ascribed events to the wrong year and remembered things incorrectly, unless Glyn Dŵr and his army had an early practice run with Cardiff. Cardiff was not one of the manors and castles assigned to Constance as her widow's dower, yet evidently she still lived there. She may be the person who sent an undated letter in French to her 'dearest and beloved cousins', telling them that she had borne 'a beautiful daughter' (*une belle fille*) on the day of composing the letter. Constance, if indeed it were she who sent this letter, added that she and the infant were in good health. [2]

Assuming that the writer of this letter was Constance, the cousins she addressed it to might have been her late husband's much older first cousin Hugh Despenser, tutor of Henry IV's pubescent eldest son the prince of Wales, and his wife Sybil. Hugh wrote his will a few weeks before Isabelle Despenser's birth, on 1 July 1400. It reveals that he and

Sybil had a daughter, Elizabeth, to whom he left £100 'for her marriage'. [3] By October 1401, however, Elizabeth Despenser had died; her aunt Anne Botiller was named as Hugh's heir in his inquisition post mortem, and this can only have been the case if he had no surviving children. Elizabeth's name implies that her great-aunt Elizabeth, Lady Despenser, née Burghersh, may have been her godmother, or perhaps it was even her great-great-aunt Elizabeth, Lady Berkeley, née Despenser (d. 1389). Her father died on 14 October 1401 in his mid-forties. Just five days before his death, Hugh was summoned to Chester to attend Henry of Monmouth, prince of Wales, and to go with him into North Wales with a company of archers. Perhaps at the same time, he was ordered to 'make inquisitions concerning treasons' in North and South Wales, though John Horspace, one of his executors, swore an oath in 1405 that this commission had never come into Hugh's hands. [4] Hugh's widow Sybil was another of his executors, and finally received her widow's dower in November 1402 after what seems a rather undue delay of over a year. [5] Sybil Despenser outlived her husband by fourteen years and died on 28 August 1415, and the manors she and Hugh had held of the inheritance of his mother Alice Hotham ultimately passed to Isabelle Despenser, granddaughter of Hugh's uncle Edward the Younger. [6]

Philip Despenser III, born in 1342 and a great-grandson of Hugh the Elder, also died in 1401, in his late fifties. His heir was his eldest son Philip IV, 36 years old, and he also had younger sons John and Robert Despenser, and a daughter, Joan, married to Sir James Ros. He left a cup to his sister Hawise, Lady Luttrell in his will, which he dictated three days before he died at Goxhill, a Lincolnshire manor he had inherited from his grandmother Margaret Goushill. To his son and heir Philip IV, Philip bequeathed a number of items for his chapel, and three books: one called *Calas*, one a romance, and one about the four Evangelists. [7]

A third English nobleman who died in 1401 was Thomas Beauchamp, earl of Warwick, less than two years after he was released from imprisonment on the Isle of Man. Warwick wrote his will on 1 April 1400, and among the bequests he left to family were a pair of paternosters made of coral with gold buckles, 'to my cousin Despenser'. [8] The identity of this Despenser cousin is not clear; perhaps he meant Henry, bishop of Norwich, or Henry's nephew Sir Hugh, who wrote his will three months after the earl. Given that Bishop Henry had been a loyal supporter of Richard II, who exiled Warwick and left his wife Margaret

Ferrers in penury, perhaps Hugh Despenser, a loyal ally of Henry IV, is a more likely recipient of the paternosters.

Warwick's son and heir Richard Beauchamp was 19 years old in 1401, two years underage. Richard added 'Lord Lisle' to his other titles by right of his wife Elizabeth, who was her late mother Margaret Lisle's heir; she was also her father Lord Berkeley's heir general, but the bulk of the large Berkeley inheritance was entailed in the male line and ultimately passed to her father's nephew James Berkeley. [9] Richard and Elizabeth had three daughters, Margaret, Eleanor and Elizabeth Beauchamp, born widely spaced over a period of at least a dozen years. Richard fought for Henry IV and his son Henry of Monmouth, who was not yet 17, at the battle of Shrewsbury in July 1403. Henry 'Hotspur' Percy, son and heir of the earl of Northumberland, and Hotspur's uncle Thomas Percy, earl of Worcester, rebelled against the king some years after supporting him in his bid for the throne in 1399, but they lost the battle. Hotspur was killed fighting and Worcester was executed afterwards, and Hotspur's father Northumberland, now in his early sixties, submitted to Henry IV at first, but not long afterwards continued the Percy rebellion.

Constance Despenser lost her father Edmund of Langley, duke of York, on 1 August 1402, when her daughter Isabelle had just turned 2 years old. The last surviving child of Edward III and Queen Philippa, Edmund was 61 when he died. His will in French still exists and names his 'very dear son of Rutland', i.e. Constance's elder brother Edward, earl of Rutland, as one of his executors, though he did not leave bequests to any of his children or grandchildren. Edward, now in his late twenties, succeeded his father as the second duke of York.

Sometime in the early 1400s, the widowed Constance had an affair with the young earl of Kent, Edmund Holland. Kent's elder brother Thomas and their uncle John had been allies of Thomas Despenser during the Epiphany Rising and like him were beheaded in January 1400, while Edmund himself, though a half-nephew of Richard II, seems to have been loyal to Henry IV. This is more likely to have been a result of pragmatism and necessity rather than conviction or genuine loyalty to the man his brother and uncle had attempted to remove from the throne. As Edmund's brother died in rebellion against the king, all his lands were forfeit, and although Henry IV did restore much of Edmund's inheritance to him over the years, he only ever held a small part of the lands as there were three dowager countesses of Kent (Edmund's sister-in-law, mother and great-aunt) whose dower had to be found for them. Edmund therefore had little choice but to make a career at court and to hope for further patronage coming his way from the king.

The earl's closeness to Henry IV, however, makes him a rather unlikely lover for Constance, who in 1405 continued her late husband's rebellion against the king by temporarily freeing the two young sons of Roger Mortimer, late earl of March, and attempting to take them to their uncle Edmund Mortimer in Wales. The two Mortimer boys had an excellent claim to the throne as the descendants of Edward III's second son Lionel, duke of Clarence, while Henry IV himself was the son of Edward's third son. This was, therefore, a direct attack on King Henry and his rule, and both Constance and her brother the duke of York were imprisoned for it in 1405. The Mortimer boys were recaptured and thereafter kept under close guard. An undated order from Henry IV to his valet John Grove, probably early in 1405 as a result of Constance's attempts to take the Mortimers to their uncle, told Grove to 'safely and securely keep … the two daughters of Lord Despenser, being for certain causes in the hands of the king'. This is the last known reference to Thomas and Constance Despenser's elder daughter Elizabeth, born c. 1394/5 or c. 1398, and she perhaps died not long afterwards. [10] A squire called Elming Leget was ordered to take Constance Despenser herself from London to Kenilworth, also to be 'safely and securely kept'. [11] Custody of Constance's son Richard, the Despenser heir, meanwhile, had been granted to his uncle the duke of York in May 1403 (this was usual and normal and does not represent Henry IV punishing Constance). [12]

Edmund Holland, earl of Kent, was born on 6 January 1383, so was a few years Constance's junior. [13] Nothing is known about their relationship or when and for how long it took place, except that it resulted in a daughter named Alianore Holland, half-sister of Richard, Elizabeth and Isabelle Despenser. An entry on the Patent Roll dated 10 January 1405 records Henry IV's permission for Kent to 'marry whomsoever he will of the king's allegiance,' so perhaps his affair with Constance was over by then. On the other hand, that entry states that Kent was 'a minor in the king's custody', when in fact he had just turned 22 and was a year past his majority, so it might be dated incorrectly. [14] Kent's eldest sister Alianore, dowager countess of March and Lady Charlton, died on 23 October 1405, and he and Constance may have named their daughter in her honour.

Constance spent several months of 1405 in captivity at Kenilworth Castle after attempting to free the Mortimer boys; perhaps she was pregnant at the time. Her lover Kent married the Italian noblewoman Lucia Visconti of Milan on 24 January 1407, which surely provides a *terminus ad quem* for his affair with Constance, especially as Constance herself was present at the wedding. [15] The chronicler of Tewkesbury Abbey thought that Constance married and had a daughter called Alianore with Thomas Fitzalan, earl of Arundel, born in 1381 and a first cousin of the earl of Kent. [16] This is a rather interesting misunderstanding which might point to a betrothal between Constance and Arundel in the early 1400s, or at least to the discussion of one. Why Constance and Kent did not marry after learning of her pregnancy is not clear. Perhaps they were unofficially betrothed and rather jumped the gun when it came to consummation, but Henry IV did not wish a loyal young nobleman to marry Thomas Despenser's widow and thus forbade the match. Or perhaps the young earl, perennially short of cash, decided that the dowry promised by Lucia's wealthy Visconti relatives made a much more enticing prospect. Kent jousted at Smithfield in 1405 and made such an excellent impression on the spectators that chroniclers commented on his valour and his great honour, and marrying a popular young nobleman high in the king's favour might have made Constance's life at Henry IV's court rather easier than it was. In the end, although she was only in her early or mid-twenties when Despenser was killed, she never married again.

Chapter 38

The Despensers were always a family who enjoyed spending time together, and Elizabeth Zouche, formerly Arundel, sister of Anne Morley, Margaret Ferrers and the late Thomas Despenser, maintained close ties to her natal family. In a letter of 31 August 1402, Lady Zouche declared her intention to 'ryde to my lady my moder,' Lady Despenser, almost certainly at Tewkesbury in Gloucestershire which was the elder Elizabeth's favourite residence. This was eighty miles from Elizabeth Zouche's Bedfordshire manor of Eaton (later called Eaton Bray) near Dunstable, where she seems to have spent much of her time; there was a room in her Eaton home called *le Batailled chambre*, as well as gardens and twenty-eight acres of woodland, and stabling for sixty horses. She also spent a lot of time at Westminster, and perhaps stayed on other occasions in a home in London which had belonged to her late second husband and was called Zouche House. Lady Zouche took a gift of gold beads with her on her visit to her mother and the *queyntest* (prettiest) paternoster which her agent could find to buy, 'wat so euer they coste', also to give to Lady Despenser. She paid thirty-eight shillings for the beads, and also purchased a fret and fillet (a head-dress of interlaced wire and a headband) of pearls for herself. Elizabeth paid over fifteen shillings for her youngest son Edward Arundel's robe to be furred, and spent twenty-six shillings and eight pence on *baudekyn* cloth (a kind of silk, possibly brocaded) for Edward and her other sons from her first marriage, John and Thomas. The Arundel boys were now aged 17, about 15 and about 12 or 13. Earlier in 1402, Elizabeth had been keen to find and hire a new butler, i.e. a cup-bearer, because 'you wyten [know] well yourself that it is harm to me that I am so long without'. [1]

Elizabeth Zouche sent letters either in English or in French as the mood took her, demonstrating the easy bilingualism of her class and era. For centuries, the English nobility had written only in French, and the many extant letters of Elizabeth's great-grandfather Hugh Despenser the Younger and uncle Henry, bishop of Norwich, are all in that language, but by Elizabeth's generation things had changed. She dictated her letters in English in a loosely-constructed idiomatic style which must have been the way she talked normally: 'and but ye may get the same man that ye spoke to me of;' 'let put them all together in the great coffer and send them home;' 'do as ye think that good is;' 'I have as lief that he be still at home;' 'and the next man that goth [goes] between I shall pay you.' She called herself 'Elyzabeth Lady Zouche' or 'E. la Zouche'. Two historians who published some of Elizabeth's letters in the 1990s talked of the 'forceful charm' apparent in them. [2] She often sent letters to an agent called John Bore, and, for all her high birth and rank, addressed him courteously and affectionately in every letter as 'dear friend' or 'right well beloved friend' ('ryth wel by loued frend'). In her letter of August 1402 announcing her intention to visit her mother, Elizabeth wrote to Bore 'I greet you well and fain [gladly] would hear of your welfare'. A touch of sarcasm appeared in a further letter to Bore when she talked about a servant of hers, the curiously-named Hoigkyn: 'As touching Hoigkyn's coming to London, I wot [know] never what he doth there, but great wages and great dispenses [expenses] he asketh for his being there'. [3]

Henry IV married his second wife Juana, daughter of King Carlos II of Navarre and widow of Duke John IV of Brittany, in Winchester Cathedral on 7 February 1403, and Queen Juana's coronation took place at Westminster Abbey soon afterwards. Most of the English nobility attended the royal wedding, and dined on roast cygnets, venison, stuffed pullets, partridges, woodcock, quails, a cake in the shape of crowned panthers and much else besides. [4] Curiously, although Henry had six children from his first marriage and an illegitimate son, and Juana had eight or nine children from her own first marriage, they had none together, although Juana was only in her early thirties and Henry in his mid-thirties in 1403. The king held a jousting tournament to celebrate his marriage, and Richard Beauchamp, earl of Warwick, was one of the English noblemen who took part.

In the early 1400s, Warwick fought in the campaign against the Welsh noble rebel Owain Glyn Dŵr ('Oweyn de Glendourdy' as his name appeared in letters sent by the king and his eldest son the prince of Wales), as did the earl of Arundel, Thomas Fitzalan. [5] Edmund Mortimer, however, brother of the late earl of March and Constance

Despenser's ally against Henry IV, joined Glyn Dŵr and married his daughter Catrin. As for Constance, she forfeited all her lands and goods on 23 February 1405 after she admitted her role in the rebellion against the king. Queen Juana petitioned her husband for custody of Constance's dower lands, and on 6 April 1405 received them. Constance's goods were restored to her on 19 January 1406, and she finally received her lands back on 15 June 1407. Her sister-in-law Philippa Mohun, much older wife of Edward, duke of York and a first cousin of Constance's mother-in-law Elizabeth Burghersh, held the former Despenser manor of Vastern in Wiltshire, and Henry IV restored it to her on 8 March 1405. [6]

Elizabeth Zouche's mother-in-law from her first marriage to John Arundel, Eleanor née Maltravers, died on 19 January 1405 at the age of about 60. Eleanor had written her will on 10 September 1404 calling herself 'Alianore Arundell'. She retained the name of her first husband John Arundel I, marshal of England (d. 1379) throughout her second marriage to Reginald Cobham, asked to be buried at Lewes Priory in Sussex with John Arundel and other members of his family, and left items to Arundel's sisters, the countesses of Hereford and Kent. [7] Elizabeth Zouche's eldest son John Arundel III was his grandmother Eleanor's heir and became Lord Maltravers on her death, and he was also the male heir of his kinsman Thomas Fitzalan, earl of Arundel, who married Beatriz of Portugal in October 1405 but was to have no children with her. Elizabeth was given custody of her late mother-in-law Eleanor's lands on 18 March 1405, to hold until her son came of age, but two months later Henry IV changed his mind and gave the lands instead to her brother-in-law Sir Richard Arundel, the only one of Eleanor Maltravers' five sons from her first marriage who outlived her. John Arundel III received his father's and grandmother's lands in November 1406, after he turned 21. [8]

Elizabeth, widowed from her much older second husband William, Lord Zouche since 1396, was involved in a legal struggle against her stepson William Zouche the younger. This was probably connected to her dower lands, and at an uncertain date Elizabeth took Zouche to court. The two had been on better terms in March 1402, however, when Zouche came to visit her and Elizabeth sent a servant to buy good-quality damask cloth and to 'bear it to the good lord' on her behalf. [9] In or a little before May 1406, their struggle took a particularly nasty turn. Zouche, so Elizabeth claimed, sent armed men to her manor of Eaton to kill her, her sons and her servants. The armed men remained there for several days, while the family barricaded themselves in. On the fourth day, Elizabeth had to send her servant John Hunte the four miles to Dunstable to buy provisions for them. Zouche's men broke Hunte's right arm then attacked the house where Elizabeth's pregnant daughter-in-law Elizabeth Talbot, who married John Arundel III sometime before 10 October 1405, was living. This attack frightened the young woman so badly that she went into premature labour, and the infant died. Elizabeth Zouche's petition stated that her daughter-in-law 'lay in peril of death,' and as Elizabeth Talbot is known to have died in 1406, the ordeal of premature childbirth must have killed her as well, soon after her mother-in-law presented the petition. Henry IV ordered William Zouche on 28 May 1406 to appear before parliament to explain himself. [10] John Arundel III married his second wife Eleanor Berkeley, mother of his two sons, in or before May 1407; their first son was born in February 1408. As for Elizabeth Zouche, the whole unpleasant episode may have convinced her to leave the manor of Eaton, as by the time of her death in April 1408 she was living at the hospital of St Mary's Priory outside Bishopsgate in London. [11] This probably points to a period of ill health before she died, and the brutal attack by her stepson and the sudden shocking loss of her daughter-in-law and grandchild may have gone some way to causing it.

As well as her daughter-in-law, Elizabeth Zouche lost her uncle the bishop of Norwich in 1406. Henry Despenser died on 23 August at the age of 65, after thirty-six years as bishop of Norwich, and was buried before the high altar in his cathedral. Sadly for posterity, he died without making a will, implying that his death was sudden. Henry's niece Anne Botiller, only daughter of his brother Hugh (d. 1374), soon followed him to the grave, and died on 3 November 1406. [12] Anne's much older husband Edward Botiller outlived her by some years and died on 10 November 1412. [13] Anne's son, mentioned in a letter of her uncle Henry Despenser, died young, her brother Hugh's only child Elizabeth was also dead, and therefore her heir by blood was her cousin Thomas Despenser's son Richard (b. 1396). Her stepfather Sir John Trussell, however, who in 1374 had abducted and married her widowed mother Alice Hotham, began a long series of lawsuits after Edward Botiller's death. Trussell claimed that his son John, younger half-brother of Anne Botiller and Hugh Despenser, was rightful heir to the Hotham estates, but they passed ultimately to Thomas Despenser's daughter Isabelle after her brother Richard died as a teenager.

Chapter 39

Sir John Arundel III and Eleanor Berkeley's son, inevitably named John, was born on 14 February 1408 at Lytchett Matravers in Dorset, a manor John III had inherited from his paternal grandmother Eleanor Maltravers. A local man called John Garland who attended the infant's baptism fell and broke his arm on his way home, and hence remembered the event twenty-one years later. Walter Russell, aged about 23, took 'two silver-gilt pots ... full of various wines' to the church for John's godparents and other attendees. [1] Just two months after the birth of her grandson, on 10 or 11 April 1408, Elizabeth Zouche died. John III, correctly said in her inquisition post mortem to be aged '22 and more', was named as her heir. [2] Elizabeth's sisters Anne Morley and Margaret Ferrers outlived her, as did her elderly mother, Elizabeth Burghersh, Lady Despenser.

Elizabeth Zouche's will of 4 April 1408, written in Latin, still exists, and she appointed five executors including her mother Lady Despenser and Richard Arundel, younger brother of her first husband. Although Elizabeth in her will named herself as 'Lady Elizabeth Zouche, late the wife of Lord William Zouche', she did not leave bequests to any of her second husband's family. This is hardly surprising, given her stepson's attack on her and her sons and daughter-in-law two years previously. Elizabeth obviously trusted and liked her first husband's brother as she appointed him as her executor, and evidently they had kept in touch during the eighteen years since John Arundel's death in 1390. That she retained a strong affection for her natal family until the end of her life is revealed by her request to be buried at Tewkesbury Abbey with her three brothers (Thomas Despenser, and Edward and Hugh, who died young) rather than with either of her husbands.

Elizabeth divided her silver vessels between her younger sons Thomas and Edward Arundel, and left Edward an altar cloth, a chalice, a 'white bed' and her coach with all its furnishings. Such coaches were extremely costly, so this was a fine gift. Thomas Arundel received a 'red bed' with coverlet and hangings, a 'red mattress' and her best blankets, and to her daughter-in-law, Edward Arundel's wife, Elizabeth left a scarlet gown furred with expensive miniver and a coverlet called 'Paunce de Grey'. (Why a coverlet had a name was not explained.) Elizabeth left nothing in her will to her eldest son John, but as he was his father's and grandparents' heir she surely thought he had no need of her possessions or money, and this does not imply her lack of affection or maternal feelings for him. She did leave generous bequests to servants, including a 'good palfrey [horse] called Bos' to her squire Simon and a white palfrey to her chaplain Master John. Her 'chief palfrey', called Lyard d'Arundel went to her brother-in-law and executor Richard Arundel. The horse's name implies that it had been a gift to Elizabeth from Richard or another member of the Arundel family in the first place. A black robe furred with expensive miniver went to a servant also called Elizabeth, and a robe of black furred worsted to another servant, Alice. Elizabeth was living at the hospital of St Mary in London when she died, and left the sisters twenty-five shillings and the prior another thirteen shillings and four pence (or one mark) in her will. [3]

Edmund Holland, the young earl of Kent who had had an affair with Elizabeth's sister-in-law Constance Despenser some years before, also died in 1408. He was killed on 15 September while assaulting the Île de Bréhat in Brittany on behalf of Henry IV's queen Juana of Navarre, formerly duchess of Brittany. The earl took off his helmet, and a crossbow quarrel struck him in the head. [4] There were now four dowager countesses of Kent – Edmund's Italian widow Lucia Visconti, his sister-in-law Joan Stafford, his mother Alice Fitzalan and his German great-aunt Elisabeth of Jülich, who was at least half a century older than Edmund yet outlived him – and whatever was left of the Kent inheritance after providing dower for all the women was shared out among Edmund's four surviving sisters and his nephew Edmund Mortimer, earl of March, as he left no legitimate children. If he made any provision for his illegitimate daughter with Constance Despenser, Alianore Holland, there is no known record of it.

Henry IV's eldest son Henry of Monmouth, prince of Wales and duke of Aquitaine and Lancaster, turned 22 in September 1408. For some years, he had been moving apart from his father politically, and setting up what amounted to a separate faction at court with young noblemen such as his kinsman Thomas Fitzalan, earl of Arundel. Henry IV himself was only 41 years old in 1408, yet already exhausted from the strain of his position and various rebellions against his rule, including two in 1405 alone. In February 1408, the 66-year-old earl of Northumberland, Henry Percy, was killed at the battle of Bramham Moor in the final stage of his long-term rebellion against the man he had helped to place on the throne in 1399. His eldest son Henry 'Hotspur' had been killed at the battle of Shrewsbury in 1403, so Northumberland's heir was Hotspur's son, inevitably also called Henry Percy, who was 15 or 16 in 1408.

Elizabeth Burghersh, who had outlived her husband Edward Despenser the Younger by thirty-four years and outlived all but two of her seven children, wrote her will on 4 July 1409. She left her eldest daughter Anne Morley her best chalice, and her other surviving daughter Margaret Ferrers of Chartley two chargers (flat dishes) and twelve silver dishes. Only two of Elizabeth's grandchildren were left bequests, Margaret's daughters Philippa and Elizabeth Ferrers: Philippa received a bed of red worsted and all the items that went with it, and Elizabeth received twelve dishes and six silver saucers. As with Elizabeth Despenser's daughter Elizabeth Zouche leaving items only to her two younger sons in her will of 1408, the bequests do not necessarily imply any lack of feeling on Lady Despenser's part for all her other grandchildren who were not left anything, but might simply mean that she thought her Ferrers granddaughters were in greater need of the items. She pardoned her son-in-law Thomas Morley and her grandson Edward Hastings the debts they owed her.

Elizabeth died on 26 July 1409 three weeks after making her will, aged about 67. She was buried as she had requested at Tewkesbury Abbey with her long-dead husband and her executed son Thomas (and, although she did not mention them in her will, also with her daughter Elizabeth Zouche and her children Edward, Hugh and Cecily Despenser who had died young). She asked for a white cross to be laid over her body and a marble stone 'with my portraiture thereon' on top of her grave. [5] Elizabeth was a great-grandmother to John Arundel IV when she died, and her eldest daughter Anne Morley became a grandmother around 1410 or 1412 when her son Edward Hastings' son John was born. [6] Elizabeth's heir to the lands she had inherited from her father Bartholomew Burghersh and grandmother Elizabeth Verdon was her grandson, Richard Despenser.

Elizabeth Despenser's godson, and her granddaughter Isabelle's future second husband, Richard Beauchamp, earl of Warwick, spent the period from 1408 to 1410 outside England. He went on pilgrimage to Rome and the Holy Land, and visited eastern Europe, where he took part in jousting tournaments and military campaigns. After his return, he became a close ally of the prince of Wales, Henry of Monmouth. Warwick received the lordship of Gower in South Wales, a territory held in the 1320s by Hugh Despenser the Younger, after the execution of the 19-year-old earl of Norfolk, Thomas Mowbray, in June 1405. Warwick's wife Elizabeth Berkeley gave birth to their eldest daughter Margaret around 1404 or 1406, and to their second, Eleanor, around 1407/9. His mother Margaret Ferrers died on 22 January 1407, and her extensive dower lands in thirteen counties and London came into his possession. [7]

Chapter 40

On 27 July 1411, the double wedding of the two young Despenser siblings took place. Richard Despenser, aged 14 years and 8 months, married Eleanor Neville, and his sister Isabelle – it was her eleventh birthday – married Richard Beauchamp of Abergavenny. Eleanor was probably the eldest of the many children of Ralph Neville and his second wife Joan Beaufort, earl and countess of Westmorland, and her youngest sister Cecily (who was not born until 1415) was the mother of two kings, Edward IV and Richard III. Eleanor herself was probably born *c.* 1397/8, so was close to her husband's age. [1] She was, like Richard Despenser himself, a great-grandchild of Edward III, and thus was her husband's second cousin. A papal dispensation for consanguinity had been granted as far back as 1 August 1408, so the Despenser-Neville marriage had been planned for at least three years. The dispensation was issued for Eleanor's sister Katherine as Richard's future bride rather than for Eleanor herself, wrongly names Richard 'son of the late Hugh Spenser', and calls both of them 'of royal race'. [2] At some point, Eleanor was substituted for Katherine.

Isabelle Despenser's new husband Richard Beauchamp, a first cousin of Richard Beauchamp the earl of Warwick, was about 14 when they wed. Via his mother Joan, Richard was a grandson of the earl of Arundel executed in 1397, and was the heir of his father William Beauchamp, Lord Abergavenny. Abergavenny was the man sent by Henry IV to seize custody of Thomas Despenser's children in January 1400, and died on 8 May 1411, a few weeks before his son married Despenser's posthumous daughter. He wrote his will on 25 April 1408, and left his only son Richard his 'best sword'. [3] Both of the young newlywed couples were too immature to live together yet, and must have remained in the custody of their adult guardians for the time being.

Robert, Lord Ferrers of Chartley, brother-in-law of Thomas Despenser, Elizabeth Zouche and Anne Morley, died on 13 March 1413, leaving his eldest son Edmund Ferrers, aged between 24 and 27, as his heir. [4] King Henry IV died exactly a week later, not quite 46 but ill and worn out before his time. His throne passed to Henry of Monmouth, eldest of his four sons and 26 years old. Henry V was crowned king of England on 9 April 1413, a day when, according to eyewitnesses, it snowed. Richard Despenser and his brother-in-law Richard Beauchamp of Abergavenny were two of the young noblemen knighted on the eve of the coronation. [5]

Sir Richard Despenser died a few months later, perhaps on 11 October 1413 at the age of only 16 – he would have turned 17 on 30 November 1413 – married but childless. What killed him at such a young age is unknown. Richard left his younger sister Isabelle as his sole heir, their other sister Elizabeth being already dead (if she had lived, she would have shared the Despenser inheritance equally with Isabelle). The date of Richard's death is not completely certain, and the chronicle of Tewkesbury Abbey states, wrongly, that he died on 7 October 1414, a date which has often been repeated ever since. [6] An inquisition taken on 31 October 1414 says that Richard died on 11 October 1413, but the document has been heavily altered and corrected and might not be trustworthy, and gets the dates of Richard's father Thomas and grandmother Elizabeth Burghersh's deaths wrong. An entry on the Patent Roll of 16 April 1414, however, states that Richard was then already dead, and he was called 'late Lord Despenser' three months later, so the date given by the abbey chronicler is certainly incorrect. [7] Richard was buried in Tewkesbury Abbey with his father, grandparents and numerous other relatives and ancestors.

Eleanor Neville, only about 15 or 16 when she lost her husband, outlived Richard by sixty years and died shortly before 6 February 1473. She kept part of the Despenser lands until her death, as was her right as a widow, and charmingly, her dower in the Worcestershire town of Upton-on-Severn included 'a third part of the garden to the west from the hay by the moat to the mulberry tree [*milberyetre*], then to the hay outside the garden ditch with a third part of the house called *berghous*'. Eleanor also received a third of Hanley Castle, including five 'great chambers' and six stone towers, which gives some idea of the size of this sadly long-vanished building. [8] Probably in early 1416, Eleanor married her second husband, Henry Percy, second earl of Northumberland. Like Eleanor herself and Richard Despenser, Henry was a descendant of Edward III, on his mother Elizabeth Mortimer's side; in fact, he was descended from

Edward's second son Lionel of Antwerp, albeit in the female line, so arguably had a better claim to the throne than Henry V. Eleanor and Henry's eldest surviving son was born in 1421, and Henry himself and no fewer than four of his and Eleanor's sons were killed fighting during the Wars of the Roses.

Isabelle Despenser came of age (14 for married women) on 27 July 1414, a few months after her brother's death. She would now hold – apart from the dower lands in the hands of her mother Constance and sister-in-law Eleanor – the Despenser inheritance, including the third of the earldom of Gloucester which had passed to her great-great-grandmother Eleanor Clare a century before, the Burghersh/Verdon lands of her grandmother Elizabeth, and the lands of her father's first cousin Hugh Despenser and his mother Alice Hotham. Her husband Richard Beauchamp's father Lord Abergavenny had held a large number of lands across England and Wales until his death in 1411, and Richard was heir to all of them, but Abergavenny's entire estate was held jointly with his wife Joan, and unfortunately for Richard, his mother outlived his father by a quarter of a century and kept all his inheritance in her own hands for the rest of her life. She outlived him too. [9] Richard, therefore, had cause to be grateful that his Despenser wife was now a considerable heiress. 'Richard Beauchamp of Abergavenny, knight, and Isabelle his wife, sister and heir of Richard, son and heir of Thomas, late Lord Despenser' petitioned Henry V to request that all of Thomas Despenser's lands currently in the hands of Isabelle's uncle the duke of York might be granted to them and the 'heirs male of Isabelle's body', Thomas's forfeiture for treason in 1400 notwithstanding. On 17 February 1415, this was granted. [10]

Richard of Abergavenny, still only about 18 years old, was appointed joint warden of 'the marches of Wales adjoining the counties of Hereford and Gloucester' on 16 June 1415. [11] Isabelle and Richard's daughter Elizabeth Beauchamp was, according to the chronicle of Tewkesbury Abbey, born at Hanley Castle on 16 September 1415 when her mother was only a few weeks past her fifteenth birthday. This chronicle is not, however, as reliable a source for the Despenser family as one might hope and often gets dates and names wrong, and evidence from various inquisitions post mortem suggests that Elizabeth was actually born *c.* 1417/18. [12] Little Elizabeth Beauchamp would be Richard and Isabelle's only child, or at least their only surviving child, and was her father's heir but not, ultimately, her mother's.

King Henry V left England in 1415, following in his great-grandfather Edward III's footsteps by claiming the French throne. The kingdom of France was in a parlous state in the early 1400s. Its king, Charles VI, who had succeeded his father Charles V in 1380 when he was barely 12, went insane in 1392, and most of the time he was entirely incapable of governing. A power struggle developed between his younger brother Louis, duke of Orléans and their uncle Philip, duke of Burgundy, and after Philip's death in 1404, Orléans carried on his rivalry against Burgundy's son and heir John the Fearless. King Henry took the opportunity to seek glory and to conquer France. He besieged Harfleur in August and September 1415, and at the battle of Agincourt on 25 October that year, annihilated the French army in what is one of the most famous English military victories in history. At Agincourt, the rearguard was commanded by Thomas, Lord Camoys, then in his mid-sixties and a great-grandson of Hugh Despenser the Elder via Hugh's youngest daughter Elizabeth.

Isabelle Despenser lost both her uncles in 1415, her mother Constance's brothers. Richard of Conisbrough, earl of Cambridge, was executed on 5 August after taking part in a hare-brained plot to put his brother-in-law Edmund Mortimer, earl of March, on the throne as the senior descendant of Edward III's second son Lionel. Constance's other brother Edward, duke of York, was killed during the battle of Agincourt, and as he had no children, his heir was his and Constance's nephew Richard of York, Richard of Conisbrough's 4-year-old son. Isabelle also lost her aunt Margaret Ferrers of Chartley, youngest of Thomas Despenser's three older sisters, when Margaret died on 3 November 1415 and was buried with her husband Robert at Merevale Abbey in Warwickshire, founded in 1148 by a Ferrers ancestor. [13] A brass of Margaret and Robert in the abbey church still exists. And Thomas Fitzalan, earl of Arundel, maternal uncle of Isabelle's husband, died on 13 October 1415, his thirty-fourth birthday. He had gone to France with Henry V, a close friend of his, but came down with dysentery and had to return to England before the battle of Agincourt. Arundel had no children from his ten-year marriage to Beatriz of Portugal, and his heirs general were his three sisters, including Isabelle's mother-in-law Joan, Lady Abergavenny. [14] The title of earl of Arundel passed to the descendants of Isabelle's late aunt Elizabeth, Lady Arundel and Zouche. As the descendants in the male line of John Arundel I (c. 1350–79), younger brother of Earl Thomas's father Richard (1346/7–97), the Arundels were Thomas's heirs male.

Two more deaths struck the Despenser family in 1416. Thomas, Lord Morley, second husband of Isabelle's aunt Anne, formerly Hastings, died on 24 September. His heir was his 23-year-old grandson Thomas from his first marriage, his son Robert having died in 1403. [15] Henry V had Thomas Morley buried in Calais where he died, though later his body was returned to England and re-interred at the priory of Austin Friars in Norwich. And Thomas Despenser's widow Constance of York died a few weeks later on 28 November 1416, aged only 40 or a little more. Constance left her daughter Isabelle, her illegitimate daughter from her relationship with the late earl of Kent, Alianore Holland, and perhaps her granddaughter Elizabeth Beauchamp, if she had already been born. The dower lands Constance had held from her marriage to Thomas Despenser passed to her daughter and son-in-law, and Richard Beauchamp of Abergavenny did homage to Henry V for them. [16] Constance was buried in Reading Abbey near her manor of Caversham, presumably by her own wish, rather than in Tewkesbury as the previous widows of Despenser lords (Eleanor Clare in 1337, Elizabeth Montacute in 1359 and Elizabeth Burghersh in 1409) had been. The Tewkesbury Abbey chronicler states that Constance was not buried until 1420, though fails to explain why. [17]

Thomas, Lord Berkeley died on 13 July 1417 at the age of 64. He was the son of Elizabeth Berkeley, herself the youngest child of Hugh Despenser the Younger, and died on the twenty-eighth anniversary of his mother's death. Thomas's only legitimate child was his daughter Elizabeth, countess of Warwick, but the problem was that much of the large Berkeley inheritance was entailed in the male line. Elizabeth and her husband Richard Beauchamp, earl of Warwick, had no mind to give up her father's large estates to her cousin James Berkeley, and took possession of Berkeley Castle shortly after Thomas's death. Warwick and Elizabeth's three daughters and their husbands enthusiastically took up the fight in later years, and the legal conflicts between the two branches of the Berkeley family would not be resolved until 1609.

Henry V and his army landed in Normandy on 1 August 1417, a few weeks after Lord Berkeley's death, and over the next few months the king of England besieged Caen and Rouen with the aim of capturing the duchy of Normandy. One English nobleman killed during the long siege of Rouen was Geoffrey Luttrell, grandson of Hawise Despenser (1344/5–1414), and the earl of Warwick was one of Henry's chief lieutenants during the campaign and captured Falaise, Domfront and Alençon. Henry was determined to conquer the entire kingdom of France, and when Rouen finally fell to him in January 1419, this enabled Henry to take his army to the gates of Paris and the conquest was well underway.

Chapter 41

On 2 June 1420, Henry V married Katherine de Valois, daughter of Charles VI, in Troyes, and it was arranged that Charles would remain king of France until his death, whereupon Henry would succeed him. Charles's only surviving son, the Dauphin Charles (b. 1403), was disinherited, though thanks in great part to the efforts of Joan of Arc, he was crowned king of France a few years later. Henry V returned to England in early 1421 after a long absence, and Katherine de Valois was crowned queen at Westminster Abbey on 23 February. The earl of Warwick acted as steward of England during the ceremony, as the deputy of the king's brother Thomas, duke of Clarence, who was in France. [1] Richard Beauchamp of Abergavenny was made earl of Worcester in the same month as the queen's coronation, a title previously held by Thomas Percy, executed in 1403. [2] Isabelle Despenser was now a countess, and in 1421, she went on pilgrimage to Canterbury, perhaps in gratitude. [3]

Thomas, duke of Clarence, fought the battle of Baugé in France on 22 March 1421 a month after his sister-in-law Queen Katherine's coronation. It proved a disaster for the English army: Clarence himself was killed, two of his stepsons were captured, and another of the English noblemen who fell was John, Lord Ros of Helmsley in Yorkshire. Ros was the son-in-law of Philip Despenser IV, being the husband of Philip's only surviving child Margery, and had fought at Agincourt in 1415 when he was only 18. [4] He and Margery had no children. Margery Despenser was pardoned on 25 June 1423 for marrying her second husband, a squire named Roger Wentworth, without royal permission. Given that she was an heiress of noble birth and Roger was not a knight nor even his father's eldest son, it must have been a love-match, and they married clandestinely. Philip Wentworth, the elder of Margery and Roger's two sons, born c. 1424 and named after her Despenser father, was the great-grandfather of Queen Jane Seymour. Margery and her children maintained an association with the Ros family: Philip Wentworth was beheaded after the battle of Hexham in 1464, where he had fought alongside Thomas, Lord Ros, nephew and heir of his mother's first husband.

When Philip Despenser IV died on 20 June 1424, Margery, then about 24 or 26 years old, became a wealthy landowner. As well as the lands she inherited from her father, her mother Elizabeth was one of the three co-heirs of the Tibetot or Tiptoft family, and these lands passed to Margery too as her parents' only surviving child; her siblings Philip, George and Elizabeth Despenser died young and were buried at the Greyfriars' church in Ipswich. [5] Ultimately, women were heirs to both lines of the Despenser family, the main branch descended from Hugh the Younger and the cadet Lincolnshire branch descended from his younger brother Philip I. Hugh the Younger's heir was his great-great-granddaughter Isabelle; Philip I's heir was his great-great-granddaughter Margery.

Sir John Arundel III, Lord Maltravers, Isabelle Despenser's first cousin, died between 21 and 27 April 1421 at not yet 36 years old. [6] His heir was his son John IV (b. 1408), who became earl of Arundel and died in 1435. The men of this branch of the Arundel family did not live long: John I drowned in 1379 probably before he reached 30, John II died in 1390 at 25, John III died at 35, and John IV at 27. Katherine de Valois, queen of England, gave birth to a son at Windsor Castle on 6 December 1421 and named him Henry after his father and grandfather. The little boy would become king of both England and France by the time he was a year old, but had inherited something of the mental instability of his maternal grandfather Charles VI of France, and did not take after his father the great warrior in any way. Henry V, who had returned to France, was never to see his little son.

English forces besieged the French town of Meaux for the entire winter of 1421/2. Richard Beauchamp, lord of Abergavenny and earl of Worcester, died during the siege, on 18 March 1422, when he was about 24 or 25 and his widow Isabelle 21. The Tewkesbury Abbey chronicler says he was hit in the head by a stone from a ballista, a large catapult-like weapon which hurled projectiles. Beauchamp's heir was his and Isabelle's daughter Elizabeth, probably about 4 years old when he died. Isabelle's second cousin John Cornwall, aged only 17, also died during the siege of Meaux: he was standing next to his father Sir John Cornwall when a cannonball fired from within the town decapitated him. [7]

Isabelle buried her husband at her family's mausoleum of Tewkesbury Abbey on 25 April 1422, and placed twelve statues as 'mourners' in the chapel she built there for Richard, which was completed and dedicated on 2 August 1438. Several of the statues were her ancestors the Clare earls of Gloucester, one was her father, and one was her great-great-grandfather Hugh the Younger. [8] Isabelle was evidently well aware of her family's history, and was not ashamed of Hugh the Younger, even though he suffered the traitor's death in 1326. She would also be buried in Tewkesbury many years later, and the inscription on her and the earl of Worcester's chapel states that she was interred 'at the right hand of her father'. For all that Thomas Despenser was summarily beheaded by a mob and, like Hugh the Younger, deemed a traitor, Isabelle was proud of the father she never had the chance to meet, and honoured his memory. Her mother Constance, and perhaps her three Despenser aunts and her grandmother Elizabeth Burghersh, must have told her all about her family history.

Henry V himself died of dysentery at the castle of Vincennes near Paris on 31 August 1422, still only in his mid-thirties. His 9-month-old son became Henry VI of England, and the infant succeeded as king of France as well on 21 October 1422 when his maternal grandfather Charles VI died. The infant king's regent (or 'protector') in England was his uncle, Henry V's youngest brother Humphrey, duke of Gloucester, and his regent in France was his other uncle, the late king's other surviving brother John, duke of Bedford. The earl of Warwick was an executor of Henry V's will, and accompanied Henry's body back to England in late October 1422. [9]

In widowhood, Isabelle Despenser spent much time at Cardiff, her birthplace, and at Hanley Castle, of which she owned two-thirds with the other third held by her sister-in-law Eleanor, countess of Northumberland. [10] Isabelle remained a widow for twenty months until 26 November 1423, when she married Richard Beauchamp, earl of Warwick, at Hanley Castle. Warwick took a break from parliament, in session at distant Westminster from 20 October to 17 December 1423, to travel to Worcestershire for his wedding. When and how Isabelle and Warwick's marriage was arranged is unclear, though on 1 July 1423 Warwick founded a perpetual chantry in a chapel in Warwickshire: two chaplains were to perform divine service daily for the young Henry VI and for 'the said earl and his wife, while alive, and after their death, for their souls'. [11] As Warwick's first wife Elizabeth Berkeley had died six months prior to this, the reference to his living wife probably indicates that he already intended to marry Isabelle. Not only was Warwick the first cousin of Isabelle's first husband, the couple themselves were third cousins, and Warwick was the godson of Isabelle's grandmother. By the laws and customs of the time, this created a spiritual affinity which, like their familial relationship, required a papal dispensation. Isabelle was also related to Elizabeth Berkeley (d. December 1422), great-granddaughter of Hugh Despenser the Younger. Richard of Warwick was eighteen and a half years Isabelle's senior, and was 41 to her 23 when they wed. As members of the rarefied higher levels of the English nobility and as relatives by blood and marriage, they must have known each other for many years.

A historian in 1973 made the extraordinarily callous comment that Elizabeth Berkeley 'presented her husband with three daughters and no son. The only service she could perform after that was to die and leave the way clear for someone more obliging'. [12] There is no doubt that the earl of Warwick, as a medieval nobleman, yearned to have a son or preferably several, but whether he saw his wife as little more than a son-making machine to be replaced by a 'more obliging' model when she failed is debatable. Countess Elizabeth's household accounts for the year 1420/21 still exist. They reveal that a woman belittled in a supposedly more enlightened age five and a half centuries later for not birthing sons was a strong and independent personality who had affectionate relationships with her daughters, relatives and numerous friends, who pursued a wide range of interests including looking after her pet bear, and who fought hard for what she believed was her rightful inheritance from her father Lord Berkeley. In 1410, in her mid-twenties, Elizabeth commissioned a translation of Boethius's famous work *On the Consolation of Philosophy.* [13]

The earl of Warwick was in France for most of the period when Elizabeth's accounts survive, and it is difficult to ascertain what kind of personal relationship they had, but Richard cared enough about Elizabeth to leave money for a 'goodly tomb of marble' to be made for her grave in his will of August 1435, a dozen years after he married Isabelle. [14] During her marriage to Richard, the lands Elizabeth Berkeley held from her parents kept their own identity rather than being subsumed into Richard's, and Elizabeth's receiver paid the incomes from them to the keeper of Elizabeth's household, not to her husband's receiver. This did not happen with the lands of Isabelle Despenser during her own marriage to Richard, perhaps because Elizabeth was 'more forceful and effective' than her widower's second wife or perhaps simply because Isabelle and Richard preferred to arrange things that way. [15] Elizabeth's heirs were her daughters Margaret, Eleanor and Elizabeth, who became countess of Shrewsbury, duchess of Somerset and Lady Latimer respectively, though Warwick had the right to keep all her lands until his own death by 'the courtesy of England'. In Elizabeth's accounts of 1420/21, her daughters were called the *juvenez dames*, 'young ladies', and the elder two, Margaret and Eleanor, were old enough to ride on horseback while little Elizabeth, only about 3, travelled in a carriage with six attendants. [16]

The marriage of Isabelle Despenser and Beauchamp of Warwick proved an extremely close and successful one, and Richard wrote a poem to his wife which he called a *Balade made of Isabelle Countasse of Warr[ewyk] and Lady Despenser, by Richard Beauchamp, Eorlle of Warrewyk*. [17] The poem contains sixty-one lines and praises the beauty of the earl's beloved *feyre lady*, and he wrote lovingly of Isabelle's *noblesse* and 'flowering youth in lustiness' which was 'grounded in virtuous *humblesse* [humility].' [18] By December 1426, Warwick owned a ship called the *Isabella*, and supposedly when he, Isabelle and their son were sailing in it and were caught in a terrific storm, he had them all lashed to the mast so that if they drowned, they would go down together. [19]

From Isabelle's side, Richard of Warwick's attractions were also obvious. The earl was hugely wealthy, and lived magnificently: in 1420/21, he spent more than £5,500, a good few million in modern money. He lent £2,000 to his widowed second daughter Eleanor, Lady Ros and future duchess of Somerset, in 1433. [20] Not only was Warwick a rich and well-connected nobleman, he was admired by all who met him, and even by an emperor. Richard II's late queen Anne of Bohemia had a brother, Zikmund (b. 1368), king of Germany, Italy, Hungary, Croatia and Bohemia and elected Holy Roman Emperor in 1433. Zikmund, who visited England in May 1416 and was made a Knight of the Garter, was so impressed with Richard Beauchamp that he exclaimed 'if all courtesy were lost, it might be found again in him,' and called him 'the father of courtesy'. Zikmund's wife Barbara of Celje (in modern-day Slovenia), also impressed with Richard, publicly did him honour by placing his motto, a bear, on her shoulder. Warwick and Isabelle were both rich and of high birth and status, were one of the great 'power couples' of fifteenth-century England, and seem, on a personal level, to have been hugely attracted to each other as well.

It is significant that Warwick referred to Isabelle in his ballad as 'countess of Warwick and Lady Despenser', as he clearly felt that her status as the Despenser heir and her family name were well worth mentioning. In 1451 long after Isabelle's death, Henry VI's government still referred to her as 'late countess of Warwick, Lady Despenser'. Her son and heir, Henry Beauchamp, duke of Warwick, was officially addressed as Lord Despenser after his mother's death, and the *Brut* chronicle and the Tewkesbury Abbey chronicle both call him Lord Despenser in his parents' lifetimes. [21] On 18 November 1423, eight days before Isabelle's wedding to Warwick, when the couple jointly made arrangements relating to manors in four counties, she referred to herself as Isabelle Despenser, countess of Worcester, using her maiden name. [22] The inscription on the chapel in Tewkesbury Abbey where she and her first husband are buried calls her 'Isabelle Despenser, countess of Warwick' not 'Isabelle Beauchamp', and in June 1423 she called herself 'Isabelle, countess of Worcester, Lady Despenser'. [23] It was most unusual for widowed noblewomen to revert to their maiden name, and doing so reveals Isabelle's great pride in her natal family.

Chapter 42

Little Elizabeth Beauchamp, Isabelle's only child from her marriage to the earl of Worcester, married in 1424 when she was no more than 9 years old and was probably younger. Her husband was Edward Neville, the youngest son of Ralph Neville, earl of Westmorland, who paid 2,000 marks (£1,333) for the marriage. Elizabeth and Edward Neville's marriage was not a particularly happy one, and Edward had a relationship with his second wife, Katherine Howard, during Elizabeth's lifetime. [1] The youngest Neville daughter, Cecily, born in 1415 and probably quite close in age to her brother Edward, was also betrothed in 1424, and her new fiancé was the greatest heir in the realm: Richard of York, born in 1411 and Isabelle Despenser's first cousin. Young Richard of York, son of an executed traitor, was fortunate enough to have two wealthy childless uncles, Edward, duke of York and Edmund Mortimer, earl of March and Ulster (d. early 1425), whose heir he was. His mother Anne Mortimer also bequeathed her descent from Edward III's second son to him, a fact which gave Richard an excellent claim to the English throne.

On 22 March 1425 at Hanley Castle, Isabelle gave birth to her son, Henry Beauchamp. [2] Henry's godparents were Joan Beauchamp, Lady Abergavenny, who was Isabelle's mother-in-law from her first marriage and little Henry's great-aunt, Humphrey Stafford, earl of Stafford, and Thomas Beaufort, duke of Exeter. Both Isabelle and Warwick called their son 'Harry'. [3] The boy must have been named in honour of the young king, Henry VI, and from the moment he was born was the sole heir to his father's earldom of Warwick and to his mother's inheritance. Little Henry Beauchamp's birth put paid to any possibility of his older half-sisters Margaret, Eleanor and Elizabeth sharing their father's earldom and lands. Henry's birth also disinherited his other older half-sister, Elizabeth Neville, from their mother Isabelle's lands, though Elizabeth remained the heir of her late father the earl of Worcester and her grandmother

Lady Abergavenny. Richard, earl of Warwick, departed from Hanley a few weeks after his son's birth to attend a parliament at Westminster which began on 30 April 1425. He and John Mowbray, earl of Norfolk, quarrelled yet again over precedence – their dispute had now endured for two decades – and Warwick lost when Norfolk was promoted from earl to duke at the end of this parliament. [4]

Ralph Neville, earl of Westmorland, father-in-law of Isabelle's daughter Elizabeth, died in October 1425 at the age of about 61. He had been married twice and had nine children from his first marriage and fourteen from his second, and ultimately had around eighty grandchildren and close to 200 great-grandchildren. His second wife Joan Beaufort, as a granddaughter of Edward III, half-sister of Henry IV and aunt of Henry V, was a powerful and well-connected woman, and was able to persuade her husband to favour her own children over his children from his first marriage to Margaret Stafford (d. 1396). Most of the family's lands and wealth went to Joan's eldest son Richard Neville (b. *c.* 1399/1400), for whom an excellent marriage to the heiress of the earldom of Salisbury was arranged. All three of Isabelle Despenser's children would marry into the huge Neville family, as did her stepdaughter Elizabeth, youngest of the earl of Warwick's three daughters from his first marriage, and as her late brother Richard also had.

As 'Lord Abergavenny', Isabelle's son-in-law Edward Neville was one of the twenty-four young noblemen summoned to Leicester on 19 May 1426 to be knighted by the 4-year-old King Henry VI. Edward was probably about 12 or 13. Henry himself had just been knighted by his uncle John, duke of Bedford, and among the other young noblemen he dubbed a knight on this occasion were two other Neville brothers and their brother-in-law Richard of York, future duke of York and earl of March; Henry Percy (b. 1421), eldest son of Richard Despenser's widow Eleanor Neville; and Elizabeth Zouche née Despenser's grandson Lord Maltravers. [5]

The earl of Warwick was made custodian of Normandy by the duke of Bedford, elder of Henry V's two surviving brothers and regent of France, at Christmas 1425. [6] Warwick, presumably with Isabelle, thereafter spent much time in France. Soon after 1 August 1426, 100 men-at-arms and 300 archers, Richard's retainers, embarked for France, though as Isabelle was heavily pregnant for the third time, she is unlikely to have crossed the Channel on this occasion. [7] Eighteen months after Henry

Beauchamp's birth, in September 1426, his sister Anne was born, her father's fourth daughter and her mother's second. [8] Anne was not an heiress at birth, but after the deaths of her brother Henry and his toddler daughter, became one of the greatest heiresses of the fifteenth century, and was the mother-in-law of Richard III. Just weeks after Isabelle gave birth to her third and last child, she lost her last aunt, who was also called Anne; perhaps Isabelle named her daughter after her. Anne Morley, née Despenser, formerly Hastings, died on 31 October 1426. She was in her sixties when she died, and her heir was her son Edward Hastings, aged 44 in 1426. She had held seven manors in Suffolk jointly with Thomas Morley as a gift of her mother Lady Despenser, and they passed to her niece Isabelle as Elizabeth's heir. [9]

Isabelle and Richard Beauchamp, earl and countess of Warwick, were a powerful and wealthy couple who between them owned a large part of the English Midlands. In the 1420s, Richard made an alliance with Isabelle's first cousin Edmund, Lord Ferrers of Chartley, another great landowner in the Midlands. Richard and Ferrers became embroiled in a conflict with Richard's aunt-in-law, and Isabelle's mother-in-law from her first marriage, Lady Abergavenny. Joan was chosen as the godmother of Isabelle and Richard's son Henry in 1425, probably an attempt at a family reconciliation, but she did her best to stir up opposition to Warwick and Ferrers in the Midlands. [10] This bad-tempered quarrelling and politicking had consequences: Joan Beauchamp claimed that on 17 March 1431, Edmund Ferrers and a large group of his men attacked her and her servants while she was lying ill in Birmingham, wounded some of her servants with arrows, and killed one. [11] The half-Despenser Edmund Ferrers had form for such behaviour; around 1413/14, he and his younger brothers Thomas and Edward fought a private war with a neighbouring family in Staffordshire called the Erdeswikes. [12] Much given to lawless and violent behaviour, Edmund Ferrers was pardoned in early 1415 for 'all treasons, murders and other offences' committed before 8 December 1414, and fought for Henry V at Agincourt in October 1415. He died on 17 December 1435 leaving his eldest son William, then 23, as his heir. [13]

Probably in the late 1420s, Isabelle Despenser commissioned the court poet John Lydgate (b. *c.* 1370) to translate the Latin work the *Fyfftene Joyes of Oure Lady* into English, and he dedicated it to 'the worshipfull Pryncesse Isabelle nowe Countasse of Warr[ewyk], Lady Despenser'. A few years later, Lydgate dedicated his work *Guy of Warwick* to

Isabelle's eldest stepdaughter, Margaret Talbot née Beauchamp, countess of Shrewsbury, whose name appeared as 'Margarite Countas of Shrowesbury, Ladye Talbot, Fournyual [Furnival] and Lisle'. Another court poet, Thomas Hoccleve (*c.* 1368–1426), had composed a work dedicated to Isabelle's uncle, her mother Constance's brother Edward, duke of York, in 1411. Lydgate and Hoccleve dedicated a number of their works to English noble ladies, but addressed the women simply and neutrally as 'my lady of March' (i.e. the countess of March) or 'my ladie Anne Countasse of Stafford' or 'the duches[s] of Bokyngham'. Only Isabelle Despenser was addressed as a 'worshipfull pryncesse'. [14]

Chapter 43

Richard Beauchamp, earl of Warwick, returned to England after his sojourn in France – he lost a third of his force while unsuccessfully besieging the town of Montargis in 1427 – and was appointed on 1 June 1428 to act as the guardian of the young king, Henry VI, now 6. He was to oversee his upbringing and education, and was given permission to chastise Henry if he fell behind in his studies. [1] Richard and Isabelle's son Henry 'Harry' Beauchamp was more than three years younger than the king, but he and Henry VI became close friends after his father was appointed as the king's guardian, and Harry grew up in the royal household. [2] In later years, the treasurer of Henry VI's household was Sir Thomas Browne (d. 1460), whose wife Eleanor Arundel was a granddaughter of Elizabeth Zouche née Despenser, being her second son Thomas Arundel's only child.

Henry VI was crowned king of England in Westminster Abbey on 6 November 1429, and the ceremony was conducted by his great-uncle Henry, Cardinal Beaufort. The young king sailed to France on 23 April 1430 with a large retinue and stayed in Rouen for sixteen months; his uncle the duke of Bedford lived there. The earl of Warwick's Household Book survives for a year from March 1431, and reveals that his eldest daughter Margaret, 'Madame Talbot', dined often with the young king during his long stay in France. Warwick's second daughter Eleanor was widowed from Thomas, Lord Ros in 1430, and several years later married Edmund Beaufort, count of Mortain and later earl of Dorset and duke of Somerset, a grandson of Edward III's son John of Gaunt and a nephew of Cardinal Beaufort. The date of the wedding is not recorded as they married clandestinely, but it probably took place not too long before 21 October 1434, when Pope Eugene IV first wrote to Eleanor and Edmund as a married couple. [3]

On Sunday, 8 April 1431, 9-year-old Henry VI dined with Isabelle Despenser and her husband, and they were entertained by musicians during the meal. In France, Isabelle must have spent a lot of time with her eldest stepdaughter Margaret Talbot, who was only about four or six years her junior and who often appears in her father's accounts at this time. Isabelle and Margaret travelled together to Paris by water from Rouen for the coronation of Henry VI as king of France in December 1431. [4] Henry's maternal uncle the Dauphin Charles, however, was making excellent progress in his campaign to become and to be recognised as king of France, and had been crowned in Reims in July 1429. Richard Beauchamp, earl of Warwick, was custodian of the city of Rouen when Joan of Arc, who had done so much to make Charles king of France, was burned there on 30 May 1431, and he was her chief jailer. As for Henry VI, he never saw his French kingdom again, and in 1461 would lose his kingdom of England as well.

Meanwhile in England, Isabelle's illegitimate half-sister Alianore launched an audacious claim in 1431 to be the heir of her late father Edmund Holland, earl of Kent, stating that Kent had married her mother Constance and that she was therefore legitimate. Kent's rightful heirs were his two surviving sisters, Margaret, dowager duchess of Clarence and Joan, dowager duchess of York, and the children of his other three sisters. All the Kent heirs worked together to reject Alianore's claim, pointing out that Constance attended Edmund's wedding to Lucia Visconti in early 1407, but did not speak up and state that the earl was already married to her. [5] Alianore's claim failed, though she did make a good marriage to the widowed James Tuchet, Lord Audley, sometime before 14 February 1430, and had children; her long-lived son Edmund Audley (1430s–1524) served as bishop of Rochester, Hereford and Salisbury. The Tewkesbury Abbey chronicle says that Isabelle Despenser arranged her half-sister's marriage to James Tuchet, and that Isabelle's son and heir Henry chose his aunt Alianore as one of his daughter's godmothers in 1444. [6]

Some years later in 1434, Isabelle and the earl of Warwick negotiated further important marriages, this time for their children Henry and Anne Beauchamp. The Beauchamp siblings' spouses were also siblings: Cecily and Richard Neville, two of the children of Richard Neville senior, earl of Salisbury, himself the eldest son of Ralph Neville and Joan Beaufort. Richard Neville junior, born in 1428 and a little younger than his bride Anne Beauchamp, was his parents' heir. The earl of Salisbury paid 4,700 marks as a marriage portion for Henry Beauchamp to wed his daughter Cecily. [7] This was the joint largest sum paid for a marriage in the entire English Middle Ages, and is an indication of how great an heir Henry was. According to the Tewkesbury Abbey chronicle, both young couples married in 1434, the year of their betrothals, though they were all still children. The weddings may have taken place in Abergavenny, home of Warwick's aunt and Isabelle Despenser's former mother-in-law, Joan Beauchamp, Lady Abergavenny. [8] The formidable and wealthy Lady Abergavenny died on 14 November 1435. Joan's heir to the manors she had inherited from her younger brother the earl of Arundel and to the extensive estates she had held jointly with her husband was her granddaughter Elizabeth Neville, Isabelle's eldest child. The jurors of Joan's inquisition post mortem all estimated Elizabeth's age as 17 or 18 in December 1435/January 1436 (except for the Herefordshire jurors, who thought she was only 16), so she seems to have been born c. 1418 when Isabelle was 17 or 18, not in September 1415 as claimed by the Tewkesbury Abbey chronicler. [9]

The earl of Warwick made his will on 9 August 1435. Richard left no items to any of his four daughters, his sons-in-law or his grandchildren, but left a 'cup of gold with the dance of men and women' to his son and heir Harry (as he called him in the will). To Isabelle, Warwick left 'all the silver vessels, bedding and household stuff which I had with her', 'all other stuff and things that I have given her since we were married,' and another four dozen silver vessels and silver basins and ewers. Warwick left all his lands and manors to his son and subsequently to the male heirs of Harry's body, and, failing Harry's male issue – Henry Beauchamp did indeed die without sons – to his daughters 'Ann, Margarett, Elenor and Elizabeth' in that order, putting his and Isabelle's daughter (not quite 9 years old) before her older half-sisters from his first marriage. [10]

In August 1435, the earl thought it possible that he and Isabelle might yet have another child; he wrote 'if God will that I have another son,' 'if it happen me to have another heir male,' and 'my younger son, if God will I have any.' As Isabelle was then only 35 years old, he may have been right, and it is perhaps curious that Isabelle bore no more children after she gave birth to Anne in September 1426, when she was 26. She only had one child with her first husband Worcester, so was perhaps not particularly fertile. There may, of course, have been miscarriages or stillbirths or infants who died young, for whom we have no record.

Chapter 44

Richard Beauchamp, earl of Warwick, was appointed lieutenant of France in July 1437 and spent the last two years of his life in France, and Isabelle Despenser was widowed for a second time on 30 April 1439 when he died at the castle of Rouen in Normandy, aged 57. Richard had appointed her as his chief executor in his will. [1] The earl's remains were taken to England for burial in early October 1439, and the gilt-bronze effigy on his tomb still exists in the Beauchamp Chapel in St Mary's Church, Warwick. King Henry VI sent 'carpenters, masons, workmen and labourers' to work on the chapel in July 1441. [2] The effigy depicts Richard in armour, clean-shaven, holding his hands up with the palms facing a foot apart as though about to pray. He has the typical short pudding-bowl haircut which English noblemen generally wore in the early fifteenth century, though his hair is delightfully curly.

Isabelle herself did not have much longer to live. She made her will in London on 1 December 1439, in English, calling herself 'Dame Isabell countesse of Warrewyk'. [3] She requested burial in Tewkesbury Abbey, in the chapel she had had built for her first husband Worcester, rather than with her wealthy and highly respected second husband, a request which reveals much about her devotion to her natal family and perhaps about her strong feelings for her first husband. Her *grete templys with the baleys*, that is, head-bands decorated with pale rubies, were to be sold for the best possible price and the money given to the abbey.

On 18 December 1439, an entry on the Patent Roll declared that Isabelle 'has long been visited with grievous bodily infirmity, so that her recovery is doubtful'. As Isabelle clearly expected to die at any moment even though she was only in her late thirties, and as her son and heir Harry Beauchamp was still only 14 years old, Henry VI's government gave custody of all her lands to nine men Isabelle trusted who would look after them until Harry came of age and would not allow any damage or waste to be done to them. [4] In her will, Isabelle left twenty marks to her attendant Elizabeth Keston, 'for the labour she hath had about me in my sickness.' [5] The names of some of her other attendants and servants appear in the will and were left bequests: Jane Newmarch, Margaret Morgan, Colyn of the chamber, Colyer, Wiltshire, Basset and Halfhide. She had kept her wedding gown – whether from her first or second marriage is not stated – which she bequeathed to 'Our Lady of Worcester', and a gold crown went to the shrine of Our Lady of Caversham. Caversham was a Despenser manor and probably where her mother Constance had died in 1416.

Isabelle died at the convent of the Minoresses near the Tower of London, also often called the Minories – where her father Thomas had once built a door directly from his house into the conventual church – on 26 or 27 December 1439. She must have been living there for a while before death. The writ to take her lands into the king's hands, and her inquisition post mortem held between January and June 1440, reveal that she owned lands in twenty-two English counties and in Wales and London. [6] Her funeral took place at Tewkesbury Abbey on 13 January 1440, and her tomb and chantry chapel can still be seen there. She had requested a cadaver effigy in her will, i.e. a depiction of herself naked, dead and decaying as a *memento mori*, with her hair swept back from her face. The inscription around the chapel reads, in Latin, 'Be mindful of the Lady Isabelle Despenser, countess of Warrewyk, who founded this chapel to the honour of St Mary Magdalene, and died in London in the Minories, A.D. 1439, on St John the Evangelist's Day [27 December]. And was buried in the choir on the right hand of her father. On whose soul may God have pity. Amen.' Among the family coats of arms which appear on the chapel, as well as the arms of the Clares and Despensers, are those of Isabelle's great-grandfather King Pedro of Castile, her great-grandfather King Edward III of England, and her grandfather Edmund of Langley, duke of York. [7] Isabelle's remains were seen during excavations in 1874/5, wrapped in a linen shroud, and her preserved hair was described as 'red-gold'. [8]

In December 1441, King Henry VI, who must have known Isabelle well and was a close friend of her son, declared that he wished to show favour to Tewkesbury Abbey because she was buried there. Rather oddly, the young king called Isabelle 'prioress of Tewkesbury'. [9] As well as Harry, Isabelle was survived by her daughter Elizabeth Neville from her first marriage, who was about 21 in 1439, her 13-year-old daughter Anne

Neville from her second marriage, and perhaps her grandsons Richard (who died young) and George Neville, future Lord Abergavenny, who may both have already been born to Elizabeth by late 1439.

Isabelle's granddaughter Anne Beauchamp, only child and heir of Harry and his wife Cecily, was born in Cardiff in February 1444, the month before Harry's nineteenth birthday. The Tewkesbury Abbey chronicler's account of little Anne's baptism is garbled, but it seems that she was named after Harry's sister because the older Anne was one of her godmothers, and that Isabelle Despenser's illegitimate half-sister Alianore Tuchet née Holland, Lady Audley, was her other godmother. [10] Harry Beauchamp was made first duke of Warwick by his friend Henry VI in 1445, but died at Hanley Castle, his birthplace, on 11 June 1446 at the age of just 21, mere months after he had come of age. One historian has speculated that he was killed by Humphrey Stafford, earl of Stafford and first duke of Buckingham (1402–60), with whom he had had a long and bad-tempered quarrel about precedence (and who was one of his godfathers). [11] On the other hand, in the fifteenth century there were numerous illnesses and infections which could carry off young and seemingly fit and healthy people.

Harry had inherited lands in no fewer than thirty-three English counties and in London and Wales from his parents, and his toddler daughter was a very great heiress. [12] He was buried in Tewkesbury Abbey with his mother and his Despenser ancestors rather than in his father's Beauchamp Chapel in Warwick. His daughter Anne died in early 1449 at barely 5 years old, and his full sister Anne Neville née Beauchamp, Isabelle Despenser's youngest child, was made his sole heir, to the disgruntlement of their older half-sisters. The question of the Despenser, Beauchamp of Warwick, Beauchamp of Abergavenny, Berkeley and Lisle inheritances, and precisely who was entitled to hold what, became endlessly complex. [13]

The title of duke which Harry Beauchamp had held so briefly died with him, and his sister Anne and her husband Richard Neville became earl and countess of Warwick. Richard Neville is famous for helping his cousin Edward IV, son of Constance Despenser's nephew Richard, duke of York, take the throne, and is known to posterity as the 'Kingmaker'. To benefit his Neville cousin, Edward IV reversed the 1400 attainder on Thomas Despenser in his first parliament as king in November 1461. As the first Yorkist king of England, Edward had an interest in presenting his three Lancastrian predecessors as usurpers, and talked of the 'persons of evil, riotous and seditious disposition, delighting in tumult and rebellious novelties' who helped Henry IV take the throne in 1399. He described Thomas Despenser as a 'noble and worthy lord' who maintained his faithful allegiance to the rightful king, Richard II. [14]

Anne and Richard Neville had two surviving children, Isabel (1451–76), named after her Despenser grandmother, and Anne (1456–85). Countess Anne (b. 1426) must have borne other children who did not live: in July 1453, Pope Nicholas V gave her permission to eat meat and eggs during Lent when she was pregnant, as she 'is weakened by former illnesses and the births of children'. [15] Her daughters Isabel and Anne Neville married Edward IV's brothers George (1449–78), duke of Clarence, and Richard (1452–85), duke of Gloucester, and when Gloucester took the throne as Richard III in 1483, Anne the younger became queen of England. George and Isabel, duke and duchess of Clarence, were both buried in Tewkesbury Abbey among Isabel's Despenser ancestors.

Isabelle Despenser was the great-grandmother of Isabel Neville and George of Clarence's son Edward (b. 1475), earl of Warwick, executed by Henry VII in 1499 after fourteen years' imprisonment in the Tower of London, and of Isabel and George's daughter Margaret Pole (b. 1473), countess of Salisbury, executed by Henry VIII in 1541. In September 1485 at the beginning of Henry VII's reign, the lands which belonged to the inheritance of Edward of Clarence, earl of Warwick, one of the Despenser and Warwick co-heirs, were called 'Spenser londes' and 'Warrewik londes'. [16] Isabelle Despenser was also the great-grandmother of Richard III's only legitimate child Edward of Middleham, who was the other Despenser co-heir but died as a child in 1484, the year before his parents. Isabelle's daughter Anne Neville née Beauchamp, countess of Warwick, despite her weakness from various illnesses and childbirth in the 1450s, outlived both her daughters and several grandchildren, and died on 20 September 1492 when she was 66. Isabelle's eldest child Elizabeth of Abergavenny died in June 1448, and Elizabeth's son and heir George Neville died on the same day as his aunt Anne, 20 September 1492.

Other than possible descendants of the Lincolnshire branch of the Despenser family – Philip Despenser IV (d. 1424) had younger brothers, John and Robert – Isabelle and her third cousin Margery Wentworth, daughter and heir of Philip IV, were the last of the Despensers. Margery outlived her elder son Philip Wentworth, executed in 1464, and died in

1478 when she was 80 or almost. Her heir was Philip's 30-year-old son, Henry Wentworth. [17] Margery probably lived long enough to see the birth of her namesake great-granddaughter, Henry's daughter Margery Wentworth, who was born *c.* 1478 and married Sir John Seymour of Wolf Hall in October 1494. There were and are numerous lines of descent from Isabelle, Margery and other women of the Despenser family: Berkeleys, Arundels, Ferrers, Hastings, Camoys, Nevilles, Wentworths, Seymours and many others.

Margery Despenser's Wentworth descendants held the title Baron Despenser until 1529, when her great-great-grandson Thomas Wentworth was created first Baron Wentworth. The barony of Despenser was revived in 1604 for the Fane family, descendants of Isabelle Despenser's daughter Elizabeth of Abergavenny. Francis Dashwood (1708–81), Chancellor of the Exchequer and founder of the Hellfire Club, son of Mary Fane, was one of Isabelle's descendants who was called Lord Despenser. In the twenty-first century, the title Lord Despenser still exists and is held as a subsidiary title by Viscount Falmouth. The family name and title, so many centuries later, live on.

Abbreviations

ANLP: Anglo-Norman Letters and Petitions from All Souls MS 182, ed. Legge
CAD: Catalogue of Ancient Deeds
CCR: Calendar of Close Rolls
CChR: Calendar of Charter Rolls
CCW: Calendar of Chancery Warrants 1244–326
CDS: Calendar of Documents Relating to Scotland
CFR: Calendar of Fine Rolls
CIM: Calendar of Inquisitions Miscellaneous
CIPM: Calendar of Inquisitions Post Mortem
CPL: Calendar of Entries in the Papal Registers: Letters
CPR: Calendar of Patent Rolls
IPM: Inquisition Post Mortem
PROME: The Parliament Rolls of Medieval England
TNA: The National Archives
TV: Testamenta Vetusta, vol. 1, ed. Nicolas

Endnotes

Introduction

1. M. Lawrence, 'Secular Patronage and Religious Devotion: The Despensers and St Mary's Abbey, Tewkesbury', *Fourteenth Century England V*, ed. N. Saul (2008), 78.
2. A.R. Meyer, 'The Despensers and the "Gawain" Poet: A Gloucestershire Link to the Alliterative Master of the Northwest Midlands', *The Chaucer Review*, 4 (2001), 413–29.
3. H.N. MacCracken, *The Minor Poems of John Lydgate*, part 1 (1911), 260.

Part 1

Chapter 1: The Slaughter of Evesham

1. *CCR 1234–7* (1908), 500; *CCR 1237–42*, 93; *CPR 1232–47* (1906), 210, 222. The identity of Hugh's mother is not known for certain, though a theory on some genealogy websites suggests that she was a daughter of Saer Quincy, earl of Winchester (d. 1219). Hugh Despenser the Elder (b. 1261), grandson of Hugh who died in 1238, was made earl of Winchester in 1322, which might (or might not) point to a relationship between the families.
2. *CCR 1242–7*, 256, 283; V. Gibbs and H.A. Doubleday, *The Complete Peerage*, 14 vols (1910–40), vol. 4, 260 note a. The Hugh Despenser who died in 1238 had an elder brother Thomas who died childless in 1218, a younger brother Geoffrey who died in 1251, and a third brother, William. Geoffrey left a son, John, who died childless in 1275. Thomas, William, Geoffrey and Hugh (d. 1238) also had a sister, Rohese or Rose, who married into the Segrave family and had descendants.
3. The Spencers of Althorp, the family of Diana, princess of Wales, are not, as often assumed, the same family as the Despensers.
4. *CPR 1258–66*, 100.
5. *CPR 1247–58*, 590.
6. *Calendar of Entries in the Papal Registers Relating to Great Britain and Ireland*, vol. 1, Papal Letters 1198–1304, ed. W.H. Bliss (1883), 431, 441; J.R. Maddicott, *Simon de Montfort* (1994), 63–4, 173–5.
7. *Complete Peerage,* vol. 4, 260.
8. *CIM*, vol. 1 (1916), 1219–1307, no. 936; *CPR 1258–66*, 359, 396. Adam was the son of Thurstan Despenser: *CChR*, vol. 1, 1226–57 (1903), 414.
9. *CIM*, vol. 1 (1904), 1256–9, no. 807; *CIPM 1216–72*, no. 389.
10. *CPR 1232–47*, 210; *CCR 1256–9*, 360.
11. A Basset sister, name unknown, married Adam Periton (d. 1266) and was the mother of Adam's three daughters and co-heirs Lettice or Hawise, Katherine and Isabel, who married into the Keynes, Paynel and Welles families. *CIPM 1216–72*, no. 633; *CIPM*

1272–91, nos. 320, 819; *CIPM 1291–1300*, no. 373. *CPL 1198–1304*, 345–6, says that Philip Basset was the uncle of the archbishop of Dublin, who was Fulk Basset or Fulk Sandford, archbishop from 1256 to 1271; Fulk's brother John Sandford was archbishop of Dublin from 1284 to 1294.

12. W. Stewart-Parker, 'The Bassets of High Wycombe: Politics, Lordship, Locality and Culture in the Thirteenth Century', King's College London PhD thesis (2013), 99–100, and see D. Carpenter, *The Battles of Lewes and Evesham, 1264/65* (1987).

13. *CIPM 1291–1300*, no. 31 (Courtenay); *CIPM 1327–36*, no. 470 (Furnival).

14. *CIPM 1307–17*, no. 116; P. Chaplais, ed., *The War of Saint-Sardos (1323–1325): Gascon Correspondence and Diplomatic Documents* (1954), 78. There is no direct evidence of Eleanor Grey's parentage, but there must have been some reason why Hugh the Younger addressed her son as his cousin.

15. *Complete Peerage*, vol. 5, 341, identifies Anne Ferrers as Hugh the justiciar's daughter, though various posts in the soc.genealogy.medieval online group state that William Ferrers married a Scottish noblewoman called Anne Durward.

16. Chaplais, *War of Saint-Sardos*, 75–7, 80, 145, 175. Hugh Despenser the Elder, his nephew Hugh Courtenay, and his brothers-in-law the earl of Warwick and Thomas Furnival, were four of the ten men who paid 1,000 marks in 1301 for Ralph Basset (d. 1343) to have his own marriage rights and seisin of his lands though he was underage: *CCR 1302–7*, 67. This also points to a family connection. For Sempringham, TNA, SC 8/34/1671, *CPR 1307–13*, 530, 598, and J. Coleman, 'New Evidence about Sir Geoffrey Luttrell's Raid on Sempringham Priory, 1312', *British Library Journal*, 25 (1999), 105, 121 (*Monseigneur Hughe le Despenser et ses soers dames en la dite priorie*). The petition does not specify Hugh the Elder or Younger, but two of Hugh the Younger's sisters were married in 1312 and the other two, born *c.* the late 1290s or early 1300s, were too young to aid and support the prior of Sempringham.

17. *CIPM 1272–91*, nos. 101, 389.

18. C. Moor, *Knights of Edward I*, vol. 3 (1930), 64–5. Hawise's paternity is not certain, and various posts on the soc.genealogy.medieval group discuss the matter.

19. *CPL 1198–1304*, 307, 312–3; *CPR 1281–92*, 479; *A Descriptive Catalogue of Ancient Deeds*, ed. H. C. Maxwell, A.4605.

20. O. de Laborderie, J. R. Maddicott and D.A. Carpenter, 'The Last Hours of Simon de Montfort' *English Historical Review*, 115 (2000), 410.

21. 'Last Hours of Simon', 394.

22. Stewart-Parker, 'The Bassets', 101 (stabbed); *Vita Edwardi Secundi Monachi Cuiusdam Malmesberiensis*, ed. N. Denholm-Young (1957), 109 (revenge); *Oxford Dictionary of National Biography*, online edition (burial).

23. A. Jobson, ed., *Baronial Reform and Revolution in England, 1258–1267* (2016), 165.

Chapter 2

1. *CPR 1258–66*, 459–60.

2. *CIPM 1216–72*, no. 807.

3. M. Morris, *The Bigod Earls of Norfolk* (2005), 221; CAD, A.537.

4. *CIPM 1272–91*, no. 101; *CCR 1279–88, 148*. Another John Despenser is mentioned in June 1306, aged '36 and more' and the heir of John of London. This John Despenser had sons John, Thomas, Nicholas and Richard and a daughter Juliana. *CIPM 1300–7*, no. 382; *CPR 1301–7*, 492; *CCR 1307–13*, 328; *CPR 1324–7*, 6. I am unaware of a family connection, if any, to Hugh the Elder.

5. *CCR 1279–88*, 6; *Calendar of Various Chancery Rolls 1277–1326* (1912), 228–9, 374; M. Lawrence, 'Rise of a Royal Favourite: The Early Career of Hugh Despenser the Elder', *The Reign of Edward II: New Perspectives*, ed. G. Dodd and A. Musson (2006), 208–9.
6. *Parliamentary Writs and Writs of Military Summons*, vol. 1, ed. F. Palgrave (1827), 569; Feet of Fines, Leicestershire, CP 25/1/123/36, no. 138.
7. *CIPM 1272–91*, no. 389.
8. Morris, *Bigod Earls*, 125.
9. *CCR 1279–88*, 88, 184; *CPR 1272–81*, 439.
10. S. Barfield, 'The Beauchamp Earls of Warwick, 1268–1369', Univ. of Birmingham MPhil thesis (1997), 19; *Annales Monastici*, ed. H. R. Luard. vol. 4 (1869), 471.
11. *CIPM 1272–91*, no. 477.
12. M. Morris, 'Edward I and the Knights of the Round Table', *Foundations of Medieval Scholarship: Records Edited in Honour of David Crook*, ed. P. Brand and S. Cunningham (2008), 66–7.
13. M. Prestwich, 'Royal Patronage Under Edward I', *Thirteenth Century England I*, ed. P.R. Coss and S.D. Lloyd (1986), 54; TNA SC 1/10/109; E 159/60, mem. 14d; *CCR 1279–88*, 462.
14. *CCR 1279–88*, 217–18, 220.

Chapter 3

1. He was there on 19 November 1294, 6 August 1297, 28 April 1298, 21 November 1299, 17 June 1301, 31 March, 11 and 29 September 1302, 24 January 1303, 29 November and 20 December 1304, sometime between 20 November 1305 and 19 November 1306, 30 November 1306, 6 December 1310, 11 September 1315, 3/4 January 1321 and possibly 14 May 1325.
2. Hugh's whereabouts and his enclosures to Vastern are in *CAD*, A.250, 3979, 4605, 4611, 4796, 4811, 4812, 4829, 4839, 4852, 4855, 4856, 4741, 5848, 9357, 12047; TNA E 42/41, SC 1/28/57; *CPR 1266–72*, 177; *CPR 1292–1301*, 42, 536; *CPR 1317–21*, 431–2; *CCW 1244–1326* (1927), 423–4, 517. TNA, C 53/111, no. 7, says that Hugh was at Portchester on 14 May 1325, though *CAD*, A.4812 is a grant by Hugh to his cook dated seventy miles away at Vastern on the same day.
3. K. Watts, 'Some Wiltshire Deer Parks', *Wiltshire Archaeological and Natural History Magazine*, 91 (1998), 90–102, at p. 91; *CIPM 1327–36*, no. 626.
4. *CAD*, A.4621, A.4741.
5. *CAD*, A.4839, A.5480; *CIPM 1272–91*, no. 819; *CPR 1266–72*, 177.
6. Stewart-Parker, 'Bassets of High Wycombe', 185, 192, 195, 352, 369; TNA, E 42/377; http://users.trytel.com/~tristan/towns/market/wiltshire/wootton.html, accessed 30 March 2019.
7. http://www.gatehouse-gazetteer.info/English%20sites/4658.html, accessed 9 April 2019; *CIPM 1427–32*, no. 706.

Chapter 4

1. Morris, 'Knights of the Round Table', 66–7; *CPR 1281–92*, 248.
2. *CPR 1281–92*, 267–8.
3. TNA, SC 1/10/133.
4. *CCR 1279–88*, 547.
5. *CPR 1281–92*, 325; Morris, *Bigod Earls,* 138, 152.

6. *CCR 1288–96*, 134; *CPR 1281–92*, 363–4, calling Alicia 'Delicia'.
7. C. Bullock-Davies, *A Register of Royal and Baronial Domestic Minstrels 1272–1327* (1986), 75; Morris, *Bigod Earls*, 138.
8. *Parliamentary Writs*, vol. 1, 569.
9. TNA, E 42/95; E 40/386.
10. TNA, C 241/15/5.
11. TNA, C 241/80/38, C 241/50/377, C 241/50/381, C 241/50/376, C 241/91/21 (£4,000 to the earl of Buchan's brother), etc.
12. CCR 1288–96, 234; *Various Chancery Rolls*, 351.
13. *CFR 1272–1307*, 339.
14. M Prestwich, *Edward I* (1988), 387, 391; *CPR 1292–1301*, 72–3, 76.
15. E 40/3185; E 42/63; *CCR 1346–9*, 40, 223–4.
16. *CAD*, A.4605, A.4741; *CPR 1292–1301*, 164; *CChR 1257–1300*, 463; *CPR 1307–13*, 255.
17. *Foedera, Conventiones, Literae*, vol. 1, 1272–1307, ed. T. Rymer (1816), 832.
18. *CPR 1292–1301*, 170, 178, 181.
19. *CAD*, A.7018; *Parliamentary Writs*, 569; *Calendar of Documents Relating to Scotland*, vol. 1, 1272–1307, ed. J. Bain (1884), no. 869; *CDS*, vol. 5 (Supplementary), no. 155.
20. *CAD*, A.7108, A.1044, A.10260; *CCR 1296–1302*, 84; *CPR 1292–1301*, 224, 233; *Foedera 1272–1307*, 849; TNA, E 30/27.
21. M. Prestwich, *Documents Illustrating the Crisis in 1297–98 in England* (1980), 72, 87, 91–2, 107; *CCW*, 75.
22. *CFR 1272–1307*, 382.

Chapter 5

1. *CPR 1292–1301*, 239.
2. Prestwich, *Documents Illustrating*, 106–7.
3. Lawrence, 'Early Career', 211–12.
4. Feet of Fines, CP 25/1/86/47, no. 343; Prestwich, *Documents Illustrating*, 168.
5. *Calendar of Early Mayor's Court Rolls, 1298–1307*, ed. A.H. Thomas (1924), 23.
6. *Vita Edwardi Secundi*, ed. Denholm-Young, 44, 114–5.
7. https://www.british-history.ac.uk/vch/herts/vol2/pp179–186, accessed 21 October 2018; TNA, SC 8/279/13926; and see also below.
8. Lawrence, 'Early Career', 214; *CIPM 1399–1405*, no. 638.
9. *CCR 1296–1302*, 324; *CAD*, A.4822, 4837, 4845, 4859, 5848, 9357; CPR 1292–1301, 536. Robert Keynes was the son of Lettice or Hawise Periton, whose mother (name unknown) was the sister of Hugh's grandfather Philip Basset.
10. *Parliamentary Writs*, 569; *CAD*, A.750; Kent History and Library Centre document no. Fa/R/s/1, available on the National Archives website (http://discovery.nationalarchives.gov.uk/).
11. T. Wright, ed., *The Roll of Arms of the Princes, Barons and Knights who Attended King Edward I to the Siege of Caerlaverock in 1300* (1864), 204.
12. Wright, *Roll of Arms*, 8.
13. *CAD*, A.3182, A.3183, A.4611, A.528, A.535, A.750.
14. *CPR 1292–1301*, 535–7, 561; *CPR 1301–7*, 30.
15. *CAD*, A.249–55.
16. He also gained possession of Sutton Mandeville, in Wiltshire but much farther south. *CAD*, A.4611, A.4803, A.4827, A.4837, A.4839, A.4852, A.4853, A.4855, A.4859; *CPR 1321–4*, 285; *CPR 1327–30*, 245; *CCR 1327–30*, 495–6; *CCR 1337–9*, 193; TNA, SC

8/49/2437, SC 8/17/848 and SC 8/209/10420; *Parliament Rolls of Medieval England,* January 1327. Stanley Abbey, near Calne, also lay a few miles from Vastern. Berwick Bassett was part of the Basset inheritance, but the abbot claimed that Philip Basset gave it to the abbey shortly before his death and that Hugh wrongfully seized it with the aid of his stepfather the earl of Norfolk.

Chapter 6

1. *CAD*, A.6278; *CIPM 1291–1300*, no. 194.
2. *CPR 1291–1302*, 179; C.M. Woolgar, *The Great Household in Late Medieval England* (1999), 15, 53, 101, 128.
3. *CIPM 1291–1300*, nos. 65, 194, 587; *CIPM 1307–17*, no. 611; *Oxford Dictionary of National Biography* (*ODNB*) entry for Robert Burnell (debts); TNA, C 241/76/246; C 241/108/64; *CCR 1307–13*, 125, 246, 550.
4. TNA, SC 8/313/E63.
5. *CIPM 1307–17*, no. 611; *CIPM 1361–5*, no, 489.
6. *CPR 1307–13*, 529; *CPR 1313–17*, 377, 514. It had belonged to Edward's great-uncle Robert Burnell, bishop of Bath and Wells: *CIPM 1291–1300*, no. 65.
7. *CPR 1292–1301*, 536; *CPR 1301–7*, 71, 85, 88; *CPR 1327–30*, 31; *CAD*, A.10, A.249–55, A.12047.
8. Feet of Fines, CP 25/1/205/15, no. 66.
9. TNA, E 39/99/61; H. Johnstone, *Edward of Carnarvon 1284–1307* (1946), 92; *CDS 1307–1357*, 392–4.
10. TNA, E 30/1675; *CCR 1307–13*, 374.
11. *CPR 1307–13*, 62.
12. *CPR 1307–13*, 528, 561, 571.
13. H. Johnstone, *Letters of Edward, Prince of Wales 1304–1305* (1931), 19–20, 107–8, 118–9, 122, 123, 133–4, 137–8.

Part 2

Chapter 7

1. Bullock-Davies, *Register of Minstrels*, 16.
2. *CChR 1327–41*, 212.
3. TNA, E 101/369/11, fo. 96v; *CCR 1307–13*, 5; *CPR 1301–7*, 443, 526–7, 536.
4. *CPR 1301–7*, 443; *CCR 1307–13*, 198, 237; *CFR 1307–19*, 54; *CCW*, 308; *CIM 1308–48*, 20, and see also below.
5. *CPR 1301–7*, 427, 441, 447.
6. *CIPM 1300–7*, no. 54.
7. *CPR 1281–92*, 497; *CPR 1292–1301*, 81.
8. *CDS*, vol. 5, no. 2583.
9. *CFR 1272–1307*, 543–4; *CCR 1302–7*, 531, 537; *CPR 1301–7*, 493.
10. Johnstone, *Letters of Edward*, 70, 75.
11. TNA, SC 1/28/114–117; *CDS*, vol. 5, no. 2600 ('Hugh son of Hugh Despenser').
12. *CFR 1272–1307*, 543–4.
13. *CChR 1300–26*, 125.
14. *CDS*, vol. 5, nos. 634, 2684.
15. *CPR 1461–7*, 310.

Chapter 8

1. TNA, C 53/94, nos. 29, 32.
2. TNA, C 53/94, nos. 31, 34.
3. Hugh did not witness the charter Edward II issued at Berkhamsted on 3 November, and was in London on 1 November: TNA, C 53/94, no. 22; *CAD*, A.523.
4. In early 1327, Lamarsh was worth £31 10s a year, Layham £35 9s, Kersey £27 6s, North Weald Bassett £40, Wix £10 and Oxcroft/Balsham around £10: *CChR 1327–41*, 2, 4; *CPR 1327–30*, 26. 'John, son of Matthew of Layham' gave Layham to Hugh Despenser, either the Elder or the justiciar, at an uncertain date: TNA, E 40/15797.
5. *The Cartulary of Chatteris Abbey*, ed. C. Breay (1999), no. 191, and TNA, SC 8/295/14716 (Kersey), SC 8/41/2044 and 2045, and SC 8/156/7789 (Layham). In September 1321, Edward II stated that Hugh the Younger held Layham: *CCR 1318–23*, 402.
6. *CChR 1226–57*, 57; *CPR 1317–21*, 208, 456. In early 1327, Ryhall was worth £60 a year: *CChR 1327–41*, 4.
7. *CPR 1321–4*, 444–5, 457; *Chatteris Abbey*, no. 191; *CPR 1232–47*, 374; *CChR 1226–57*, 407.
8. http://www.wykes.org/wix.html, accessed 30 March 2019; F. Underhill, *For Her Good Estate: The Life of Elizabeth de Burgh* (1999), 90 (Elizabeth Despenser); https://www.british-history.ac.uk/vch/suff/vol2/pp107–108 (Kersey), and https://www.british-history.ac.uk/vch/essex/vol2/pp154–155 (Latton), both accessed 9 April 2019.
9. TNA, SC 8/33/1646; *CIPM 1327–36*, nos. 306, 502; *CIPM 1352–60*, no. 639; *CAD*, A.527; *CPR 1370–4*, 82.
10. *CPR 1317–21*, 208.
11. *CFR 1307–19*, 8, 10; *CIPM 1307–17*, no. 44; *CIPM 1317–27*, no. 275.
12. *CCR 1396–9*, 83–4. Among others, N. Fryde, *The Tyranny and Fall of Edward II 1321–1326* (1979), 114–5, and Underhill, *Good Estate*, 7, confuse Isabella Despenser with her husband's first wife Isabella Valence (d. October 1305), half-niece of Henry III. John Hastings' marriage to Isabella Valence was planned by 4 March 1269 when they were young children, and they received a papal dispensation to wed on 15 July 1275. *CPR 1266–72*, 323; *CPL 1198–1304*, 450.
13. *CIPM 1307–17*, no. 471; *CP*, vol. 6, 667; T. Sharp, *Illustrative Papers on the History and Antiquities of the City of Coventry* (1871), 198; *CPL 1305–41*, 70, 104. 'Jonetta' appears in *CPR 1292–1301*, 314. Hastings' younger daughter Elizabeth, probably born 1297, married Roger, Lord Grey of Ruthin, and his second son John was the father of Laurence Hastings, earl of Pembroke (1321–48).
14. *Roll of Arms...Caerlaverock*, 23.
15. *CIPM 1327–36*, no. 646.
16. *CCR 1396–9*, 83–4.
17. *CPR 1330–4*, 313.
18. *CCR 1307–13*, 11, 109.
19. *CFR 1307–19*, 14; the other was the lord of Castillon in Gascony.
20. TNA, C 53/94, nos. 11, 13, 14, 17, 18, 20.
21. *CPR 1307–13*, 196, 273, 280, 305, 330; *CCR 1307–13*, 185.
22. *CPR 1307–13*, 51; *Vita*, 4.
23. *CCW*, 275 (married); *CIPM 1291–1300*, no. 209 (Margaret's age); E 40/3185 (Philip). Edward I granted Margaret's marriage rights to Sir Fulk Fitzwarin, her grandfather, in June 1299: *CPR 1292–1301*, 422.
24. *CCR 1307–13*, 493.
25. *The Anonimalle Chronicle 1307 to 1334*, eds. W.R. Childs and J. Taylor (1991), 132.

26. TNA, C 53/96, nos. 32–6, *CPR 1307–13*, 179–81 (Elder); *CChR 1300–26*, 130 (Younger).
27. *CCR 1307–13*, 173, 198.
28. *CPR 1307–13*, 512.

Chapter 9

1. *CCR 1307–13*, 198, 237; *CFR 1307–19*, 54; *CCW*, 308; *CIM 1308–48*, no. 69.
2. *Issues of the Exchequer*, ed. F. Devon, 124, and see my *Edward II and Hugh Despenser the Younger: Downfall of a King's Favourite*, 34–5, 158.
3. TNA, C 53/96, no. 3; *CAD,* A.215.
4. TNA, C 53/97; *CAD,* A.4811.
5. *Annales Londonienses 1195–1330*, in W. Stubbs, ed., *Chronicles of the Reigns of Edward I and Edward II*, vol. 1 (1882), 200.
6. TNA, C 53/98, nos. 29 and 30, and C 53/99. The only charter he did not witness that year was no. 16, dated 16 April 1313 at Windsor.
7. *CPR 1307–13*, 203; *CCR 1307–13*, 190, 323, 514; *CFR 1307–19*, 50; *CIPM 1307–17*, no. 212. Wambrook was a manor Elizabeth had inherited from her father John Hertrigg, whom Despenser the Elder, as justice of the forest, indicted for killing a stag in Windsor forest in or before October 1305: *CPR 1301–7*, 381.
8. *CPR 1307–13*, 464, 509.
9. *Foedera 1307–27,* 187.
10. *CPR 1307–13*, 512, 528, 561, 571; *CCR 1307–13*, 561; *CPR 1313–17*, 7; C 53/99.

Chapter 10

1. See his entry in the *ODNB*, and M. Lawrence, 'Power, Ambition and Political Rehabilitation: The Despensers, *c.* 1281–1400', Univ. of York DPhil thesis, 2005, 41–2.
2. *CAD*, A.7428; Feet of Fines, CP 25/1/286/34, nos. 5, 6; TNA, C 53/99, no. 17.
3. TNA, C 53/99, nos. 12–14, 20; *CPR 1307–13*, 558–9.
4. *CPR 1307–13*, 582; *CCR 1307–13*, 583.
5. *CIPM 1307–17*, no. 412; *CCR 1307–13*, 525; Sharp, *History and Antiquities of Coventry,* 197–8. Hastings' son-in-law William Huntingfield died later in 1313, and Edward II gave the marriage of Hastings' 7-year-old grandson Roger Huntingfield and custody of his lands to Hugh Despenser the Younger on 9 October 1313, though rescinded the grant: *CFR 1307–19*, 181, 203, 223, 242, 278.
6. *CIPM 1307–17*, no. 472; TNA, C 134/34/5; *CFR 1307–19*, 179. His father-in-law Ralph Goushill had died at the same age in August 1294 when his daughter Margaret was also mere months old: *CIPM 1272–91*, no. 607; *CIPM 1291–1300*, no. 209.
7. *CIPM 1422–7*, nos. 308, 312; *CCR 1422–9*, 159.
8. *PROME*.
9. TNA, E 40/10237.
10. *CIPM 1272–91*, nos. 592, 739; *CIPM 1307–17*, no. 272; *CCR 1288–96*, 19, 62, 68, 102–3; *CPR 1281–92*, 280; *CPR 1292–1301*, 156; *CChR 1300–26*, 228–9. Guy St Amand was 'aged 17 at the feast of the Purification, 13 Edward I', which gives a date of birth around early February 1268; Amaury's proof of age says that he turned 21 around mid-Lent 1289, which gives a date of birth in March 1268. John St Amand was either 27, 30, 32 or 34 in August/September 1310.
11. *CPR 1292–1301*, 570; *CPR 1301–7*, 392; *CFR 1307–19*, 74, 84; *CCR 1318–23*, 200; *Complete Peerage*, vol. 11, 298.

12. *CPR 1301–7*, 389, 392, 420; *England and Her Neighbours, 1066–1453: Essays in Honour of Pierre Chaplais*, ed. M. Jones and M. Vale (1989), 142.
13. *CIPM 1327–36*, no. 286; *CPR 1313–17*, 265. Amaury was already married to his wife Joan by 22 April 1330 when he was 15: Feet of Fines, CP 25/1/286/226, no. 56.
14. BCM/A/2/19/7 (Berkeley Castle Muniments); *CPR 1330–4*, 141 (executors). TNA, SC 8/30/1492 is a petition by John St Amand dating to 1320, which spells his name 'Johan de Seint Amaund'.
15. *The Chronicle of Lanercost 1272–1346*, ed. H. Maxwell (1913), 208 (Younger); *Anonimalle*, 89 (Elder).
16. TNA, SC 8/261/13014; *CDS*, vol. 5, nos. 1713, 1716, 2961, 2969, 2974.
17. *Vita*, 57–8.

Chapter 11

1. *CCR 1313–18*, 263–4; Feet of Fines, CP 25/1/285/28, no. 50.
2. *CFR 1307–19*, 268, 271; *Year Books of Edward II*, vol. 25, Part of Easter, and Trinity, 1319, ed. J.P. Collas (1964), 130–32.
3. TNA, C 53/101 and 102.
4. *CCW*, 423–4.
5. *CPR 1313–17*, 309, 407; TNA, SC 8/177/8843.
6. *CIPM 1307–17*, no. 538, p. 353.
7. TNA, C 53/102, no. 12.
8. Feet of Fines Sussex, CP 25/1/285/30, no. 123.
9. *CFR 1272–1307*, 349 (the manor was Flockthorpe, a deserted medieval settlement); C. Bullock-Davies, *Menstrellorum Multitudo: Minstrels at a Royal Feast* (1978), 186 (knighting).
10. V. Gibbs, 'The Battle of Boroughbridge and the Boroughbridge Roll', *Genealogist*, new series, 21 (1905), 224.
11. *An Abstract of Feet of Fines for the County of Sussex*, vol. 3, 1308–1509, ed. L.F. Salzman (1916), nos. 1614, 1659; Feet of Fines, CP 25/1/205/19, no. 18.
12. H.G.D. Liveing, *Records of Romsey Abbey* (1906), 164; *CIPM 1352–60*, no. 634; *CIPM 1370–3*, no. 173.
13. *CIPM 1370–3*, no. 173. Thomas Camoys died on 28 March 1421 at about 70, and his heir was his grandson Hugh Camoys: *CIPM 1418–22*, nos. 749–53.
14. *CPR 1324–7*, 21; *CIPM 1317–27*, no. 515.
15. *CChR 1300–26*, 469.
16. *CPR 1343–5*, 462; *CPR 1348–50*, 573; *CCR 1374–7*, 449; *CPR 1385–9*, 335; Feet of Fines, CP 25/1/207/29, no. 26; *CAD*, B.3718; *John of Gaunt's Register*, ed. S. Armitage-Smith, vol. 1 (1911), 1371–1375, no. 739.
17. *CFR 1319–27*, 16; *CPR 1317–21*, 426, 449.
18. *CPR 1317–21*, 325, 366; C 134/61/1; *CIPM 1317–27*, nos. 138, 676.
19. *CAD*, nos. A.4980, A.8019; *CIPM 1317–27*, no. 310. See also *CIPM 1291–1300*, no. 360; *CIPM 1307–17*, no. 421; *CIPM 1317–27*, no. 62; *CIPM 1352–60*, no. 384; *CCR 1323–7*, 223; *Complete Peerage*, vol. 4, 371–2; *Complete Peerage*, vol. 12B, 199.

Chapter 12

1. *CPL 1342–62*, 164.
2. *CPL 1305–41*, 231.

3. *Monasticon Anglicanum*, ed. W. Dugdale, vol. 2 (new edition, 1819), 62; R. Allington-Smith, *Henry Despenser the Fighting Bishop* (2003), viii, 4, but see *CChR 1300–26*, 448–51, 466.
4. TNA, E 101/380/4, fo. 20v: *vne sele...p' Johan le Despens' fuitz mons' Hugh le Despens' le fuiz.*
5. T. Stapleton, 'A Brief Summary of the Wardrobe Accounts of the Tenth, Eleventh and Fourteenth Years of King Edward the Second', *Archaeologia*, 26 (1836), 340.
6. *A Survey of London Reprinted From the Text of 1603*, ed. C.L. Kingsford (1908), 178.
7. *CIPM 1336–46*, no. 337 ('the feast of St Cuthbert, 14 Edward II').
8. TNA, E 101/379/17, mem. 2; Society of Antiquaries of London MS 122, 43.
9. TNA, SC 8/259/12929; *CCR 1318–23*, 150–1. John Berenger was born *c.* 1304 (*CIPM 1336–46*, no. 27) and was the same age as Elizabeth herself.
10. *Complete Peerage*, vol. 9, 142.
11. *CFR 1307–19*, 380, 388, 394; *CPR 1317–21*, 387, 582.
12. *Calendar of Wills Proved and Enrolled in the Court of Husting, London*, part 1, 1258–1358 (1889), 315.
13. *CPR 1317–21*, 262, 271; *CCR 1318–23*, 123.
14. *CPR 1317–21*, 269.
15. *CDS*, vol. 5, no. 3250.
16. Gascon Rolls C 61/33, nos. 106, 118, 122, 125, 131–2, 134–5, available at gasconrolls.org; *CPR 1317–21*, 422, 426, 429, 449.
17. *CPR 1317–21*, 467–8, 473.
18. TNA, SC 8/56/2759, 60, 61 and 62, and SC 8/162/8098; *CPR 1317–21*, 440–1, 510; *CPR 1321–4*, 132, 181.

Chapter 13

1. *Anonimalle*, 92–3; *Chronicon Galfridi le Baker de Swynbroke*, ed. E.M. Thompson (1889), 10.
2. Cited in S. Phillips, *Edward II* (2010), 98.
3. *CCR 1318–23*, 541–2; *CPR 1321–4*, 164–9, 249, 372, 378, 444–5.
4. *CCR 1318–23*, 543–4; *CPR 1321–4*, 164–70. In 1321, Hugh held seventeen manors in Wiltshire, six in Gloucestershire, five in Dorset, five in Hampshire, two in Berkshire, six in Oxfordshire, three in Buckinghamshire, four in Surrey, one in Cambridgeshire, two in Huntingdonshire, four in Leicestershire, one each in Yorkshire and Lincolnshire, five in Cheshire and five in Warwickshire.
5. *CPR 1321–4*, 164–5, 387–8.
6. J.C. Davies, 'The Despenser War in Glamorgan', *Transactions of the Royal Historical Society*, 9 (1915), 58; see also S.L. Waugh, 'The Profits of Violence: The Minor Gentry in the Rebellion of 1321–1322 in Gloucestershire and Herefordshire', *Speculum*, 52 (1977), 843–69.
7. TNA, SC 8/7/301.
8. *Vita*, 115–16; *CCR 1318–23*, 507; TNA, SC 8/17/833, SC 8/40/1970 and SC 8/7/327; *The Brut or the Chronicles of England*, part 1, ed. F.W.D. Brie (1906), 214; *Anonimalle*, 100; *Annales Paulini 1307–1340*, in Stubbs, *Chronicles*, vol. 1, 300.
9. Gibbs, 'Boroughbridge Roll', 224.
10. *Anonimalle*, 106.
11. *CChR 1300–26*, 443–4; *CPR 1321–4*, 128. Despite his closeness to the king, however, the new earl had to petition Edward II sometime between 1322 and 1326 regarding unpaid debts: TNA, SC 8/42/2093.

12. See *Downfall of a King's Favourite*, 103–10, and my article '"We Might be Prepared to Harm You": An Investigation into Some of the Extortions of Hugh Despenser the Younger', *Journal of the Mortimer History Society*, 2 (2018), 55–69.

13. *CPR 1330–4*, 404; SC 8/176/8753; TNA, SC 8/59/2947; *Downfall of a King's Favourite*, 92–3.

Chapter 14

1. *CCR 1318–23*, 577, 609; *CPR 1321–4*, 184.
2. Society of Antiquaries of London Manuscript 122, 42, 69.
3. *CDS 1307–57*, no. 809.
4. TNA, E 101/380/4, fo. 10v.
5. *CChR 1300–26*, 448–51; TNA, E 101/380/4, fo. 20v.
6. See the many letters to and from Hugh in Chaplais, *War of Saint-Sardos*.
7. TNA, E 101/380/4, fo. 16v.
8. *CPR 1321–4*, 235; Hampshire Feet of Fines, CP 25/1/206/27, no. 48; *CCR 1369–74*, 543.
9. TNA, E 101/380/4, fo. 30v.
10. He was appointed keeper of the peace in Bedfordshire in May 1329, for example: *CPR 1327–30*, 430.
11. *CPR 1324–7*, 86; TNA, C 53/111, no. 11.
12. *Vita*, 135.
13. TNA, C 53/111, nos. 7, 9 10, 11, 12A; TNA, E 101/380/4, fo. 29v.
14. E.B. Fryde, 'The Deposits of Hugh Despenser the Younger with Italian Bankers', *Economic History Review*, 2nd series, 3 (1951), 361; TNA, E 101/380/4, fo. 16r.
15. TNA, E 101/380/4, fo. 16r.
16. *CIPM 1317–27*, no. 618; *CIPM 1327–36*, no. 276; *CFR 1319–27*, 357–8; *CCR 1330–3*, 162.
17. *Calendar of Memoranda Rolls, Michaelmas 1326–Michaelmas 1327*, no. 763; the visit is undated, but Edward was briefly at Hadleigh on 22 July 1325.
18. SAL MS 122, 38; *Vita*, 140.
19. *Vita*, 142–3.
20. TNA, C 53/112, nos. 13, 24.
21. *CPR 1324–7*, 215.
22. SAL MS 122, 53.
23. *CIPM 1317–27*, no. 710.
24. SAL MS 122, 63; Despenser the Elder witnessed a royal charter on 22 May, TNA, C 53/112, no. 4.
25. SAL MS 122, 64, 80; *CPR 1324–7*, 276, 311; *CFR 1319–27*, 389.

Chapter 15

1. *Annales Paulini*, 312–13; *Croniques de London*, ed. G.J. Aungier (1844), 50.
2. *CPL 1342–62*, 164, 254.
3. SAL MS 122, 82.
4. *CFR 1319–27*, 421; SAL MS 122, 88.
5. *CFR 1319–27*, 416.
6. *Croniques de London*, 51.
7. *Annales Paulini*, 317–18; *Brut*, 240.
8. *CCR 1323–7*, 655.
9. *Brut*, 239–40.
10. See *Downfall of a King's Favourite*, 150–3.

Endnotes

Part 3

Chapter 16

1. *CChR 1327–41*, 2–4; *CPR 1324–7*, 339–40; *CPR 1327–30*, 33; *CFR 1327–37*, 7–8; *CPR 1330–4*, 523–4; *CCR 1396–9*, 278–9, 284–5, 298–9.
2. *CPR 1338–40*, 50; *CPR 1343–5*, 131.
3. *CIM 1348–77*, no. 699.
4. *CPR 1327–30*, 14, 20, 32; *CCR 1323–7*, 654.
5. One exception is that Isabella Hastings acknowledged a debt of just under £300 to Queen Isabella in June 1328 (*CCR 1323–7*, 394), though this may have been entirely above board.
6. *Memoranda Rolls*, no. 437; *CCR 1323–7*, 624; *CPR 1327–30*, 22. An inquisition of 1331 stated that Eleanor married Laurence, but this is surely an error: *CIPM 1327–36*, no. 391 (p. 292).
7. *CCR 1323–7*, 620; *CCR 1327–30*, 16, 275–6; *CPR 1327–30*, 243.
8. *CPR 1327–30*, 37–9.
9. *CPR 1327–30*, 171, 175.
10. *Admissions to Trinity College, Cambridge*, ed. W.W. Rouse Ball and J.A. Venn, vol. 1 (1916), 88, 91, 92.
11. *Complete Peerage*, vol. 3, 466.
12. *CFR 1319–27*, 348; *CCR 1327–30*, 352.
13. *PROME*, November 1330 parliament.
14. *CIPM 1336–46*, no. 239; *CPR 1338–40*, 482; *CPR 1343–5*, 242; Lawrence, 'Power, Ambition', 212.
15. *CFR 1383–91*, 346. The elder William's heir was his son Alan, born 1317, whose mother was Alice Toeni (d. 1324), widow of Hugh the Younger's uncle Guy Beauchamp, earl of Warwick (d. 1315).
16. *CPR 1374–7*, 438.

Chapter 17

1. K. Warner, 'The Adherents of Edmund of Woodstock, Earl of Kent, in March 1330', *English Historical Review*, 126 (2011), 779–805.
2. *CCR 1330–3*, 175.
3. *CPR 1327–30*, 455, 514; *CPR 1330–4*, 69, 84, 123. Alina was at Westminster on 9 February and 21 April 1331: Feet of Fines, CP 25/1/194/11, nos. 35, 42.
4. *CIPM 1327–36*, no. 286; *CCR 1327–30*, 132–3, 139; *CPR 1330–4*, 151.
5. *CPR 1354–8*, 587.
6. TNA, SC 8/42/2091 and 2092; *CCR 1330–3*, 325–6; *CPR 1330–4*, 246; *PROME*, September 1331.
7. *PROME*.
8. DL [Duchy of Lancaster] 10/261; *CChR 1327–41*, 200; *CPR 1330–4*, 333; *CFR 1327–37*, 323–4.

Chapter 18

1. *CPR 1330–4*, 278.
2. M. Vale, *The Princely Court* (2001), 311–13.
3. *CPR 1330–4*, 267, 342, 377, 462; *CPR 1334–8*, 494; *CPR 1367–70*, 219; *CPR 1374–7*, 147.

4. *CPR 1330–4*, 273, 277.

5. *Collectanea et Topographica et Genealogica*, vol. 4, eds. F. Madden, B. Bandinel and J.G. Nichols (1837), 390, 394; *CPR 1330–4, 462*; *CDS*, vol. 5, nos. 1841, 1869, 1938, 3322. Alan Tesdale was said in the parliament of January 1327 to have been Hugh the Younger's chamberlain, though Clement Holditch held this position in 1325/26. John Botiller was Hugh the Younger's steward.

6. P. Dryburgh, 'Living in the Shadows: John of Eltham, Earl of Cornwall (1316–36)', *Fourteenth Century England IX*, ed. J. Bothwell and G. Dodd (2016), 41–2.

7. *Register of Edward the Black Prince*, vol. 4 (1933), 68.

8. *CIPM 1327–36*, no. 646.

9. *CIPM 1347–52*, no. 47; *CIPM 1399–1405*, no. 883.

10. *CFR 1327–37*, 459.

11. 'A Fragment of an Account of Isabel of Lancaster, Nun of Amesbury, 1333–4', ed. R.B. Pugh, in *Festschrift zur Feier des zweihundertjährigen Bestandes des Haus-, Hof- und Staatsarchivs*, vol. 1, ed. L. Santifaller (1949), 489–91, 495–8; *CFR 1327–37*, 431–2.

Chapter 19

1. *CDS 1272–1307*, no. 1011.

2. *CIPM 1352–60*, no. 333, gives the date of their wedding and the date of birth of their eldest son. In about 1328/30, Anne's brother Henry Ferrers had married Edward Despenser's cousin Isabella Verdon, daughter of his mother Eleanor's sister Elizabeth Burgh, and Elizabeth perhaps had something to do with the marriage of her nephew and her son-in-law's sister.

3. *CDS*, vol. 5, no. 3455.

4. *CIPM 1327–36*, no. 559; *CPR 1313–7*, 402; *CPR 1321–4*, 324; *CPR 1330–4*, 63, 440; *CCR 1333–7*, 272–3; *PROME*, December 1332; TNA, SC 8/11/525.

5. *CIPM 1413–18*, nos. 629–30; *CPR 1446–52*, 37.

6. *CCR 1346–9*, 86; *CPR 1348–50*, 412. Blanche of Lancaster (d. 1380) was the eldest child of Maud Chaworth, older half-sister of Hugh Despenser the Younger and his brother Philip I.

7. *Petitions to the Pope 1342–1419*, ed. W.H. Bliss (1896), 364. Henry was also said by the pope to be 'in his tenth year' on 2 August 1354 and in his twenty-seventh year on 3 April 1370 (i.e. still 26), though as these ages place his date of birth more than nine months after his father's death in September 1342, they are impossible.

8. *Petitions to the Pope 1342–1419*, 261; *CPL 1362–1404*, 83.

9. N. Saul, *Richard II* (1997), 102; *ODNB*, citing the St Albans chronicler Thomas Walsingham; Allington-Smith, *Fighting Bishop*, 91; A.K. McHardy, *The Reign of Richard II: From Minority to Tyranny* (2012), 98.

10. Underhill, *For Her Good Estate*, 90.

11. *CPR 1334–8*, 464. Confusingly, this grant refers to the two women as 'daughters of Hugh Despenser the Elder', but this probably means that their brother Huchon was now deemed 'Hugh the Younger', at least to the clerk who recorded this grant. There is no evidence that Hugh the Elder had daughters called Joan and Eleanor, but plenty of evidence that the two women were Hugh the Younger's daughters.

12. *CIPM 1336–46*, no. 132; *CFR 1337–47*, 25.

13. *CPR 1334–8*, 461–2.

14. *CPR 1343–5*, 571.

15. *CPR 1334–8*, 550.

16. *CDS*, vol. 5, nos. 3617, 3634 (it happened again in 1341: nos. 3734–5).
17. TNA, SC 1/54/28.
18. *CPR 1330–4*, 110.
19. *CPR 1334–8*, 464; *CCR 1337–9*, 273.
20. *CCR 1337–9*, 521, Elizabeth and Maurice were married by 28 September 1338: *CIPM 1413–18*, no. 816.
21. J. Smyth, *Lives of the Berkeleys* (1883), vol. 1, 366.
22. *CPL 1305–41*, 541.
23. Underhill, *Good Estate*, 90; Smyth, *Lives*, 366.

Chapter 20

1. W. de Gray Birch, *A History of Margam Abbey* (1897), 307–8; *CCR 1343–6*, 483.
2. *CCR 1349–54*, 322; *CFR 1356–68*, 109; *CPR 1361–4*, 411; *CIPM 1361–5*, no. 459.
3. *CIPM 1347–52*, no. 244.
4. *CPL 1305–41*, 553. Giles' proof of age is in *CIPM 1327–36*, no. 691. His mother Margaret was the sister and co-heir of Gilbert Clare of Thomond (1281–1307), the first husband of Huchon's aunt Isabella Hastings, and was a first cousin of Huchon's mother Eleanor.
5. TNA, C 143/269/9; *CPR 1343–5*, 268. The other seven manors were Martley and Bushley, Worcestershire; Burford, Oxfordshire; Stanford-in-the-Vale, Berkshire (now in Oxfordshire); Ashley, Hampshire; Rotherfield, Sussex; Sodbury, Gloucestershire.
6. *CPR 1327–30*, 85; *CPR 1338–40*, 183. Alina held Compton Dando as a lifetime gift of Ingelram Berenger: *CCR 1313–18*, 264.
7. *CPR 1321–4*, 30; *CPR 1338–40*, 201; *CPR 1340–3*, 216; *CPR 1343–5*, 268; *CFR 1356–68*, 284; TNA, SC 8/195/9741A and B. Huchon's widow Elizabeth held Martley between 1349 and 1359: *CCR 1349–54*, 17–18; *CIPM 1352–60*, no. 523.
8. *CPR 1338–40*, 50.
9. 'Plea Rolls for Staffordshire, 20 Edward II', in *Staffordshire Historical Collections*, vol. 10, part 1, ed. G. Wrottesley (1889), 74–5; Birmingham Archives MS 3688/189; *CCR 1313–8*, 264.
10. *CPR 1334–8*, 550; *CPR 1340–3*, 194, 328; *CDS*, vol. 5, no. 1985.
11. Underhill, *Good Estate*, 52–3, 88–9.

Chapter 21

1. *CDS*, vol. 5, nos. 1985, 3734–5. John of Eltham, earl of Cornwall, whom Huchon had previously served, died in Scotland in 1336.
2. *CIPM 1336–46*, no. 395; Lawrence, 'Power, Ambition', 50; *Early Lincoln Wills 1280–1547*, ed. A. Gibbons (1888), 16.
3. *CIPM 1336–46*, no. 395; *CFR 1337–47*, 301. Huchon was still in Brittany with Edward III on 20 January 1343, and the king praised his 'good service' on 19 November 1342. *CFR 1337–47*, 309; *CPR 1436–41*, 163.
4. *CCR 1339–41*, 223.
5. *CIPM 1361–5*, no. 544.
6. *Early Lincoln Wills*, 23. Hawise was named after her great-grandmother Hawise FitzWarin, mother of Margaret Goushill, who may still have been alive when she was born.
7. *CPL 1342–62*, 588.
8. *Early Lincoln Wills*, 56–7, 99; *CIPM 1384–92*, nos. 1008–9; *CIPM 1392–9*, nos. 1062–3; *CIPM 1413–18*, nos. 154–6; *CIPM 1418–22*, nos. 30–2.

9. *CPR 1334–8*, 464; *CPR 1343–5*, 138, 158; *CCR 1337–9*, 501; *CCR 1349–54*, 285; *CCR 1381–5*, 267–8; *CFR 1383–91*, 86–7, 262–3, 287.
10. *CPR 1343–5*, 571.
11. *CPL 1342–62*, 164, 254.
12. *CCR 1343–6*, 483.
13. M. Burtscher, *The Fitzalans, Earls of Arundel and Surrey* (2008), 43.

Chapter 22

1. *CCR 1346–9*, 86; *CFR 1347–56*, 208; *CPL 1342–62*, 528.
2. *ODNB*.
3. *CIPM 1352–60*, no. 253; *CIPM 1361–5*, no. 322.
4. *CPR 1345–8*, 485–513; G. Wrottesley, *Crécy and Calais From the Original Records in the Public Record Office* (1898), 6, 31–40. The *Brut*, 539, says Huchon took part 'as an erle [earl]'. Philip Despenser II, b. 1313, had a son called Hugh, but he was only born in 1346/7, and the late Edward Despenser the Elder's second son Hugh was born *c.* 1337/8 and was far too young to fight in 1346.
5. M. Livingstone and M. Witzel, *The Road to Crécy: The English Invasion of France, 1346* (2005), 256–9.
6. *CPR 1345–8*, 158, 477.
7. *CPR 1348–50*, 550.
8. *CPR 1343–5*, 378 (steward); *CIPM 1336–46*, no. 469 (attorney); *CIPM 1347–52*, no. 47.
9. *Testamenta Eboracensia: Or, Wills registered at York*, vol. 1, ed. J. Raine (1836), 38–9.
10. *ODNB*.
11. *CIPM 1347–52*, no. 428; *CFR 1347–56*, 109.
12. *CCR 1349–54*, 33.
13. *CFR 1347–56*, 109.
14. Guy Bryan outlived his and Elizabeth's sons Guy the younger (d. 1386) and Philip (d. 1387), and his heirs on his death in 1390 were their granddaughters Philippa and Elizabeth. *CIPM 1384–92*, nos. 211, 352–5, 959–62.
15. *CFR 1347–56*, 208, 378–9; *CPR 1348–50*, 290.
16. *CIPM 1347–52*, nos. 216–17.

Part 4

Chapter 23

1. *CPR 1348–50*, 296; F. Devon, *Issues of the Exchequer*, 163.
2. *CPR 1348–50*, 573; Feet of Fines, CP 25/1/206/25, no. 47.
3. *CCR 1349–54*, 471, 478–9.
4. *CFR 1347–56*, 287; *CIPM 1347–52*, no. 637.
5. *CPR 1348–50*, 516, 518.
6. *CPR 1334–8*, 487; *CPR 1340–3*, 84; *CPR 1350–4*, 299. John Hotham the younger held Fyfield in Essex jointly with Ivetta, with remainder to her brother Henry, later first Lord Scrope of Masham: *CIPM 1347–52*, no. 637, and see http://www.british-history.ac.uk/vch/essex/vol4/pp46–52, accessed 18 January 2019.
7. For example, *CCR 1349–54*, 478. John's father Peter Hotham was presumably the bishop's brother.
8. *CPR 1350–4*, 149; *CCR 1349–54*, 428.
9. *CIPM 1374–7*, no. 56; *CIPM 1377–84*, nos. 220–3.

10. A.R. Bell, A. Curry, A. King and D. Simpkin, *The Soldier in Later Medieval England* (2013), 109.
11. *CIPM 1399–1405*, nos. 601–8.
12. *CIPM 1327–36*, no. 82.
13. *CIPM 1374–7*, no. 56; *CPR 1389–92*, 9; *CDS*, vol. 5, no. 4381; *CCR 1399–1402*, 436–7. Alice's great-uncle John Hotham, bishop of Ely, held Bonby by September 1318: *CCR 1318–23*, 11–12. In 1475, Bonby was given to Edmund Skern, great-great-great-grandson of Alice's first cousin Maud Hotham: *CPR 1467–77*, 520.
14. *CCR 1349–54*, 478–9; *CCR 1364–8*, 425–6.
15. *ODNB*.
16. *CPR 1370–4*, 324.
17. *ODNB*; *Early Lincoln Wills*, 44.

Chapter 24

1. *CIPM 1365–9*, no. 217.
2. R.C. Palmer, *English Law in the Age of the Black Death* (1993), 397 (I owe this reference to www.soc.genealogy.medieval); *CPR 1367–70*, 321.
3. *A Survey of London*, 178.
4. *Register of the Black Prince*, vol. 4, 163, 165.
5. *CPR 1358–61*, 301; medievalsoldier.org, accessed 11 March 2019.
6. *CPL 1362–1404*, 27.
7. *ODNB*.
8. *CIPM 1352–60*, no. 333; *CPR 1354–8*, 637; *CPR 1358–61*, 244; *CCR 1364–8*, 38–9; *CPR 1374–7*, 219.
9. *CIPM 1352–60*, no. 523; *CCR 1349–54*, 11, 17–18, 31; *Monasticon Anglicanum*, vol. 2, 62.
10. W.A. Shaw, *The Knights of England: A Complete Record from the Earliest Time*, vol. 2 (1906), 10. Thomas was still overseas in August 1362: *CAD*, A.13638.
11. *ODNB*.
12. *CPR 1334–8*, 252–3; *CPR 1354–8*, 135; *A Short Calendar of the Feet of Fines for Norfolk*, part 2, 1307–1485, ed. W. Rye (1886), 325.
13. *CIPM 1361–5*, no. 47; *CFR 1356–68*, 193, 211–2; *CFR 1369–77*, 326; *CFR 1377–83*, 303, 321, 363–4; *Feet of Fines for Norfolk*, ed. Rye, part 2, 331.
14. *CFR 1377–83*, 303, 321, 364; *CCR 1381–5*, 167–8; *CIPM 1377–84*, no. 587; *CCR 1349–54*, 89; TNA, C 131/14/2, C 131/184/9 and C 241/133/184.
15. *CPR 1377–81*, 404.

Chapter 25

1. *Register of the Black Prince*, vol. 4, 478.
2. *CIPM 1361–5*, no. 489; *CFR 1356–68*, 277, 284; *CPR 1350–4*, 533.
3. *CAD*, A.11046.
4. *Chronica Johannis de Reading et Anonymi Cantuariensis, 1346–1367*, ed. J. Tait (1914), 175–6.
5. *CFR 1356–68*, 344.
6. Cited in Lawrence, 'Power, Ambition', 32.
7. *CPR 1361–4*, 529.
8. L.J.A. Villalon and D.J. Kagay, *To Win and Lose a Medieval Battle: Nájera (April 3, 1367), A Pyrrhic Victory for the Black Prince* (2017), 312, 318, 347, 348, 419, 593.

Chapter 26

1. *CIPM 1365–9*, no. 131.
2. *CPR 1367–70*, 34, 58.
3. T. Guard, *Chivalry, Kingship and Crusade: The English Experience in the Fourteenth Century* (2013), 73.
4. *CPL 1362–1404*, 27.
5. A.S. Cook, *The Last Months of Chaucer's Earliest Patron* (1916), 37–46.
6. *Last Months*, 64, 72–3.
7. *Testamenta Vetusta*, vol. 1, 70–1.
8. W. Caferro, 'Edward Despenser, The Green Knight and the Lance Formation: Englishmen in Florentine Military Service, 1366–1370', *The Hundred Years War (Part III): Further Considerations*, ed. L.J.A. Villalon and D.J. Kagay (2013), 98–9; medievalsoldier.org, accessed 11 March 2019.
9. Lawrence, 'Power, Ambition', 37.
10. *CPR 1370–4*, 260, 285 (Lombardy); *CIPM 1392–9*, no. 148.
11. Allington-Smith, *Fighting Bishop*, 13.
12. *CPL 1362–1404*, 28.
13. M.A. Devlin, 'An English Knight of the Garter in the Spanish Chapel in Florence', *Speculum*, 4 (1929), 270–81.

Chapter 27

1. He was in England on 23 April 1363, 30 September 1363, 10 February 1364, 20 March 1367, 26 October 1367, 6 October 1370, probably 12 December 1370, August 1372, 10/20 April, 14/20 May and 19 June 1373, 26 June, 18 November and 28 December 1374. *CAD*, A.167, A.11046; *CPR 1361–4*, 328; *CPR 1370–4*, 283–8; *CPR 1374–7*, 30, 31, 371, 438; *CPR 1381–5*, 15; *CPR 1389–92*, 397; *Cartae et Alia Munimenta quae ad Dominium de Glamorgancia Pertinent*, vol. 4, 1333; Feet of Fines, CP 25/1/141/133, no. 12, and CP 25/1/125/66, no. 295. Edward was in Viterbo, Italy on 8 May 1370: *CPR 1399–1401*, 432.
2. Lawrence, 'Power, Ambition', 66.
3. *CPR 1377–81*, 564; *CP*, vol. 4, 276; medievalsoldier.org, accessed 11 March 2019.
4. *Monasticon Anglicanum*, 62.
5. *Monasticon Anglicanum*, 62.
6. *CIPM 1422–7*, no. 774.
7. *John of Gaunt's Register 1371–75*, no. 1778.
8. *CPR 1377–81*, 538.
9. John I's IPM of February/May 1380 gives his eldest son's date of birth: *CIPM 1377–84*, nos. 179–89. *CFR 1413–22*, 166–7, lists the Arundel siblings in what must be birth order: Joan, countess of Hereford; Richard, earl of Arundel; Alice, countess of Kent; John I; and lastly Thomas, archbishop of Canterbury, who was 20 years old in August 1373. John I and Eleanor Maltravers were already married or betrothed on 4 August 1357 and certainly married by 9 February 1359: *CPR 1354–8*, 595; Feet of Fines, CP 25/1/288/47, no. 637. She was the heir of her grandfather John, Lord Maltravers, and at his IPM in February 1364 was said to be 19 years old: *CIPM 1361–5*, no. 592. As well as their eldest son and heir John II, John I and Eleanor had younger sons Richard, William, Edward and Henry and daughters Joan and Margaret; see *TV*, 95.
10. Saul, *Richard II*, 18.

11. *CPR 1377–81*, 538; *CFR 1405–13*, 112–13. King's Stanley was held by Adam Despenser in the thirteenth century: *CChR 1226–57*, 414.
12. *CIPM 1365–9*, no.140; *CIPM 1374–7*, no. 105; *CIPM 1377–84*, nos. 311–15; *CIPM 1384–92*, no. 340; *CPR 1374–7*, 350, 358; *CCR 1374–7*, 395–6, 414–15, 423; *CPR 1377–81*, 443; *CCR 1381–5*, 4, 36.
13. *TV*, 175; *Anglo-Norman Letters and Petitions from All Souls MS 182*, ed. M.D. Legge (1941), no. 45; *CIPM 1413–8*, nos. 34–42.
14. *CIPM 1374–7*, no. 209.
15. *CPR 1370–4*, 283, 285, 287, 329, 481–2; *CPR 1374–7*, 94–5; *CPR 1381–5*, 15; *CPR 1389–92*, 397; *ODNB*; D. Nicolle, *The Great Chevauchée: John of Gaunt's Raid on France 1373* (2011). Edward was in England on 19 June 1373: Feet of Fines, CP 25/1/125/66, no. 295.
16. *CPR 1377–81*, 186, calling Thomas 'Edward'.
17. *John of Gaunt's Register 1379–83*, ed. E.C. Lodge and R. Somerville (1937), 50.

Chapter 28

1. Caferro, 'Green Knight', 98–101.
2. *CPR 1377–81*, 222.
3. TNA, C 241/155/32; Allington-Smith, *Fighting Bishop*, 4.
4. *CPL 1362–1404*, 135–6.
5. *CIPM 1374–7*, no. 56; *Early Lincoln Wills*, 98; *CFR 1369–77*, 275.
6. *CPR 1374–7*, 15, 34–5; http://www.historyofparliamentonline.org/volume/1386–1421/member/trussell-sir-john-1349–1424, accessed 1 October 2018.
7. *CCR 1377–81*, 200, 214–5, and see the History of Parliament page above.
8. History of Parliament page; *CIPM 1377–84*, nos. 220–3; *Early Lincoln Wills*, 98.
9. Bell et al, *Soldier in Later Medieval England*, 109.
10. *CFR 1369–77*, 308, 326; *CIPM 1374–7*, no. 208; he died on 'Thursday after the Assumption last'. John Coroner came from Leverington in Cambridgeshire: *CPR 1367–70*, 152; *CCR 1369–74*, 340.
11. *CIPM 1374–7*, no. 209.
12. *Early Lincoln Wills*, 44.

Part 5

Chapter 29

1. TNA, SC 8/106/5275 and SC 8/158/7884; *CPR 1385–9*, 416; *CFR 1377–83*, 46.
2. TNA, SC 8/107/5316; SC 8/85/4206.
3. *CPR 1374–7*, 492–3; *CCR 1374–7*, 413, 511, 551.
4. *CPR 1377–81*, 92.
5. *CCR 1385–9*, 339; TNA, C 241/175/82, C 131/203/42 and 43, and SC 8/113/5634.
6. medievalsoldier.org, accessed 11 March 2019 (Edmund alive 1381); *CP*, vol. 1, 243–4 note d (descendants); *John of Gaunt's Register 1371–1375*, nos. 181, 1607 (Deincourt); B.W. Greenfield, 'Meriet of Meriet and of Hestercombe', *Proceedings of the Somersetshire Archaeological and Natural History Society*, 28 (1882), 99–215 (at 154–5, 160–1). For the legal case of 1382, see Douglas Richardson's post 'List of Children for Sir Edmund de Arundel & Sibyl de Montagu' on soc.genealogy.medieval, and http://www.medievalgenealogy.org.uk/cp/arundel.shtml, both accessed 8 March 2019. For Philippa Sergeaux and her family, see *CIPM 1392–9*, nos. 421–3, 1093; *CIPM*

1399–1405, nos. 31–8. In 1396, Philippa officially surrendered any claim to Arundel lands: *CCR 1396–9*, 72. Her second husband was Sir John Cornwall (d. 1443), who married secondly John of Gaunt's daughter Elizabeth of Lancaster in 1400. Elizabeth Arundel's first husband Leonard Carew was born on 23 April 1342 (*CIPM 1361–5*, no. 613) and her second, John Meriet, on 24 March 1346 (*CIPM 1365–9*, no. 269).

7. Lawrence, 'Power, Ambition', 175.
8. *CFR 1377–83*, 175, 204; *CIPM 1377–84*, nos. 220–3; *Early Lincoln Wills*, 98.
9. *CPR 1377–81*, 410.
10. *CPR 1381–5*, 130–1.
11. *CPR 1377–81*, 404.
12. *CChR 1300–26*, 448–51, 466.
13. *John of Gaunt's Register 1379–83*, 50.
14. *CPR 1377–81*, 225; *CPR 1381–5*, 364. Thomas was a great-great-great-grandson of Edward I, and Constance was Edward's great-great-granddaughter, making them third cousins once removed.
15. *CPR 1405–8*, 16, 227.
16. *CPR 1377–81*, 564.
17. *The Chronica Maiora of Thomas Walsingham, 1376–1422*, trans. D. Preest (2005), 96–101; *The Anonimalle Chronicle 1333–81*, ed. V.H. Galbraith (1927), 131–2; *Historiae Vitae et Regni Ricardi Secundi*, ed. G. Stow (1977), 57. Elizabeth's brother-in-law Sir Hugh Hastings intended to go to Brittany with John Arundel I in 1379: A. Goodman, 'The Military Subcontracts of Sir Hugh Hastings, 1380', *English Historical Review,* 95 (1980), 115.
18. *CPR 1377–81*, 452–3.
19. *CCR 1381–5*, 597 (Burley); *Chronica Maiora*, 145–6 (Henry).
20. *CChR 1341–1417*, 230; *CIM 1348–77*, no. 969.
21. *CIPM 1377–84*, nos. 335–8; TNA, C 136/14/7; *CFR 1377–83*, 260.
22. *Early Lincoln Wills*, 98.
23. TNA, C 143/357/19.
24. *CIPM 1377–84*, no. 335; *CFR 1377–83*, 277–8; *CPR 1401–5*, 64. Edward's widow Elizabeth Burghersh held one-third of Essendine in dower. Essendine is four miles from Stamford.
25. *CFR 1377–83*, 256; *CPR 1377–81*, 225. Buckland and Singleborough passed to Edward the Elder in 1334 from Idonea Leyburne: *CIPM 1327–36*, no. 559.

Chapter 30

1. *Chronica Maiora*, 145–7.
2. *CIPM 1399–1405*, nos. 489–509, 855.
3. *CFR 1377–83*, 303; *CFR 1383–91*, 86–7; *CIPM 1377–84*, nos. 587–90; J. Weever, *Antient Funeral Monuments* (1631), 487. *CIPM 1377–84*, nos. 581–6, is Amaury St Amand's IPM; his son Amaury, aged '30 and more' or '40 and more', was his heir.
4. *Somerset Medieval Wills 1383–1500*, ed. F. W. Weaver (1903), 289. Elizabeth married Wyth before 29 May 1372: *Wykeham's Register*, vol. 2, ed. T.F. Kirby (1899), 162–3.
5. *CPR 1381–5*, 140–1, 257.
6. *CIPM 1336–46*, nos. 199, 283, 374; *CIPM 1352–60*, nos. 537, 559, 595.
7. *ANLP*, no. 55 (p. 103).
8. *CIPM 1405–13*, nos. 1036–43.
9. *CCR 1385–9*, 614.
10. TNA, SC 8/182/9094. By the time of Hugh's death in 1401, he and Sybil no longer held Little Barford; his IPM states that he held nothing in Bedfordshire. *CIPM 1399–1405*, no. 608.

11. https://www.british-history.ac.uk/vch/beds/vol2/pp206–209, accessed 3 March 2019.
12. TNA, C 41/173/98 (debt); *Early Lincoln Wills*, 98 (Hugh's will of 1400, mentioning Elizabeth; Hugh's sister Anne was named as his heir when he died in 1401 so Elizabeth must have died before her father).
13. *CIPM 1384–92*, nos. 406–7, 897; *CIPM 1399–1405*, nos. 528, 854, 883–4. The infant's godfathers were John, abbot of Selby and Thomas, abbot of Drax. Edward was the heir of his great-uncle John Hastings (1329/31–93), elder son of Hugh Hastings I (d. 1347) and grandson of Isabella Despenser (d. 1334).

Chapter 31

1. *Foedera 1377–83*, 84, 164; *Issues of the Exchequer*, 222–3; *PROME*; McHardy, *Reign of Richard II*, 110–13; Allington-Smith, *Fighting Bishop*, 54–78.
2. *CPR 1381–5*, 502.
3. *CIPM 1384–92*, nos. 951–2; *CIPM 1399–1405*, nos. 1116–23. Ditton was the manor where John Arundel II's grandparents Richard, earl of Arundel and Eleanor of Lancaster married in February 1345, and in 1385 was held by Margery, Lady Molyns. Datchet had formerly been a Despenser manor, forfeited by Hugh the Elder in 1326, and in 1385 was also held by Lady Molyns. Elizabeth's husband went on campaign to Scotland in March 1384, aged 19, and fought overseas in 1387 and 1388. His younger brother William Arundel fought overseas in 1390. See medievalsoldier.org, accessed 11 March 2019.
4. Goodman, 'Military Subcontracts', 115.
5. *CIPM 1384–92*, nos. 406–7; *CIPM 1422–7*, nos. 774–80; Norfolk Record Office MR 317A 242 × 5, available on the National Archives website.
6. A. Luttrell, 'English Levantine Crusaders, 1363–1367', *Renaissance Studies*, 2 (1988), 143–53, at 150 note 61.
7. *ANLP*, nos. 297, 307, pp. 360–1, 372–3. At least one of the letters was written after September 1399, as it refers to Philippa's brother Henry, who became king of England that month, as Bishop Henry's 'very sovereign liege lord'.
8. *Oeuvres de Froissart*, ed. K. de Lettenhove, vol. 11 (1870), 327.
9. *CPR 1381–5*, 274; *CPR 1385–9*, 92; *CCR 1385–9*, 496–7, 614; *CPR 1389–92*, 11, 49, 119, 168; *CDS*, vol. 5, nos. 4118, 4162, 4207–14; *Issues of the Exchequer*, 234; *The Diplomatic Correspondence of Richard II*, ed. E. Perroy (1933), no. 61; *Soldier in Later Medieval England*, 109, 135; Feet of Fines CP/25/1/278/145, no. 3; TNA, E 101/73/2/31 and C 148/129; medievalsoldier.org, accessed 11 March 2019. Hugh was in England on 4 December 1384, 26 April 1385 and 24 October 1385, and was sent to Flanders on 24 November 1385: *CPR 1381–5*, 487, 502; *CPR 1385–9*, 41, 92.
10. *CPR 1389–92*, 481.
11. H.E.L. Collins, *The Order of the Garter 1348–1361: Chivalry and Politics in Late Medieval England* (2000), 64, 101; *Soldier in Later Medieval England*, 27.
12. *CPR 1385–9*, 416.

Chapter 32

1. McHardy, *Reign of Richard II*, 264–5.
2. *CIPM 1384–92*, nos. 792–5.
3. *The Westminster Chronicle 1381–1394*, ed. and trans. L.C. Hector and B.F. Harvey (1982), 440–1.

4. *Early Lincoln Wills*, 25; P. Payne and C. Barron, 'The Letters and Life of Elizabeth Despenser, Lady Zouche (d. 1408)', *Nottingham Medieval Studies*, 4 (1997), 131; *CPR 1399–1401*, 168.
5. *CCR 1389–92*, 213, 370; *CPR 1389–92*, 430; *CFR 1383–91*, 333.
6. *CIPM 1392–9*, no. 701.
7. *CPR 1374–7*, 134, 147; *CChR 1341–1417*, 230; *CIM 1348–77*, no. 969.
8. *CCR 1381–5*, 623.
9. *CCR 1396–9*, 232; *CPR 1401–5*, 340.
10. Payne and Barron, 'Letters and Life', 150.
11. *CPR 1377–81*, 494.
12. *CPL 1362–1404*, 375.
13. Another reason may have been Bishop Henry's feud with the prior of Walsingham, Norfolk, at the end of the 1380s: Thomas Morley was appointed one of the custodians of the priory after Henry removed the prior. *CPR 1389–92*, 36, 73–4; TNA, SC 8/212/10588 and SC 8/215/10750. Henry was the supervisor of the will of Thomas Morley's father William (1319–79), so had known the Morley family for a while; *ODNB*.
14. *CFR 1383–91*, 346.
15. *CPR 1389–92*, 413; M. Lawrence, ''Too Flattering Sweet to be Substantial'? The Last Months of Thomas, Lord Despenser', *Fourteenth Century England IV*, ed. J.S. Hamilton (2006), 147–8 note 11.
16. TNA PROB 11/153, *TV*, 134–5.
17. *CIPM 1413–18*, no. 624; *CPR 1391–6*, 302; *CPR 1401–5*, 321; *CPL 1398–1404*, 544.
18. *CCR 1399–1401*, 55.
19. Lawrence, 'Flattering Sweet', 149, 156–7, for the inventory; my translations.
20. *CPR 1399–1401*, 223–4. A censer was a container for burning incense; *agnus dei* means 'lamb of god', and was a small disc of wax impressed with the figure of a lamb and blessed by the pope, often worn suspended around the neck.
21. *CPR 1391–6*, 341.
22. *CPR 1391–6*, 384, 386, 483.
23. *CPR 1391–6*, 384, 427, 483; *CCR 1392–6*, 204–5; Saul, *Richard II*, 472–3 (itinerary).
24. *CChR 1341–1417*, 347–8.
25. *ANLP*, no. 3 (pp. 47–8). Elizabeth Zouche's sister-in-law from her first marriage, Margaret Arundel, had been an attendant of Anne of Bohemia, and on 11 August 1394 a few days after the queen's funeral, Richard II gave Margaret a grant of 40 marks a year in gratitude for her good service to her. *CPR 1391–6*, 518.

Chapter 33

1. Lawrence, 'Power, Ambition', 67.
2. *CIPM 1392–9*, nos. 701–40; *CCR 1396–9*, 3.
3. *Early Lincoln Wills*, 93.
4. *CIPM 1399–1405*, nos. 2, 884.
5. *CPR 1399–1401*, 336; *Cardiff Records*, vol. 1, ed. J.H. Matthews (1898), 31–2. Thomas was at Sherston in Wiltshire on 1 October 1396, *CPR 1399–1401*, 182–3. The Despensers' manor of Sherston had two 'watermills which cannot grind in summer': *CIPM 1352–60*, no. 523.
6. *Monasticon*, vol. 2, 62.
7. *CPR 1396–9*, 588.

8. *ANLP*, nos. 43, 318 (pp. 91, 383–4). Elizabeth Audley was a daughter of Henry, Lord Beaumont (d. 1340), and the widow of Nicholas, Lord Audley (*c.* 1328/9–91). Elizabeth made her will on 30 September 1400 and died on 27 October 1400: *TV*, 152; *CIPM 1399–1405*, no. 477. Her heir was Henry Beaumont, b. 1381, great-grandson of her brother John Beaumont (1317/18–42). Her older sister Isabella, duchess of Lancaster (*c.* 1315/20–1359/60), was the mother-in-law of John of Gaunt from his first marriage, and the maternal grandmother of King Henry IV.

9. *CCR 1402–5*, 522.

Chapter 34

1. *CPR 1396–9*, 245.
2. *CChR 1341–1417*, 369.
3. *CPR 1396–9*, 219, 224.
4. Saul, *Richard II*, 473; A. Dunn, *The Politics of Magnate Power in England and Wales 1389–1413* (2003), 140.
5. Philippa's mother Joan Burghersh, Lady Mohun, who died in 1404 when she was at least 80, was the sister of Elizabeth's father Bartholomew, d. 1369. Philippa was the youngest of three daughters, and her eldest sister Elizabeth Mohun was countess of Salisbury by marriage to William Montacute. *CFR 1399–1405*, 308–9, 321.
6. *ODNB*.
7. *CPR 1396–9*, 520, 545.

Chapter 35

1. Dunn, *Politics of Magnate Power*, 141.
2. *ODNB*.
3. *ANLP*, no. 287 (pp. 347–8).
4. *CCR 1399–1402*, 13; *CPR 1399–1401*, 92, 271; TNA, E 101/320/21 and 22.
5. *ANLP*, nos. 228, 237 (pp. 294–5, 303).
6. *CCR 1396–9*, 28.
7. *PROME*.
8. *Chronicles of the Revolution, 1397–1400: The Reign of Richard II*, ed. C. Given-Wilson (1993), 160.
9. *ODNB*; Lawrence, 'Too Flattering Sweet', 154.

Chapter 36

1. *Foedera 1397–1413*, 120.
2. *Chronicque de la Traison et Mort de Richart Deux Roy Dengleterre*, ed. B. Williams (1846), 243–4.
3. *CIPM 1413–18*, nos. 278–9; *Brut*, 361; *Chronicles of the Revolution*, 228. His widow Constance's IPM in Wales in 1416 gives 13 January 1400 as the date of Thomas's death, but the jurors in Nottinghamshire and Wiltshire gave the 5th: *CIPM 1413–18*, nos. 621–2, 625.
4. *CPR 1399–1401*, 188, 197, 223–4, 226.
5. *CPR 1399–1401*, 330; *CPR 1401–5*, 321; *CIPM 1413–18*, no. 624; TNA, E 199/27/8 and SC 8/342/16111.
6. *CCR 1399–1402*, 41; *TV*, 174.

7. Lawrence, 'Flattering Sweet', 155.
8. *CPR 1399–1401*, 216.
9. *ANLP*, no. 45 (pp. 92–3).
10. *ANLP*, nos. 1, 64 (pp. 45–6, 113–5); Allington-Smith, *Fighting Bishop*, 124–5.
11. *ODNB*.
12. *CFR 1399–1405*, 48, 104; *CPR 1399–1401*, 204–5.
13. Shaw, *Knights of England*, vol. 1, 129.
14. *ANLP*, no. 62 (pp. 110–12); Allington-Smith, *Fighting Bishop*, 128–9.

Part 6

Chapter 37

1. *CIPM 1413–18*, no. 184.
2. Constance's dower lands are listed in *CPR 1405–8*, 4 (she held the castles of Llantrisant and Kenfeg, but not Cardiff); *ANLP*, no. 225 (p. 291); the index ascribes the letter to Constance.
3. *Early Lincoln Wills*, 98–9.
4. Cheshire Archives DLL 1/6, on the National Archives website; *CCR 1401–5*, 516.
5. *CIPM 1399–1405*, nos. 601–8; TNA, C 1/6/334 (executor); *CCR 1402–5*, 122 (dower); *CFR 1399–1405*, 154, 166 (lands and heir). *CCR 1413–19*, 242, says wrongly that Hugh died on 12 December 1399.
6. *CIPM 1413–18*, no. 392; *CCR 1413–19*, 228; *CFR 1413–22*, 225–6, 228, 241.
7. *CPR 1381–5*, 562; *CPR 1399–1405*, 84, 135; *CIPM 1399–1405*, nos. 416–18; *CIPM 1413–18*, nos. 154–6; *Early Lincoln Wills*, 99; J. Gage, *The History and Antiquities of Suffolk: Thingoe Hundred* (1838), 8.
8. *TV*, 153–5.
9. *Complete Peerage*, vol. 8, 54. In later years, Richard was also given the title of count of Aumale.
10. *Monasticon*, 62.
11. *Issues of the Exchequer*, 300.
12. *CPR 1401–5*, 235; TNA, SC 8/172/8595.
13. *CIPM 1399–1405*, nos. 974–80.
14. *CPR 1401–5*, 478.
15. *PROME*, January 1431 parliament.
16. *Monasticon*, 62.

Chapter 38

1. Payne and Barron, 'Letters and Life', 131, 134–5, 138, 149–52 (modernised spelling).
2. E. Rickert, 'Some English Personal Letters of 1402', *The Review of English Studies*, vol. 8, no. 31 (1932), 258–9; 'Letters and Life', 143, 149–52 (modernised spelling).
3. 'Letters and Life', 150–1, modernised spelling.
4. I. Mortimer, *The Fears of Henry IV: The Life of England's Self-Made King* (2007), 260.
5. *ANLP*, nos. 230, 235 (pp. 296, 300).
6. TNA, SC 8/231/11526; *CCR 1401–5*, 435–6; *CCR 1405–9*, 207; *CPR 1401–5*, 496; *CPR 1405–8*, 4, 107.
7. E.H. Martin, *A History of the Manor of Westhope, Co. Salop* (1909), 21, wrongly identifying Eleanor Maltravers as her mother-in-law Eleanor of Lancaster, countess of

Endnotes

Arundel, who died in 1372. Alice, countess of Kent (*c.* 1348/9–1416), John Arundel I's sister, was the mother of Constance Despenser's lover Edmund Holland.

8. *CFR 1399–1405*, 303, 309–10; *CCR 1405–9*, 164.
9. Payne and Barron, 'Letters and Life', 148.
10. TNA, SC 8/23/1109; SC 8/153/7637; *Rotuli Parliamentorum*, vol. 3 (1783), 565–6; *CPL 1404–15*, 71.
11. 'Letters and Life', 144.
12. *CFR 1405–13*, 78; *CFR 1413–22*, 226.
13. *CIPM 1405–13*, nos. 1036–43; *CFR 1405–13*, 247, 257; *CCR 1413–19*, 242; *CFR 1413–22*, 226; some of these entries say that he died on 3 March.

Chapter 39

1. *CIPM 1427–32*, no. 312.
2. *CIPM 1405–13*, no. 389; *CFR 1413–22*, 120.
3. 'Letters and Life', 137, 144–5.
4. *ODNB*.
5. *TV*, 174–5; Lawrence, 'Power, Ambition', 151. *CCR 1413–19*, 241–2, and *CIPM 1413–18*, no. 625, both say that Elizabeth died on 26 July 1411, but it was certainly 26 July 1409: *CFR 1405–13*, 124.
6. *CIPM 1437–42*, 46–7.
7. *CIPM 1405–13*, nos. 278–91.

Chapter 40

1. Ralph Neville and Joan Beaufort married *c.* November 1396. The chronicle of Tewkesbury Abbey says that Richard Despenser's wife Eleanor was their eldest daughter, though wrongly calls her 'Elizabeth': *Monasticon*, 62. The next Neville sister was Katherine Mowbray, duchess of Norfolk, old enough to give birth in September 1415 so almost certainly born before 1400, and the eldest brother was Richard, earl of Salisbury. Unless he was named after a godfather, Richard Neville's name implies that he was born before Richard II's deposition in September 1399. Eleanor Neville married Richard Despenser in July 1411 and Katherine married John Mowbray in January 1412, which tends to confirm that Eleanor was older than Katherine, unless perhaps they were twins.
2. *CPL 1404–15*, 128–9.
3. *CIPM 1405–13*, nos. 844–60 (Richard Beauchamp was 'aged 14 years and more' in June 1411); *TV*, 171–2. William Beauchamp of Abergavenny and the earl of Arundel's daughter Joan had a daughter, Joan the younger (d. 1430), who married James Butler, earl of Ormond, and was the great-great-grandmother of Henry VIII's second queen, Anne Boleyn. Another daughter, Elizabeth, is mentioned in Abergavenny's will.
4. *CIPM 1413–18*, nos. 34–42; *CFR 1405–13*, 248.
5. Shaw, *The Knights of England*, vol. 1, 129; *CP*, vol. 1, 26; *ODNB* (snow).
6. *Monasticon*, 62. *CP*, vol. 4, 282, copies this date though does not cite the source.
7. *CIPM 1413–18*, nos. 278–9, 632; *CCR 1413–19*, 133–4, 175; *CPR 1413–16*, 192–3, 263. Northamptonshire Archives W(A) box 1/parcel XI/no. 5/d, available on the National Archives website, is the inquisition.
8. *CIPM 1413–18*, no. 632 (dower, and see also *CPR 1446–52*, 87); *CFR 1471–85*, 38 (death).

9. *CIPM 1405–13*, nos. 844–60.
10. TNA, SC 8/32/1575; *CPR 1413–16*, 286.
11. *CPR 1413–16*, 347.
12. *Monasticon*, 63; *CP*, vol. 1, 27; *CIPM 1432–7*, nos. 214–15, 500–19.
13. *Monasticon*, 62.
14. *CPR 1416–22*, 238–9; *CIPM 1413–18*, nos. 654–71.
15. *CIPM 1413–18*, nos. 594–6.
16. *CIPM 1413–18*, nos. 621–31; *CCR 1413–19*, 339–40; *CFR 1413–22*, 145, 185.
17. *Monasticon*, 62–3.

Chapter 41

1. *Foedera 1420–41*, 63.
2. *CP*, vol. 1, 27.
3. M. Lawrence, 'Secular Patronage and Religious Devotion: The Despensers and St Mary's Abbey, Tewkesbury', *Fourteenth Century England V*, ed. N. Saul (2008), 89; J.C. Ward, *English Noblewomen in the Later Middle Ages* (1992), 145–6.
4. *CIPM 1413–18*, no. 237; *CIPM 1418–22*, nos. 836–54; *CPL 1398–1404*, 609; J. Barker, *Agincourt: The King, the Campaign, the Battle* (2005), 227, 283.
5. *CPR 1422–9*, 136, 183; *CIPM 1422–27*, nos. 307–12; *CP*, vol. 4, 291 note f; Weever, *Antient Funeral Monuments*, 487.
6. *CIPM 1418–22*, nos. 811–23.
7. *Monasticon*, 63; Barker, *Agincourt*, 159; *CPR 1436–41*, 562; *CCR 1454–61*, 230. John Cornwall was the son of Elizabeth of Lancaster, Constance Despenser's first cousin. There is no IPM for Beauchamp of Worcester, presumably because he never held his inheritance as it was all in his mother's hands.
8. *Monasticon*, 63; Lawrence, 'Secular Patronage', 89.
9. *ODNB*.
10. She was in Cardiff on 4 May and 13 June 1423, for example: *CPR 1446–52*, 268; *Cardiff Records*, vol. 1, 37–8.
11. *CPR 1422–9*, 136.
12. K.B. McFarlane, *The Nobility of Later Medieval England* (1973), 193.
13. C. Ross, 'The Household Accounts of Elizabeth Berkeley, Countess of Warwick, 1420–1', *Transactions of the Bristol and Gloucestershire Archaeological Society*, 70 (1951), 81–105; *The Cultural Patronage of Medieval Women*, ed. J. Hall McCash (1996), 233.
14. *TV*, 232; 'The Last Will and Testament of Richard Beauchamp, Earle of Warwicke and Aumarle', in *Historia Vitae et Regni Ricardi II Angliae Regis*, ed. T. Hearne (1729), 243.
15. Ward, *English Noblewomen*, 109–10.
16. Ross, 'Household Accounts', 87, 89.
17. H.N. MacCracken, 'The Earl of Warwick's Virelai', *Publications of the Modern Language Association of America*, 22 (1907), 597–607.
18. 'Virelai', 605–6, modernised spelling.
19. *CPR 1422–9*, 385; *Brut*, 472.
20. Ross, 'Household Accounts', 105; *CCR 1429–35*, 249.
21. *CPR 1446–52*, 148, 451; *Brut*, 472; *Monasticon,* 63.
22. Feet of Fines CP/25/1/291/65, no. 15.
23. *Cardiff Records*, vol. 1, 37–8.

Chapter 42

1. *ODNB*. She was called 'Elizabet Bieuchamp, damsel, of the diocese of Worcester' on 13 September 1423: *CPL 1417–31*, 305, 309. Edward Neville's eldest sister Eleanor, later countess of Northumberland, married Elizabeth's uncle Richard Despenser in 1411. Edward's mistress and second wife Katherine Howard was a granddaughter of Thomas Mowbray (d. 1399), first duke of Norfolk, and sister of John Howard, duke of Norfolk, killed fighting for Richard III at Bosworth in 1485.
2. *CIPM 1437–42*, nos. 307–25. The chronicle of Tewkesbury Abbey (*Monasticon*, 63) gives 22 March 1424 as his date of birth, but this was only four months after Isabelle and Warwick's wedding.
3. *The Fifty Earliest English Wills in the Court of Probate, London, 1387–1439*, ed. F.J. Furnivall (1882), 118; 'Last Will and Testament', *Historia Vitae et Regni*, 244–5.
4. *PROME*.
5. *ODNB*; Shaw, *Knights of England*, 130–2; R.A. Griffiths, *The Reign of King Henry VI: The Exercise of Royal Authority, 1422–1461* (1981), 80–1.
6. *ODNB*.
7. *CPR 1422–9*, 361; *CCR 1422–9*, 277.
8. *Monasticon*, 63.
9. *CIPM 1422–7*, nos. 774–80; *CFR 1422–30*, 136.
10. *ODNB*.
11. SC 8/295/14702.
12. *Collections for a History of Staffordshire*, ed. The William Salt Archaeological Society, new series, vol. 12 (1909), 124.
13. *CP*, vol. 5, 317–8; *CIPM 1432–7*, nos. 480–89.
14. McCash, *Cultural Patronage of Medieval Women*, 246–7.

Chapter 43

1. *Foedera 1420–41*, 399; D. Grummitt, *Henry VI* (2015), 83.
2. J. Watts, *Henry VI and the Politics of Kingship* (1999), 196.
3. *CPL 1427–47*, 514–15, and see *CPL 1431–47*, 465. Henry VI pardoned them for the unlicenced marriage in March 1438, *CPR 1436–41*, 160. Thomas Ros (d. 1430) was the younger brother and heir of John Ros (d. 1421), first husband of Margery Despenser, later Wentworth.
4. https://www.historytoday.com/ct-allmand/coronations-henry-vi, accessed 27 April 2019.
5. *PROME*, 1431 parliament.
6. *Monasticon*, 62–3, and see also below. *CPL 1427–47*, 175, states that Alianore and James married in the knowledge that they were related within prohibited degrees, but did not consummate their marriage until after they had received papal absolution. James was born in Derby on 26 December 1397: *CIPM 1418–22*, no. 670.
7. McFarlane, *Nobility*, 87.
8. *Monasticon*, 63; R. Davies, *Lords and Lordship in the British Isles in the Late Middle Ages* (2009), 152, says that a Warwick wedding took place in Abergavenny in 1435/6, though the details are garbled: the book claims that the earl of Warwick's sister Anne (he had no sister of this name) married Lord Despenser (who was Warwick and Isabelle's son Henry Beauchamp).
9. *CIPM 1432–7*, nos. 500–19. Joan dictated a long will twenty months before her death: *TV*, 224–30.
10. 'Last Will and Testament', *Historia Vitae et Regni*, 240–49.

Chapter 44

1. *CPR 1436–41*, 363; *TV*, 231–3.
2. *CPR 1436–41*, 574.
3. *Fifty Earliest English Wills*, 116–19.
4. *CPR 1436–41*, 360; *CFR 1437–45*, 77, 233.
5. *Earliest English Wills*, 118 (modernised spelling).
6. *CFR 1437–45*, 104–5; *CIPM 1437–42*, nos. 307–30.
7. *Complete Peerage,* vol. 1, 27. The *Brut* chronicle (p. 475) states wrongly that Isabelle was buried in Warwick next to her second husband.
8. W.E. Hampton, *Memorials of the Wars of the Roses: A Biographical Guide* (1979), 68.
9. *CPR 1441–6*, 29.
10. *Monasticon*, 63. Confusingly, the chronicle talks of 'Lady Anne, sister of Lady Isabelle the countess, and aunt of Lord Henry', and the wife of 'Lord Hugh Audley'. Alianore's husband was actually called James Tuchet, Lord Audley.
11. C. Hardyment, *Malory: The Knight who Became King Arthur's Chronicler* (2005), 240.
12. *CFR 144–52*, 2–3; *CIPM 1442–7*, nos. 433–60.
13. Hicks, 'Despenser Forfeitures', especially 184, 187; M. Hicks, 'Cement or Solvent? Kinship and Politics in Late Medieval England: The Case of the Nevilles', *History*, 83 (1998), 42–3.
14. *PROME*.
15. *CPL 1447–55*, 151.
16. *CPR 1485–94*, 6, 64.
17. *CP*, vol. 4, 292.

Select Bibliography

Primary Sources

A Descriptive Catalogue of Ancient Deeds, ed. H.C. Maxwell, 6 vols. (1890–1915)
Adae Murimuth Continuatio Chronicarum, ed. E.M. Thompson (1889)
Anglo-Norman Letters and Petitions from All Souls MS 182, ed. M.D. Legge (1941)
Annales Londonienses 1195–1330, in ed. W. Stubbs, *Chronicles of the Reigns of Edward I and Edward II*, vol. 1 (1882)
Annales Monastici, ed. H.R. Luard. vol. 4 (1869)
Annales Paulini 1307–1340, in Stubbs, *Chronicles*, vol. 1
The Anonimalle Chronicle 1307 to 1334, eds. W.R. Childs and J. Taylor (1991)
The Anonimalle Chronicle 1333–81, ed. V.H. Galbraith (1927; reprinted 1970)
The Brut or the Chronicles of England, 2 parts, ed. F.W.D. Brie (1906–8)
Calendar of Chancery Warrants, 1244 –1326, 1 vol. (1927)
Calendar of the Charter Rolls, 1226 –1417, 5 vols. (1903–16)
Calendar of the Close Rolls, 1234–1441, 50 vols. (1898–1937)
Calendar of Documents Relating to Scotland, 1272–1509, 5 vols., ed. J. Bain (1884–8)
Calendar of Early Mayor's Court Rolls, 1298–1307, ed. A.H. Thomas (1924)
Calendar of Entries in the Papal Registers Relating to Great Britain and Ireland: Papal Letters, ed. W.H. Bliss and J.A. Twemlow, 1198–1455, 10 vols. (1893–1915)
Calendar of the Fine Rolls, 1272–1452, 16 vols. (1911–39)
Calendar of Inquisitions Post Mortem, 1216–1447, 26 vols. (1906–2010)
Calendar of Memoranda Rolls (Exchequer): Michaelmas 1326–Michaelmas 1327 (1968)
Calendar of the Patent Rolls, 1232–1441, 44 vols. (1891–1907)
Calendar of Various Chancery Rolls 1277–1326 (1912)
Calendar of Wills Proved and Enrolled in the Court of Husting, London, parts 1 and 2, 1258–1358 and 1358–1688 (1889–90).
Cardiff Records, vol. 1, ed. J.H. Matthews (1898)
Cartae et Alia Munimenta quae ad Dominium de Glamorgancia Pertinent, vols. 3 and 4 (1910)
Chronica Johannis de Reading et Anonymi Cantuariensis, 1346–1367, ed. J. Tait (1914)
The Chronica Maiora of Thomas Walsingham, 1376–1422, trans. D. Preest (2005)
The Chronicle of Adam Usk, 1377–1421, ed. C. Given-Wilson (1997)
The Chronicle of Lanercost 1272–1346, ed. H. Maxwell (1913)
The Chronicle of Pierre de Langtoft, vol. 2, ed. T. Wright (1868)
Chronicles of the Revolution, 1397–1400: The Reign of Richard II, ed. C. Given-Wilson (1993)
Chronicon Galfridi de Baker de Swynebroke, ed. E.M. Thompson (1889)

Chronicque de la Traison et Mort de Richart Deux Roy Dengleterre, ed. B. Williams (1846)

Collectanea Topographica et Genealogica, vol. 4, eds. F. Madden, B. Bandinel and J.G. Nichols (1837)

Croniques de London, ed. G.J. Aungier (1844)

The Diplomatic Correspondence of Richard II, ed. E. Perry (1933)

Documents Illustrating the Crisis of 1297–98 in England, ed. M. Prestwich (1980)

Early Lincoln Wills 1280–1547, ed. A. Gibbons (1888)

Feet of Fines for various counties, available at http://www.medievalgenealogy.org.uk/fines/counties.shtml

The Fifty Earliest English Wills in the Court of Probate, London, 1387–1439, ed. F.J. Furnivall (1882)

Flores Historiarum, vol. 3, ed. H.R. Luard (1890)

Foedera, Conventiones, Literae, 1272–1441, 10 vols., ed. T. Rymer (1816–20)

'A Fragment of an Account of Isabel of Lancaster, Nun of Amesbury, 1333–4', ed. R.B. Pugh, in *Festschrift zur Feier des zweihundertjährigen Bestandes des Haus-, Hof- und Staatsarchivs*, vol. 1, ed. L. Santifaller (1949), 487–98

The Gascon Rolls Project at www.gasconrolls.org

Gesta Edwardi de Carnarvon Auctore Canonico Bridlingtoniensi, in ed. W. Stubbs, *Chronicles of the Reigns of Edward I and Edward II*, vol. 2 (1883)

The Henry III Fine Rolls Project at https://finerollshenry3.org.uk/home.html

Historia Vitae et Regni Ricardi Secundi, ed. G. Stow (1977)

Issues of the Exchequer, ed. F. Devon (1837)

John of Gaunt's Register 1371–75, ed. S. Armitage-Smith (1911)

John of Gaunt's Register 1379–83, ed. E.C. Lodge and R. Somerville (1937)

Knighton's Chronicle 1337–1396, ed. G.H. Martin (1995)

'The Last Will and Testament of Richard Beauchamp, Earle of Warwicke and Aumarle', in *Historia Vitae et Regni Ricardi II Angliae Regis*, ed. T. Hearne (1729), 240–9

Le Livere de Reis de Britanie e le Livere de Reis de Engletere, ed. J. Glover (1865)

National Archives records, especially SC 1 (Ancient Correspondence), SC 8 (Ancient Petitions), C 53 (Charter Rolls), E 101 (Accounts Various)

Oeuvres de Froissart, ed. K. de Lettenhove, vol. 11 (1870)

The Parliament Rolls of Medieval England, ed. C. Given-Wilson et al (2005)

Parliamentary Writs and Writs of Military Summons, vol. 1, ed. F. Palgrave (1827)

Petitions to the Pope 1342–1419, ed. W.H. Bliss (1896)

Register of Edward the Black Prince, vol. 4 (1933)

The Reign of Richard II: From Minority to Tyranny, ed. A.K. McHardy (2012)

The Roll of Arms of the Princes, Barons and Knights Who Attended King Edward I to the Siege of Caerlaverock, ed. T. Wright (1864)

Rotuli Parliamentorum, vols. 1–4, 1272–1439 (1767–83)

Royal Charter Witness Lists for the Reign of Edward II 1307–1326, ed. J.S. Hamilton (2001)

A Short Calendar of the Feet of Fines for Norfolk, part 2, 1307–1485, ed. W. Rye (1886)

Society of Antiquaries of London MS 122

A Survey of London. Reprinted From the Text of 1603, ed. C.L. Kingsford (1908)

Testamenta Eboracensia: Or, Wills Registered at York, vol. 1, ed. J. Raine (1836)

Testamenta Vetusta: Being Illustrations from Wills, vol. 1, ed. N. Harris Nicolas (1826)

Vita Edwardi Secundi Monachi Cuiusdam Malmesberiensis, ed. N. Denholm-Young (1957)

Select Bibliography

The War of Saint-Sardos (1323–1325): Gascon Correspondence and Diplomatic Documents,
ed. P. Chaplais (1954)

The Westminster Chronicle 1381–1394, ed. and trans. L.C. Hector and B.F. Harvey (1982)

Year Books of Edward II, vol. xxv, Part of Easter, and Trinity, 1319, ed. J.P. Collas (1964)

Secondary Sources

Allington-Smith, R., *Henry Despenser: The Fighting Bishop* (2003)

Barfield, S., 'The Beauchamp Earls of Warwick, 1268–1369', Univ. of Birmingham MPhil thesis (1997)

Barker, J., *Agincourt: The King, the Campaign, the Battle* (2005)

Bell, A.R., A. Curry, A. King and D. Simpkin, *The Soldier in Later Medieval England* (2013)

Bullock-Davies, C., *Menstrellorum Multitudo: Minstrels at a Royal Feast* (1978)

Bullock-Davies, C., *A Register of Royal and Baronial Domestic Minstrels 1272–1327* (1986)

Burtscher, M., *The Fitzalans, Earls of Arundel and Surrey* (2008)

Caferro, W., 'Edward Despenser, The Green Knight and the Lance Formation: Englishmen in Florentine Military Service, 1366–1370', *The Hundred Years War (Part III): Further Considerations*, ed. L. J. A. Villalon and D. J. Kagay (2013), 85–103

Clarence Smith, J. A., 'Hastings of Little Easton', *Transactions of the Essex Archaeological Society*, third series, vol. 2, part 1 (1966), 1–13

Coleman, J., 'New Evidence about Sir Geoffrey Luttrell's Raid on Sempringham Priory, 1312', *British Library Journal*, 25 (1999), 103–28

Collins, H.E.L., *The Order of the Garter 1348–1361: Chivalry and Politics in Late Medieval England* (2000)

Cook, A.S., *The Last Months of Chaucer's Earliest Patron* (1916)

Davies, J.C., 'The Despenser War in Glamorgan', *Transactions of the Royal Historical Society*, 9 (1915), 21–64

Davies, J.C., 'The First Journal of Edward II's Chamber', *English Historical Review*, 30 (1915), 662–80

Devlin, M.A., 'An English Knight of the Garter in the Spanish Chapel in Florence', *Speculum*, 4 (1929), 270–81

Dodd, G., and A. Musson, eds., *The Reign of Edward II: New Perspectives* (2006)

Dryburgh, P., 'The Career of Roger Mortimer, First Earl of March', Univ. of Bristol PhD thesis, 2002

Dryburgh, P., 'Living in the Shadows: John of Eltham, Earl of Cornwall (1316–36)', *Fourteenth Century England IX*, ed. J. Bothwell and G. Dodd (2016), 23–47

Dunn, A., *The Politics of Magnate Power in England and Wales 1389–1413* (2003)

Fryde, E.B., 'The Deposits of Hugh Despenser the Younger with Italian Bankers', *Economic History Review*, 2nd series, 3 (1951), 344–62

Fryde, N., *The Tyranny and Fall of Edward II 1321–1326* (1979)

Gage, J., *The History and Antiquities of Suffolk: Thingoe Hundred* (1838)

Gibbs, V., 'The Battle of Boroughbridge and the Boroughbridge Roll', *Genealogist*, new series, 21 (1905), 222–5

Gibbs, V., and H.A. Doubleday, *The Complete Peerage*, 14 vols. (1910–40)

Goodman, A., 'The Military Subcontracts of Sir Hugh Hastings, 1380', *English Historical Review*, 95 (1980), 114–20

Griffiths, R.A., *The Reign of King Henry VI: The Exercise of Royal Authority, 1422–1461* (1981)

Guard, T., *Chivalry, Kingship and Crusade: The English Experience in the Fourteenth Century* (2013)

Hall McCash, J., ed., *The Cultural Patronage of Medieval Women* (1996)

Hallam, E.M., *The Itinerary of Edward II and his Household, 1307–1327* (1984)

Hamilton, J.S., 'Charter Witness Lists for the Reign of Edward II', in ed. N. Saul, *Fourteenth Century England I* (2000), 1–20

Hardyment, C., *Malory: The Knight who Became King Arthur's Chronicler* (2005)

Hicks, M., 'An Escheat Concealed: The Despenser Forfeitures, 1400–61', *Proceedings of the Hampshire Field Club and Archaeological Society*, 53 (1998), 183–9

Hicks, M., 'Cement or Solvent? Kinship and Politics in Late Medieval England: The Case of the Nevilles', *History*, 83 (1998), 31–46

Holmes, G.A., 'The Judgement on the Younger Despenser, 1326', *English Historical Review*, 70 (1955), 261–7

Holmes, G.A., 'A Protest Against the Despensers, 1326', *Speculum*, 30 (1955), 207–12

Johnstone, H., *Edward of Carnarvon 1284–1307* (1946)

Johnstone, H., *Letters of Edward, Prince of Wales 1304–1305* (1931)

Laborderie, O. de, J. R. Maddicott and D.A. Carpenter, 'The Last Hours of Simon de Montfort', *English Historical Review*, 115 (2000), 378–412

Lawrence, M., 'Power, Ambition and Political Rehabilitation: The Despensers, c. 1281–1400', Univ. of York DPhil thesis, 2005

Lawrence, M., 'Rise of a Royal Favourite: The Early Career of Hugh Despenser the Elder', *The Reign of Edward II: New Perspectives*, ed. G. Dodd and A. Musson (2006), 205–19

Lawrence, M., 'Secular Patronage and Religious Devotion: The Despensers and St Mary's Abbey, Tewkesbury', *Fourteenth Century England V*, ed. N. Saul (2008), 78–93

Lawrence, M., 'Too Flattering Sweet to be Substantial? The Last Months of Thomas, Lord Despenser', *Fourteenth Century England IV*, ed. J. S. Hamilton (2006), 146–58

Liveing, H.G.D., *Records of Romsey Abbey* (1906)

Martin, E.H., *A History of the Manor of Westhope, Co. Salop* (1909)

Meyer, A.R., 'The Despensers and the "Gawain" Poet: A Gloucestershire Link to the Alliterative Master of the Northwest Midlands', *The Chaucer Review*, 4 (2001), 413–29

Moor, C., *Knights of Edward I*, 5 vols. (1929–32)

Morris, M., *The Bigod Earls of Norfolk* (2005)

Morris, M., 'Edward I and the Knights of the Round Table', *Foundations of Medieval Scholarship: Records Edited in Honour of David Crook*, ed. P. Brand and S. Cunningham (2008), 57–76

Morris, R., 'Tewkesbury Abbey, the Despenser Mausoleum', *Transactions of the Bristol and Gloucestershire Archaeological Society*, 93 (1974), 142–55

Mortimer, I., *The Fears of Henry IV: The Life of England's Self-Made King* (2007)

Mortimer, I., *1415: Henry V's Year of Glory* (2009)

Mortimer, I., *The Perfect King: The Life of Edward III, Father of the English Nation* (2006)

Oxford Dictionary of National Biography, online edition, http://www.oxforddnb.com/

Payne, P. and C. Barron, 'The Letters and Life of Elizabeth Despenser, Lady Zouche (d. 1408)', *Nottingham Medieval Studies*, 4 (1997), 126–56

Phillips, S., *Edward II* (2010)

Prestwich, M., *Documents Illustrating the Crisis in 1297–98 in England* (1980)

Prestwich, M., 'Royal Patronage Under Edward I', *Thirteenth Century England I*, ed. P.R. Coss and S. D. Lloyd (1986), 41–52

Select Bibliography

Rickert, E., 'Some English Personal Letters of 1402', *The Review of English Studies*, vol. 8, no. 31 (1932), 257–63

Ross, C., 'The Household Accounts of Elizabeth Berkeley, Countess of Warwick, 1420–1', *Transactions of the Bristol and Gloucestershire Archaeological Society*, 70 (1951), 81–105

Saul, N., 'The Despensers and the Downfall of Edward II', *English Historical Review*, 99 (1984), 1–33

Saul, N., *Richard II* (1997)

Shaw, W.A., *The Knights of England: A Complete Record from the Earliest Time*, vol. 2 (1906)

Smyth, J., *The Lives of the Berkeleys* (1883; written before 1640)

Stapleton, T., 'A Brief Summary of the Wardrobe Accounts of the Tenth, Eleventh and Fourteenth Years of King Edward the Second', *Archaeologia*, 26 (1836), 318–45

Stewart-Parker, W., 'The Bassets of High Wycombe: Politics, Lordship, Locality and Culture in the Thirteenth Century', King's College London PhD thesis (2013)

Thompson, E.M., 'The Pageants of Richard Beauchamp, Earl of Warwick, Commonly Called the Warwick MS', *The Burlington Magazine for Connoisseurs*, 1 (1904), 150–64

Underhill, F., *For Her Good Estate: The Life of Elizabeth de Burgh* (1999)

Warner, K., 'The Adherents of Edmund of Woodstock, Earl of Kent, in March 1330' *English Historical Review*, 126 (2011), 779–805

Warner, K., *Downfall of a King's Favourite: Edward II and Hugh Despenser the Younger* (2018)

Warner, K., *Edward II: The Unconventional King* (2014)

Warner, K., '"We Might be Prepared to Harm You': An Investigation into Some of the Extortions of Hugh Despenser the Younger', *Journal of the Mortimer History Society*, 2 (2018), 55–69

Waugh, S.L., 'For King, Country and Patron: The Despensers and Local Administration, 1321–1322', *Journal of British Studies*, 22 (1983), 23–58

Waugh, S.L., 'The Profits of Violence: The Minor Gentry in the Rebellion of 1321–1322 in Gloucestershire and Herefordshire', *Speculum*, 52 (1977), 843–69

Wrottesley, G., *Crécy and Calais From the Original Records in the Public Record Office* (1898)

Index

(Women are indexed under their maiden names)